MICRO

SMALL ACTIONS, BIG IMPACT

SKILLS

MICRO SKILLS

SMALL ACTIONS, BIG IMPACT

ADAIRA LANDRY, MD
RESA E. LEWISS, MD

HANOVER
SQUARE
PRESS

Recycling programs for this product may not exist in your area.

ISBN-13: 978-1-335-01329-3

MicroSkills

Hanover Square Press
22 Adelaide St. West, 41st Floor
Toronto, Ontario M5H 4E3, Canada
HanoverSqPress.com
BookClubbish.com

Printed in U.S.A.

To my mom and dad, who taught me my very first words.

—Adaira Landry

To my family.

—Resa E. Lewiss

MICRO
SMALL ACTIONS, BIG IMPACT
SKILLS

TABLE OF CONTENTS

INTRODUCTION

When we told our colleagues, friends, and family we were writing a book to help people navigate the workplace, they asked, "Oh, is it for doctors?" "Nope," we replied. "Oh, it's for women?" And again, we replied "Nope."

This book is for everyone. And yet, we believe early-career professionals will benefit the most. Because your entry point into the workforce is where you need a primer to guide you. This is a time when we can feel most lost—waiting for someone to hand over all of the answers.

We cannot state our first piece of advice more clearly. Do not expect someone to save you or your career. You, yes you, are completely responsible for the health of your career. Of course you may find and build relationships with your people—people who listen, guide, and support. But nobody is losing sleep over whether or not your presentation was perfect. And nobody is anxious or stressed over whether or not you get that promotion. In fact, no one is more interested in your career than you. And that is the way it should be.

Why does the truth—that you drive your own success—cause so much apprehension?

Because the best strategies for success in the workplace are not so much taught as they are expected to be known. Worse still, there is a pervasive myth that some people have "it," and some don't. The characteristics of successful people—competence, ambition, humility, dependability, good communication—are often wrongly considered innate traits, rather than larger skills that can be dissected and learned in smaller pieces—what we call MicroSkills.

MicroSkills: Small Action, Big Impact is our personal and heartfelt gift to you. *MicroSkills* is built on a core and easy-to-learn premise: that every big goal, complicated task, healthy habit, and, yes, even what we think of as core character traits, can be broken down into simple, measurable skills that are easily understood, practiced, and incorporated. Consider this book a collection of privileged information, full of efficient solutions you want as early as possible in your career. *MicroSkills* is designed to feel immediately accessible—we do not want you to wait until the last page to feel its impact.

Our promise is simple: if you buy this book on a Friday, you will be better at your job by Monday.

As award-winning educators and physicians, we have shared our expertise in outlets, such as *Fast Company, Forbes, CNBC, Nature, Science, Slate, STAT News, USAToday*, the *Harvard Business Review, Teen Vogue, Vogue,* the *New York Times*, and the *Philadelphia Inquirer.* We have witnessed how effective the

MicroSkills principles can be, not only in our own demanding careers but also in the lives and careers of the hundreds of students and early-career professionals we have taught and mentored. We have spoken on stages, such as TEDMED, and as invited lecturers at academic institutions, such as Brown, Columbia, Cornell, Harvard, Johns Hopkins, Northwestern, University of Pennsylvania, and Stanford.

Allow us to introduce ourselves. Adaira Landry, MD, MEd is an assistant professor at Harvard Medical School. She studied and trained at UC Berkeley, UC Los Angeles, NYU, and Harvard. She has a decade of experience mentoring students and early-career professionals. When not caring for patients in the emergency department, she mentors college students across the United States and is an advisor for Harvard Medical School students. She is a healthcare contributor for Forbes Magazine. She has been a consultant for tech start-ups and is a cofounder of a nonprofit, Writing in Color—an organization that teaches people of color the craft of writing through free courses led by writers of color. She is also a mom to three little girls.

Resa E. Lewiss, MD, is a professor of emergency medicine. She trained at Brown University, the University of Pennsylvania School of Medicine, the National Institutes of Health, and Harvard Emergency Medicine. She has over twenty-five years of experience championing peers, students, and professionals at all stages of their careers. She is an early adopter and an internationally renowned pioneer in the field of clinical ultrasound, and innovative medical education. A TEDMED speaker and Times Up Healthcare founder, Resa is committed to diverse, equitable and inclusive workplaces. As the creator, founder, and producer of *The Visible Voices Podcast*, she designs conversations focused on health care, equity, and current trends. As a physician healthcare design consultant, her focus has been ultrasound hardware and workflows. She's helped to redesign the built environment of a Harvard ICU and an infectious diseases unit in Malawi.

It has not been a straightforward or easy path for either of us. There was no book that blueprinted the specific skills we needed. We achieved our goals by using a trove of MicroSkills that we learned and compiled thanks to disparate published content, experiences, observations, and each other. We do not want your journey to be as challenging as ours has been. We want you to attain your desired success and to use this book as a compass to get there quicker. Rest assured that as physicians we emphasize self-care and self-compassion throughout the book. Thus, we provide a blueprint to tackle common workplaces challenges while not sacrificing your own well being.

In preparing to write this book, we took a hard look at the self-help and professional-development industry. We listened to lectures, attended workshops, and read books and articles about the workplace. We spoke with contacts from a range of industries: business, medicine, marketing, tech, law, graphic design, education, retail, and the arts. We discovered overarching themes as well as a large gap. Books promise so much value and proclaim that ostensibly anyone can apply their teachings. And yet we know this to not be the case. Despite their best intentions, many of the lessons fall flat.

Why is that?

Most source materials, despite their claim of accessibility for all people, start from a premise that narrows their relatability. We witnessed authors, coaches, professors, and executives, make assumptions about the privilege and capabilities of their audience. Assumptions about the reader's expendable income, the size of their network, their amount of free time, their confidence in engaging a supervisor, their mental health, and their personal identifiers—like ability, age, gender, and race. It is unfortunate that, in a reader category that promises to help the masses, the majority of books are authored by white men who, if not born into wealth, at least had access to the network, time, and institutions to help them obtain it. There is nothing inherently wrong with authors sharing the wisdom they have. We find, however, that the *assumptions* some authors make can lead to inadvertently skipping vital steps, teachings, or resources others need to access opportunity. For the reader who does not have the bandwidth, network, or disposable income, many books produce feelings of inadequacy, shame, confusion, overwhelm, and discouragement.

So we wrote the book we wish we had when we were starting our professional journey.

MicroSkills aims to avoid preconceived notions about where you are. Each chapter is structured in the same format so you can learn our approach and practice until it becomes rote. Our objective? To mitigate assumptions, by using four teaching tools:

1. Personal Vignettes: These anecdotes serve an emotional function to reach you, the reader. Stories connect humans. And we want you to vicariously connect with our experiences and see yourself in these stories. Each MicroSkill is based on a real story from our lives and illustrates the skill we want to teach.

2. Addressing the Need for Change: We don't want you to change for the sake of changing. We want you to believe you need to grow and be motivated to evolve in a way that makes you better at work. Each MicroSkill explains the stakes: the effects if you adopt the skill, the effects if you don't.

3. Normalizing the Difficulty of Change: We are exquisitely aware of how easy it is accept the status quo. But we want you to avoid stagnating and adopting a universal "good enough is good enough" attitude. Each MicroSkill identifies why that particular skill is hard to learn and integrate. We try to remove assumptions about your education, experience, access, and interest.

4. Critical Actions: We did not write a book of theoretical concepts. We instead teach you the small steps, the "how-tos" of being better at work. By breaking a MicroSkill down into critical actions you are able to see the pieces that make the whole. Follow action A, and B, and C. See how they build upon each other. Explore the critical actions for any MicroSkill and discover where gaps that need attention lie.

We believe identifying, learning, and integrating MicroSkills will help you navigate any challenge. For example, in the emergency department, we use MicroSkills to take better care of patients. Think about a patient who is not breathing and their heart has stopped pumping. They need CPR. Taking care of that patient requires a collection of MicroSkills: assign team members a role at the bedside, prioritize the medications to give, do chest compressions according to a certain rate and rhythm, check for a pulse after a measured amount of time, and keep calm throughout the high stress moment.

We also have used MicroSkills to navigate careers in academic medicine. Why would we need such skills? Like many other fields, our industry is a place where women are less likely to be designated as leaders, promoted as professors,[1] or selected as award recipients.[2] It's a simultaneously demanding and discouraging path. Like the lack of salary equity in other fields, women physicians don't receive the same salary as men physicians for equivalent work.[3] Although the majority of students in USA medical schools are women[4] and 80% of the healthcare workforce is women, leadership roles do not reflect this. Women have barely gained representation as chairs or deans in the past 25 years.[5] Resa was the first woman professor of emergency medicine in the department she joined in 2017. The lack of equity is compounded with even worse statistics when we consider intersectional identities. For example, less than 6% of physicians in the United States identify as Black.[6] Adaira was the sole Black woman fellow and then sole Black woman faculty in her department for six years. The persistent underrepresentation of physicians of color is disheartening. In medicine, 40% of women move to part-time practice or leave medicine altogether within six years of completing their training.[7] A 2023 study showed that the median age of attrition for women emergency medicine physicians is 45.6 years whereas for men it is 59 years.[8] So survival in our professional environment goes beyond grit and passion. To advance, we had to strategically navigate and deeply comprehend the workplace that has been infiltrated with systemic ways to oppress our growth and inclusion.

Using MicroSkills, we help you dismantle the architecture of success down to its foundation and building blocks. Had we known this strategy earlier, we would have moved further, faster, and more efficiently.

Readers may ask why we did not write a designated chapter or section of the book dedicated to diversity, equity, and inclusion. Just as in the workplace, where there is no separate chapter for being a woman, gay, Black, low-income, or disabled, we decided to integrate the impact of personal identity throughout the book. You will see those aspects of who we are throughout the entire read. We share our perspectives, the way we see the world, and the way the world sees us. We deliver strategic advice and illustrative stories that are helpful for anyone, especially those who feel disadvantaged based on their identity.

When we were brainstorming and writing the framework for *MicroSkills*, we kept returning to these three truths:

TRUTH #1: TIME CAN ONLY BE SPENT.

As emergency medicine physicians, we never save time. If a task is no longer necessary, we immediately use those saved minutes on something else. No matter how we see it, every minute matters. In fact, seconds matter when it comes to saving a life. But even if your job does not involve life-or-death situations, the fact remains that every one of us is constantly spending time on work or thinking about how we will spend our time on work. If a task is no longer required, time can never go back into a savings account for later. Something else fills the void.

TRUTH #2: THE WORLD IS NOT EQUAL.

Everyone comes to the table with varying experiences and resources. Any group of peers will have differences in education, knowledge, money, personal identities, responsibilities at home, and networks. Some people get a copy of what we call the *workplace playbook* from family or friends. Many people don't get a copy and have to figure out survival and success independently. While MicroSkills cannot solve the global inequities in and of the workplace, they can equip readers with the tools to accurately assess their own strengths and weaknesses, what they have access to, and what they lack. By taking the initiative to level off an inequality with skills acquisition, you begin to gain confidence navigating the workplace.

TRUTH #3: LEARNING IS LIMITLESS IF IT IS ACCESSIBLE.

Very few things in this world are as limitless as our capacity to learn. In the workplace, an openness to learning only strengthens you, your expertise, and your trajectory. Access to knowledge can in itself feel prohibitive, e.g. limited funds, home responsibilities, disabilities, etc. There is no way *MicroSkills* will teach you everything about the workplace. But it will show you the power of recognizing and resolving your own knowledge gaps to make success more accessible.

The workplace is complicated because you do not work in a vacuum. There are three pillars to any workplace: the self, the team, and the work. All three are important to consider as you read this book. Some of the strategies and skills we suggest are relevant to the self: how you prioritize your calendar and opportunities on your plate. Some are related to how you interact with the team: communicating clearly, providing support. The rest guide you on how to consider and complete your work: meeting timelines and building expertise.

This book will undoubtedly shape your career. But we need to normalize one last thing—improvement at work does not require deep pain, constant self-sacrifice, or physical, mental, or spiritual exhaustion. As physicians we want to uphold your physical, mental, and social health as you strive towards your goals. Using both compassion and strategy, *MicroSkills: Small Actions, Big Impact* focuses on you and supports your journey to be better at work.

1

MICROSKILLS FOR SELF-CARE

RESA

During my four years of emergency-medicine residency, I never ate a real meal on shift. This was not just a Resa thing. This was an everyone thing. The culture essentially convinced us there was no time to eat. And that same culture led us to believe we should not take care of ourselves. I watched my peers and the faculty go eight or ten hours without eating or drinking. I tried, but I could not last that long without eating. I remember being hungry while caring for critically ill patients. I'd feel jittery and short tempered on the telephone with consultants all out of hunger. I developed a workaround that kept me from disappearing too long from the department or from getting in trouble: Each shift, I raced to the coffee shop. I'd grab a room temperature bagel and a small coffee. Then I'd inhale the bagel while speed walking back to the department and sip the coffee for the rest of the shift. That was my meal.

All of us want to be healthy and fully present at work. We want to thrive and not merely survive. Merriam-Webster defines self-care as health care provided by oneself often without the consultation of a medical professional.[9] And when nobody is modeling this for us, self-care probably does not come naturally. We may not inherently practice intensive and deliberate self-care because baked into the culture of many workplaces is self-sacrifice and a denial of biological functions: eating, drinking, using the bathroom, taking time off when sick, and getting adequate sleep.

We have this nagging feeling that when you think of self-care, you imagine retail therapy, vacations, and mostly pampering the physical body. While this is a part of the equation, these comprise a small part of how we define self-care. Emotional and mental healing and protection are much more important goals. Self-care is about creating a sense of purpose and movement toward feeling good in and outside the workplace. It is about creating boundaries, and holding these without fearing repercussions.

THIS IS **ALSO** SELF CARE

Self-care is about creating a sense of purpose and movement toward feeling good in and outside the workplace, and it can look different for everyone.

This may come as a surprise, but doctors are not particularly healthy or stellar at taking care of themselves. We are great at helping others. But we are not good at asking for help, delegating tasks, or pausing to relax. Depression, substance use disorders, and suicide rates are higher among physicians. Reportedly men physicians have a 40% higher rate of death by suicide than age matched men and women physicians have 130% higher rate than age matched women.[10] Many state medical boards ask intrusive mental health questions as part of the approval process for state licensure.[11] And stigma in discussing mental-health diagnoses and shame surrounding physicians seeking treatment remain.[12] Such circumstances perpetuate doctors neglecting themselves. We know this denial of self-care is not just in medicine. And we believe that self-care can be learned and practiced using MicroSkills.

So why open a book about navigating the workplace with a chapter on self-care? Because you need to keep this harsh truth in mind: you might love your job but your job will not love you back. Your company, institution, job will not love you back.[13] You may love your colleagues. And those same people may care deeply about you. All of these things can be true. But your job, the job itself, is not your family. Since your job will not love you back, we want you to define what makes a meaningful life outside of work and recognize that you have needs and fulfillment, that go beyond the professional.

In this chapter we cover nine MicroSkills to improve your self-care.

MICROSKILLS FOR SELF-CARE:

1. Nourish relationships with people you trust.
2. Recognize the value of gratitude and demonstrate appreciation of others.
3. Make yourself an award-winning sleeper.
4. Protect your ability to deliberately rest.
5. Manage your personal finances.
6. Monitor your personal hygiene and physical health.
7. Off-load routine tasks that bring no joy or purpose.
8. Place and organize everything on a calendar.
9. Set limits on time spent in meetings.

THE MICROSKILL:

1. NOURISH RELATIONSHIPS WITH PEOPLE YOU TRUST

WHAT IS THE ACTUAL SKILL?

Identify and recruit your personal board of directors.

ADAIRA

Doctors fear giving patients the wrong dosage of medicines. That fear became my reality when I was a junior resident. The patient was in cardiac arrest (their heart was not beating and they were not breathing). In the resuscitation room, the medical team members were shouting over each other and bumping into each other. My supervisor ordered a medication. The nurse gave me a syringe filled with 3 times the amount of medicine the patient needed. I assumed the dose was what my supervisor had ordered. She assumed I would know to give only what the patient needed. In the end, I administered the wrong dose. The patient was already dead before I gave the medicine—I did not cause them to be more or less dead. Yet, I felt terrible because it was a mistake. Patients dying from cardiac arrest never feels good even when the CPR and resuscitation go smoothly. Add in a medical error and the trauma to the soul is amplified. I called a different doctor colleague to talk about the error at the end of my shift. I trusted that this person would not judge me, or point a finger or try to teach me a hard lesson. I was right. They let me talk. They listened and offered words which consoled me. And I felt better.

WHY DO WE NEED THIS SKILL?

It is hard living a healthy life in isolation. And similarly hard to work in isolation. It is the people, both at work and outside work, who you need to help you stay healthy. There are "blue zones" in the world, areas with the highest number of centenarians. One of their core principles is building community and connecting with others.[14] Throughout this book, when we talk about your "personal board of directors" we are talking about individuals with whom you have a level of respect and trust.[15] They are there, sitting at your table, to help you succeed and support you when you struggle. Your personal board can be peers—who are at the same level, training, rank as you. Some of these board members fill the role of "failure friend." In medicine, we call failure friends when we have a particularly traumatic patient case and we feel we failed.[16] Failure friends are people you call when you don't get the job you wanted or your 360 evaluation is not stellar. Your board members sit at your table and can provide honest feedback even when the conversation is difficult. These people offer varied skills and perspectives to fill in your gaps to help you learn and grow.

WHY IS THIS SKILL HARD TO ACHIEVE?

- Keeping your guard up makes it difficult to approach people when you really need help.
- Investing in your community takes time, energy, vulnerability, and emotional intelligence.
- You can gauge people incorrectly and disappointingly realize they are neither trustworthy nor interested in helping you.

WHAT ARE THE CRITICAL ACTIONS FOR THIS MICROSKILL?

IDENTIFY YOUR TRUSTED PEOPLE: Ask yourself: Who would I call in case of emergency at work? Who helps me feel better each and every time we interact? Do I have someone in my corner who is particularly good with conflict and difficult conversations? Who has a calm maturity and wisdom I wish to emulate? Who do I trust to not turn my crisis into gossip? People who respond to your call—or always get back to you—and who make you feel good and safe are examples of board members for your table.

ALWAYS GROW YOUR NETWORK: Think of an always growing table composed of a personal board of directors. Keep open seats at that table. Ask yourself: Do I need help in a certain area or aspect of life, e.g. running a meeting, setting an agenda, time management? Always be willing to bring good people on and offer them a seat. Knowing this prevents you from taxing any one person too much or too often. We also want to normalize that relationships ebb and flow as your skills grow and your needs shift.

Always keep open seats at your table and be willing to bring good people into the mix. This prevents you from taxing one person too much or too often.

SET PRACTICAL EXPECTATIONS: This group of people is dynamic. Someone close to you today may be unavailable for various reasons next year. Do not expect the relationships to be constantly active. Ask them how they like to communicate: phone calls, emails, texts. Do they want you to reach out directly or go through an assistant? Never assume you can call, email, or text someone at all hours unless they give you that go ahead.

SCHEDULE ROUTINE CHECK-INS: Reach out, keep in touch, and spend time with your people: invite them for a chat, a meal, or a walk. Talk with them and be sincere in your interest in getting to know them. Remind yourself that vulnerability helps them get to know you. Ask questions, give updates, and ask them if it's okay to keep in touch going forward.

GIVE. DON'T JUST TAKE: Consider how you could potentially be helpful to your board of directors: send them opportunities they might want, nominate them for awards, email their boss a note of recognition, invite them to a networking event, say "thank you."

PRIORITIZE DIVERSITY: Diversify your portfolio—your board does not need to be full of people who look like you or do the same work. Get to know people much older, much younger, and people with whom you do not share gender or racial concordance. You can learn from people with other life experiences and values.

RESPOND TO VIOLATIONS OF TRUST: There is always the risk that your confidential conversations are shared. If you find yourself in a situation where your trust was violated, assess the reasons why. There is a chance, especially if repetitive behavior, that the person violating your trust is not a healthy part of your self care or your team. Consider a direct conversation and hear them out. Then decide if you want the person to remain at your table or not.

THE MICROSKILL:

2. RECOGNIZE THE VALUE OF GRATITUDE AND DEMONSTRATE APPRECIATION OF OTHERS

WHAT IS THE ACTUAL SKILL?

Regularly say and show your *Thank yous*.

RESA

I remember the patient encounter when I learned how to lead an "end of life" discussion with the family. I was a resident and a patient with metastatic breast cancer came into the emergency department. She was weak, thin, in a lot of pain, and dying. The senior physician and I gathered her family in the room reserved for difficult conversations, and I watched him skillfully lead them in decisions for her "end of life." Everyone seemed relieved and at peace. Years later I was on shift as the senior physician and I admitted a patient with cancer from the emergency department to the hospital. He had cancer and needed intravenous antibiotics for an infection. He and his partner were friendly and appreciative. Soon thereafter, he came to the emergency department, only I did not recognize him. His cancer had advanced and he had lost a lot of weight. He was weak with low blood pressure, and barely able to talk. He was dying. His partner recognized me and in a friendly, unconcerned manner said she was going to go eat and offhandedly she asked if he would be admitted to the hospital. (It's common that people do not comprehend how sick their loved ones are.) I walked her into a private room and held the difficult conversation I had witnessed the senior physician hold years prior. "He is very very sick today. You should not leave for too long. You should call the children and ask them to come to the hospital." One of the emergency nurses told me that the partner came to find me the next day to express her thanks for the conversation. I wrote a letter to that senior physician thanking him for what he taught me. He kept that letter and told me he re-reads it from time to time.

WHY DO WE NEED THIS SKILL?

Many of us are taught to be polite: hold open a door, say please and thank you. However, gratitude goes deeper than pleasantries. It's not simply a phrase. Gratitude is a conscious behavior and an attitude. And it benefits you as well as its recipient(s). A gratitude practice can positively affect your sleep and your ability to experience joy.[17] Gratitude is associated with feeling more optimistic, more generous and less isolated. Gratitude benefits your mental health and enhances your relationships with others.

WHY IS THIS SKILL HARD TO ACHIEVE?

- Gratitude takes effort, thought, and practice. You may be busy. You may forget. You may take people for granted.
- Perhaps you may simply not value gratitude.
- Workplaces and leaders do not always model a gratitude practice.
- It's easy to focus and dwell on the negative aspects of life.

WHAT ARE THE CRITICAL ACTIONS FOR THIS MICROSKILL?

PRACTICE GRATITUDE: Slow down, notice your environment and think about people from whom you learn valuable lessons. Nourish the relationships with the people who are sources of support. Thank them. Write down or say aloud the people, situations, objects, and concepts for which you are thankful at a certain time daily or weekly. Adaira often does this at the dinner table where she asks her family, "What's one part of today that you are really glad happened?" Keep a mental, digital, or hardcopy list where you highlight daily moments of gratitude. This can happen anywhere anytime: when you drive, exercise, or meditate. Start with one thing—maybe three things—for which you are grateful.

TRACK YOUR *THANK YOU'S*: Notice how many times you say *thank you* in a day. Are there missed opportunities? Are there more people in your life you could authentically thank and show appreciation to? Are there people you could contact now and say words of gratitude?

VALUE THE THANK-YOU NOTE: More valuable than saying "thank you," consider showing it more intentionally. This could be a handwritten thank-you note. A text. An email after a meeting or chat. Be concrete and convey what specifically you recognize about the person and what they did. "Thank you for calling out that joke as disrespectful and unprofessional and being an upstander. I was uncomfortable and froze in the moment." You do not need to show your appreciation through a material gift. That being said, if sending a book, flowers, or ice cream feels right, go for it.

THE MICROSKILL:

3. MAKE YOURSELF AN AWARD-WINNING SLEEPER

WHAT IS THE ACTUAL SKILL?

Develop sleep habits that support your physical, mental, and emotional health.

RESA

I came late to the "*sleep is health*" mindset. Emergency medicine as a profession is perfect for someone who functions well on little sleep and is both a late night and an early morning person. And sleep deprivation is baked into the "training to be a doctor" culture. Shifts start and end at all hours. Driving home after overnight shifts, I remember hoping for no red lights so I would not nod off when coming to a red light or stop sign. In New York City, I stood up during subway rides home after overnight shifts because sitting down meant accidentally waking up in Queens and missing my stop in Manhattan. My attitude and relationship to sleep changed when I recovered from overnight shifts more slowly and it took days to feel back to myself. I really started paying attention to my ability to think clearly, my mood, and how I felt in my body. I also read about sleep science and hygiene. Sleep is now on the top health priorities list for me.

WHY DO WE NEED THIS SKILL?

Most of us need seven to nine hours of sleep per day.[18] Start paying attention. If you do not commit to a regular sleep schedule and routine, you will notice: body fatigue, mind fatigue, moodiness, irritability, decreased productivity and less thought clarity. Sleep deprivation has real health risks: stress, obesity, and depression.[19] Even if you would like a full nights rest, an early-morning meeting culture—common in the workplace—may affect your ability to get a healthy amount of rest.[20]

WHY IS THIS SKILL HARD TO ACHIEVE?

- Good sleep habits are not celebrated, and some people boast about getting by on little sleep.
- You have deadlines, responsibilities, stressors, and digital stimulation that cut into sleep.
- Stressors at home and/or work can potentiate insomnia.
- You mistakenly think that alcohol, stimulants, and medications aid your sleep.[21]

WHAT ARE THE CRITICAL ACTIONS FOR THIS MICROSKILL?

ADJUST YOUR MINDSET: Calm your onerous system. Identify and remove what activates rather than calms your mind, e.g. the night time news, scrolling on social media, stressful discussions with colleagues or family, etc.

DECOMPRESS EMOTIONS: Slow deep breathing stimulates melatonin release and relaxes your body by decreasing sympathetic tone.[22] Try a gratitude practice. Say aloud or write down that for which you are grateful.[23] Consider relaxation or meditation apps, e.g. Headspace or Calm.

TAKE BREAKS FROM STRESS: Home life can be stressful. Forgive yourself for going to bed with dishes in the sink or the kids' lunches unprepared. You can't do it all and we aren't asking you to. Write down your next day to-do list a few hours before bed, so it's off your mind. If the day looks stressful, see what can be postponed or cancelled. Instead, spend time building connections with the people in your personal life who you care about and care about you. Or spend time alone.

MIND THE CLOCK: Try to go to sleep and awaken at the same time each day. This includes weekends. Avoid all-nighters that leave you in front of the screen stressed about work. If the nature of your job requires you to stay up for 20-hour stretches, working on spreadsheets until 3am, pause and ask yourself, "Is this making me happy? Is this good for me? What is causing me to push myself so hard and often?"

ADJUST THE AMBIENT TEMPERATURE: The room should not be too warm or too cold. It is very hard to sleep when shivering from cold or sweating from heat.

MINIMIZE NOISE AND SOUND: Sound and light affect your sleep.[24] If you struggle with sleep, try to keep the room dark, quiet, and relaxing. A dark room can also improve your mental health.[25] Blackout curtains are a favorite window treatment for emergency doctors who work night shifts. Eye masks are very effective. White-noise machines work for some. Electronics, e.g. phones and laptops, can be distractors so remove these at least an hour before sleep.

AVOID STIMULATING FOODS AND DRINKS: Large meals, alcohol, and/or caffeine can make it difficult to fall asleep or to stay asleep. Not to mention they can activate or worsen stomach-acid reflux. Avoid these close to bedtime.[26]

UNDERSTAND THE IMPACT OF MEDICATIONS: A large topic, but we will keep it brief. Melatonin works for some—not all—people. This hormone is made in the brain in response to darkness. It also comes in a bottle. If you think you need something other than over-the-counter aids intended for sleep, speak with your regular doctor. Alcohol and pain medications should not be used to fall asleep.

EXERCISE REGULARLY: Exercise is best during the day for some and at night for others. If you exercise at night, keep it easy so that you aren't full of adrenaline as your head hits the pillow. Overall, working out can contribute to more restful sleep.[27]

TRY DIFFERENT ROUTINES: Don't keep doing the same nightly routine if it's not working. Adaira likes to lift her arms up and make small slow circles to tire her muscles, and she uses a fan every night (even in the Boston winters). Resa believes in a hot shower or bath. There is no single routine that works for everyone so try different strategies.

THE MICROSKILL:

4. PROTECT YOUR ABILITY TO DELIBERATELY REST

WHAT IS THE ACTUAL SKILL?

You should be as intentional and deliberate about resting as you are about working.

RESA

Early on, I had fully subscribed to a mindset of *the more you work, the more you accomplish.* I believed in burning the midnight oil and forgoing sleep and rest in general. The culture of academic medicine had not really provided another model. In the days with an eight-hour shift, I would lecture or schedule meetings before or after a shift. In days without shifts, I would teach workshops, write papers, and more. I remember pivoting when I read the evidence supporting "deliberate rest." The thought is that being deliberate in taking time away from work, i.e. deliberately resting, allows a person to be more productive and efficient during periods of working. I came to realize I was not working efficiently or in a way that was healthy, restorative, or prioritizing self-care. I saw my own productivity soar when I ensured daily exercise, walks in nature, naps, pleasure reading, sharing meals, and spending time with close friends.

WHY DO WE NEED THIS SKILL?

Deliberate rest is healthy and helps you be more present, productive, and efficient.[28] Alex Soojun-Kim Pang in his book *Rest* writes, "Rest is not something that the world gives us. It's never been a gift. It's never been something you do when you've finished everything else. If you want rest, you have to take it. You have to resist the lure of busyness, make time for rest, take it seriously, and protect it from a world that is intent on stealing it."[29] The concept of deliberate rest may seem indulgent or a luxury. We also realize this MicroSkill may be easier said than done.

The term "second shift" refers to the household responsibilities and childcare that occur after a full day in the workplace.[30] These duties fall disproportionately on women. We also note that single parents also struggle to rest after their workday. It is hard to deliberately rest when drowning in mandatory obligations. This is more reason why when you need rest, and the opportunity is there, you take it.

Deliberate rest is not scrolling on social media or bingeing on movies. These media stimulate, stress, and seize your chance to relax, reflect, question, and debrief. Adaira deliberately rests on weekends: she limits her desk work and focuses on family time and gardening. Resa deliberately rests every morning by waking up early for yoga and meditation. We need to be thoughtful and intentional about our activities when not working. We cannot work all the time: it's not healthy, and frankly it backfires in terms of being productive.

WHY IS THIS SKILL HARD TO ACHIEVE?

- You are addicted to work and find comfort in being productive.
- You fear missing out, not seeing an email, not meeting a project deadline, or losing a competitive edge.

- Deliberate rest is not possible due to limited resources or mandatory obligations.

WHAT ARE THE CRITICAL ACTIONS FOR THIS MICROSKILL?

PICK ONE BEHAVIOR CHANGE: No need to to revamp your life overnight. Try one change at a time. Pick one new way to deliberately rest. Allow yourself a nap or sit in silence, rather than sitting at the desk and pushing through another document. Go for a walk with friends and return to writing the work proposal with a calmer, clearer mind. Take a bath after walking the dog.

PROTECT YOUR DELIBERATE REST: Prioritize these periods and know that you do not need to explain yourself to other people. For instance, you don't have to tell someone you can't go to the evening work event because you scheduled a meal with friends. But many of us would feel uncomfortable just replying, "No." If that is the case simply say, "I am so sorry, I can't join. I have a conflict." The more you see the value of intentionally resting, the easier it will be for you to create boundaries with the team and workplace. And the more ready you will be to return to work.[31]

REIGN IN EMAIL: It's easy to feel on the clock at all times. If your job doesn't require 24/7 availability, then set up an out of office message. Ask people to send an email during certain hours. Or, you may add a line to your email signature that says something such as "*I do not access email outside of my working hours (M–F, 9am–5pm). I will respond during those times.*"

THE MICROSKILL:

5. MANAGE YOUR PERSONAL FINANCES

WHAT IS THE ACTUAL SKILL?

Organize and monitor your personal finances.

ADAIRA

I graduated residency with over $284,000 in student loans. Many of them were high interest loans, at 8% and 9%. For four years in residency, I literally paid zero attention to my loans. And when I graduated I thought, "hmm, I wonder how much money I owe?" Gulp. I was shocked. And my fiancé (now husband) was also very shocked! I decided to get rid of that stress (the loans, not the fiancé). I learned so much about student loans and decided there were paths that were financially advantageous (such as student loan forgiveness) and there were paths that were psychologically advantageous (pay off as soon as I can). I got out of debt very strategically and had a plan to tackle high interest loans first. It took me 3 years and I paid off my loans. Of course, I had a huge privilege—a physician's salary and I had no kids at the time, so I could work a significant amount of overtime. I lived off cup-of-noodles and barely took vacation. Seriously. While I don't recommend this path to everyone, it was still a huge lesson to mind my money. Never again have I neglected my financial obligations.

WHY DO WE NEED THIS SKILL?

Developing healthy financial habits will position you for financial independence—a state where you feel the freedom to make personal and professional choices at your own discretion (e.g. retire at an early age, travel, buy a vacation home, work part-time). For instance, Adaira strategized her finances beginning at age twenty-five. By thirty-five, she was able to decrease her emergency department shift responsibility from full time to part time—that's seven shifts a month from twelve shifts. Taking care of your finances now creates room for you to take risks later.

WHY IS THIS SKILL HARD TO ACHIEVE?

- Finances seem overwhelming, so you may procrastinate, not know where to start, and avoid engaging altogether.
- You lack a financial cushion from generational or inherited wealth.
- You lack financial literacy as personal finance isn't yet universally taught at school.
- You don't feel freedom is achievable due to competing demands, such as student loans, a mortgage, rent, childcare.
- You might not be driven by money so building a strategy is not a priority.

WHAT ARE THE CRITICAL ACTIONS FOR THIS MICROSKILL?

ADDRESS THE PROBLEM: The stress of finances can cause you to avoid the topic and that may put you in worse shape. Avoidance will not make financial troubles go away. Talk to people you trust who can help you manage the overwhelm. Recruit a finance expert onto your personal board of directors. There are many ways to gain comfort with managing money. And remember that financial problems need not be resolved in a single day.

PERFORM DEBT INVENTORY: Everyone has a different relationship to debt. It's often influenced by how you were raised and how you saw the adults in your life relate to money.[32] As scary as it may be, you should keep track of your debt. Take an inventory: credit cards, personal loans, student loans, car payments. Everything. Some debt may be necessary, such as a mortgage or student loans. And some debt may be forgiven via various programs through the government or your employer.[33] Before you make plans, understand the landscape of your debt.

LOWER THE COST OF LIVING: We'd love for you to be able to afford anything you want. But this is not the reality for many. As a result, brainstorm ways to save. Due to exorbitant mortgage values, many early-career professionals struggle to buy real estate. A reasonable alternative is to rent alone or with roommates, or live with family at no or low cost.[34] As a result, many move in with family or roommates. Moving to a city with a lower cost of living is an option for some, but not all. We also acknowledge that it doesn't feel fair to have to uproot your life because of financial restrictions. Use public transportation to save car and other travel costs. Ask your supervisor for a raise, e.g. "Given growing costs of living and my consistent contribution to the company, can we find a time to discuss my salary and options for an increase?" Check with employee benefits for discounts or subsidies. If you need to borrow money, speak with trusted family and friends.

SEEK FINANCIAL ADVICE: Read books. Watch videos. Speak with people in your circle who are financially literate. Join online personal finance interest groups. For instance, there are finance groups on social media that specifically focus on "FIRE," which stands for Financial Independence, Retire Early, strategic saving and spending to gain financial freedom and early retirement.[35] At all times, be mindful of misinformation. In the digital world, digest the content and then read the comments that follow which often discuss the accuracy of an entry. If working with a financial advisor, ask the person if they are a fiduciary financial advisor, which means they are bound by law to act in your best interest. Mind any red flags with financial advisors including high fees, a sense of urgency about spending, and a strong promise of guaranteed high returns.[36]

STREAMLINE MONEY TRANSFERS: Direct deposit is your friend. Make it automatic, even if it's a small amount. And direct that money to high interest loans first, e.g. credit-card debt or personal loans. Download your bank's mobile app and submit checks electronically to avoid depositing in person. Set up recurring bills to be paid automatically, e.g. monthly mobile and monthly internet bills. Check your credit-card statement and work towards paying it full monthly.

GROW AN EMERGENCY FUND: Emergencies can be quite costly. And unpredictable. You cannot predict health emergencies or family members falling ill, or other reasons to need extra money. Start small and save enough to cover one month's expenses. Then, keep saving until you have up to three, then six months' worth of expenses covered.

MEET WITH BENEFITS REPRESENTATIVES: Companies and organizations, especially large ones, have staff that specialize in finance for employees. You may be part of an association—a union or guild—with similar employee financial support. Research your benefits: disability and other insurance, retirement, and defined periods of leave, such as sick or family leave. Seek out cost savings benefits e.g. transportation pre-tax monthly payments, or even discounted parking or museum tickets.

CONTRIBUTE TO A RETIREMENT ACCOUNT: The earlier you start the better. And the more you can maximize your contribution the better. The simplest first step is to see what type of retirement account your job offers: 401K, 403b, Roth, pension, etc. If your job contributes an extra percentage to your retirement—called *matching*—take advantage of this offer. It's as close to free money as you'll get. Companies typically partner with a retirement-portfolio company (e.g. Fidelity, Vanguard, TIAA, Prudential) and suggest plans for enrollment based upon your age and risk tolerance.

UNDERSTAND AND SECURE INSURANCE: There are at least six key types of insurance: health, disability, life, umbrella, property, and automobile. If you don't own a car, you don't need automobile insurance. If you live with your parents and they are insured, you might not need your own property insurance. Be cautious if someone mentions *whole life insurance*—it's debated and commonly considered a scam.[37] You often have narrow windows of time in each year to enroll in these benefits or have to experience a so-called qualifying event (e.g. birth of a child or marriage), which is why it's so important to ask your supervisors or onboarding administrators when you get hired.

LIFE:
to protect your dependents if you die

HEALTH:
to protect your body

DISABILITY:
in case your ability to go to work changes

PROPERTY:
to protect your belongings and your home

UMBRELLA:
in case someone gets hurt (e.g. slips on your property)

AUTOMOBILE:
for vehicular accidents

There are at least six key types of insurance: life, health, disability, property, umbrella, and automobile.

THE MICROSKILL:

6. MONITOR YOUR PERSONAL HYGIENE AND PHYSICAL HEALTH

WHAT IS THE ACTUAL SKILL?

Maintain your cleanliness and health.

RESA

I remember working a few shifts in the emergency department with one medical student. She dressed neatly and seemingly with intention. However, she had very strong body odor. Patients made comments when she left their room as the smell lingered. After the third shift, nurses pulled me aside and told me I had to speak with her. I had never initiated this type of sensitive and potentially difficult conversation. I first spoke with a colleague with experience broaching sensitive matters. They told me to speak kindly starting with a check in on their well-being. The student was open to the conversation. We talked. She was in a good mental health state. We chatted about her home, access to soap, hot water, and clothes laundering facilities. She was unaware of the odor, and once I gave her that heads-up, she told me she knew what to do. She corrected the issue, the odor went away, and there were no further comments.

WHY DO WE NEED THIS SKILL?

Hygiene, grooming, and neatness of appearance are not vain. They speak to how you think about, respect, and take care of the self. We want you to feel healthy and good at work. Since we are not the fashion police, please style your hair and clothing based on how you feel suitable for work. We are also not asking anyone to conform to a cis, hetero, white standard of professional aesthetic. What we are suggesting are fundamental actions to care for the self. That being said—and we aren't proud this reality exists—we want you to know that conventional attractiveness may drive popularity or promotion.[38] In fact, one survey showed that 86% of employees and 80% of managers associated how you dress with your ability to be promoted. We will defer to you on the aesthetic you prefer. Our job, as authors, advisors, and mentors, is to share the reality: our appearance, in its authentic form or not, does matter in the workplace.[39]

WHY IS THIS SKILL HARD TO ACHIEVE?

- Maximizing sleep or prioritizing morning duties (e.g. pets or kids) takes priority over personal grooming.
- It may feel uncomfortable or self-indulgent to dedicate time to your appearance and health.
- You don't have a stable living or economic situation, making hygiene an objective challenge.
- You struggle with physical limitations or your mental health which make preparing for the day difficult.
- You lack insurance: no benefit plan through your work for mental health, dental or eye care.

WHAT ARE THE CRITICAL ACTIONS FOR THIS MICROSKILL?

SIMPLIFY YOUR ROUTINE: Moving tasks such as picking out clothing, washing hair, and laundry to weekends or evenings can reduce the amount of effort needed before starting the workday. If you dread taking care of clothing, avoid purchasing clothing that requires more upkeep. Consider packing lunch before sleeping (which is often cheaper than day-of delivery or take-out). Fresh vegetables, fruits, nuts, hummus are all quick meals that are easy to prepare, though we recognize they are costly.[40] We want to normalize that what we are suggesting are fundamental actions to care for the self. These are organizational steps to be healthy which severely impacts the rest of your life and career.

ESTABLISH A HEALTH-CARE TEAM: Outpatient doctors have different types of visits for "new patients" versus "established patients." New-patient visits are longer in length and harder to get. This holds true for dentists, and Ob-Gyn doctors, and more. This is why when you have a bad headache or back pain, and you call for a new doctor appointment, the wait is three, four, or six months. But if you establish a primary-care physician now, it is typically faster to get in the office for a shorter visit, when you have an acute complaint later.

PRACTICE DENTAL HYGIENE: The American Dental Association recommends keeping teeth and gums healthy to prevent tooth decay.[41] Brush your teeth twice and floss once daily, use fluoride and mouthwash, and visit a dentist on a regular basis. These habits also help prevent bad breath. Avoid tobacco as it harms the teeth and the tongue, causes gum disease, and contributes to bad breath.[42] We get that sugary foods like candy and soda can taste good; however, they also cause tooth decay.

CLEAN YOUR BODY, HAIR, AND CLOTHING: Bathing helps remove dead skin cells, bacteria, and oils. Clean areas more prone to sweat or strong odor, such as in the groin and armpits. Wash your hands at work. Washing hair is a part of this hygiene regimen. However, every head of hair is different. We don't ask you to change what is healthy and protective for your hair type. Launder and iron your clothes as needed. Go easy on cologne, perfume, and essential oils. Check if your work has a "no-scent" policy. We want you to strike a balance: don't let your appearance be the only thing people think about when they discuss you.

THE MICROSKILL:

7. OFF-LOAD ROUTINE TASKS THAT BRING YOU NO JOY OR PURPOSE

WHAT IS THE ACTUAL SKILL?

Strategically remove tasks that drain your time and energy.

ADAIRA

As a mom and a wife, I initially felt like a failure when I hired a house cleaner. I had assumed I'd be able to personally manage clinical shifts, kids, marriage, and other home obligations. But the mess was piling up all over my house. And so was my stress. I am of the sort where I need a clean house. And a dirty or really messy house makes me uncomfortable. So I hired a professional. I was so embarrassed the first time I let her in my house. Toys, laundry, and cereal were everywhere. But when I returned home later that day and saw the results, I jokingly texted her, *Um, would you like to move in?* She was that life-changing. It was worth every penny. And yes, the cleaning fee was not something I could always afford. But when I had the income, it saved me hours and hours of time. It decreased my stress levels tremendously. I can't believe I suffered for so long.

WHY DO WE NEED THIS SKILL?

Many of us believe we can do it all, do it all well, and do it better than anyone else. The reality: it's just not possible. And your health suffers when you live this way. Working long hours has been shown to increase the risk of strokes and heart attacks.[43]

Off-loading tasks is not just a practice of removing duties, but a mindfulness exercise in considering how your time could be better spent addressing your personal health. By off-loading the work that drains you, you can decrease stress and feel more joy. This shift also leaves more space to focus on your professional growth.

WHY IS THIS SKILL HARD TO ACHIEVE?

- You feel guilty offloading work to other people.
- Admitting that you are overwhelmed requires vulnerability and can feel embarrassing.
- You have financial obligations (e.g. student loans, childcare, or rent) that make additional expenditures prohibitive.
- You don't know how to off-load work from your plate.

WHAT ARE THE CRITICAL ACTIONS FOR THIS MICROSKILL?

ADD PERSPECTIVE: Consider the reason you are off-loading items on your plate. Instead of just rationalizing *These tasks are boring or useless*, finish the sentence with *and I don't have as much time to spend with myself/family/friends/exercising/hobbies as I could.* Doing this early often helps you understand why you need to free up time.

NORMALIZE VULNERABILITY: No one has it all together. The celebrities, politicians, executives, colleagues you might admire and respect for seeming "polished" or "in control" also do not have it all together. At least not by themselves. Tell yourself, "I cannot do this alone." And feel confident saying it because many others can relate to that sentiment. It's not just you. We promise.

REDISTRIBUTE RESOURCES: Take inventory of expenses that cost you financially. If they are optional and draining you, even slightly, then it's time to off-load. A good rule: cancel all of those elective expenses that drain the bank and are unused. For example, the subscription to magazines you do not read and film channels you do not watch could be monies used for a house cleaner, or food delivery service. Reallocate or save the money for later.

IDENTIFY WORK TO OFF-LOAD: Unsure where to start? Get inspiration from others. Ask the people who seem to be organized and accomplishing it all, "What tasks do you off-load, delegate or hire?" Think about chores that you dread and give you no sense of purpose. Focus on those. Start small. There are four ways to off-load: automate, delegate, outsource, and streamline tasks.

AUTOMATE:
set the bulk of the work upfront so it's easier to do next time (i.e. autopay bills).

DELEGATE:
identify someone on the team who can do the work (i.e. ask children to do chores).

OUTSOURCE:
bring in an external party to complete the work (i.e. hire a gardener).

STREAMLINE:
cut out unnecessary steps (i.e. unsubscribe to emails to get less in the inbox).

Think about chores that you dread and that give you no sense of purpose, and focus on off-loading those tasks.

TALK TO YOUR SUPERVISOR: Tasks and projects you might offload could be at home or at work. If the items in your workplace have limited value, respectfully discuss how you are spending your time and the impact of that effort. Mention specifics to help build your argument. Of note, you are not obligated to have a solution. However, having a few ideas often helps when trying to create change.

STATE THE ISSUE WITH A TASK	OFFER A CONCRETE ALTERNATIVE TO THE TASK
"Can we talk about the weekly meeting notes I email? I surveyed the group, and no one seems to read them. They take a good bit of time, which I could use for other tasks."	"One option would be to rotate so everyone takes a turn at taking notes. Another is I could just send out a high-level summary with focused action items. That would cut down on the time spent. Lastly, we could record meetings so if someone misses, they can just listen later."

THE MICROSKILL:

8. PLACE AND ORGANIZE EVERYTHING ON THE CALENDAR

WHAT IS THE ACTUAL SKILL?

Organize everything on a calendar and don't rely on your memory.

ADAIRA

As a mom of three little kids, a busy professional, and wife to a husband in tech—I have a lot of activities, meetings, parties, conferences, and vacations on the calendar. There is literally no way I'd function without checking my calendar every day. However, the big day for my family is Sunday. After the kids go to bed my husband and I go through our calendars for the week. Literally day by day so that it's all scheduled—pick up/drop off for the kids, my shifts, which birthday parties we will attend (and which we must miss), and all of the practices (violin, ballet, circus, etc.). My brain would be mush if I tried to even rely on my memory. When I was earlier in my career I had less on my plate—less responsibilities overall. So I never had a calendar. But as soon as responsibilities arrived I started to organize and I highly recommend the same to anyone with a busy life. Unloading all of this information on to a calendar lightens my mind and allows self-care to be a high priority.

WHY DO WE NEED THIS SKILL?

Reducing cognitive load and protecting your time is important for self-care. Have you ever missed a meeting or double-booked a time slot because you did not check all your calendars? We have too. Neuroscientists have determined that we can only keep track of 4 items at a time.[44] If carefully and intentionally placed, a calendar can be an excellent way to manage your commitments and leisure time. And it's not just for work: remembering someone's birthday is as straightforward as learning the date, placing it on a calendar and selecting the "repeat annually" option.

WHY IS THIS SKILL HARD TO ACHIEVE?

- This skill asks you to be organized and intentional.
- You question the efficiency of the upfront effort to do this.
- You have numerous unlinked and unintegrated calendars. And you are intimidated by the effort it would take to consolidate them.
- The software functionality can be confusing.

WHAT ARE THE CRITICAL ACTIONS FOR THIS MICROSKILL?

CONSOLIDATE CALENDARS: If you use more than one calendar, try to combine them. Have a one calendar goal. Most calendar programs allow you to automatically forward and sync them.

MAKE YOUR CALENDAR ACCESSIBLE: If you need to refer to your calendar often, consider making it accessible. Synchronize to your phone, your laptop, and from the cloud. Be mindful: having your calendar immediately available can disrupt your deliberate rest. For this reason, Adaira does not keep any calendar apps on her phone.

CREATE A READABLE CALENDAR: Do not overflow the calendar so much that nothing can be found. Filling every hour of the calendar e.g., "go to gym" or "buy groceries" may add clutter to the day's agenda. Color codes are great and keep different and recurrent meetings and tasks visually distinct.

ADD DETAILS TO CALENDAR EVENTS: Title the entry clearly so you know what the appointment is without looking back to email. Add details in the meeting description: pertinent websites, links, notes from prior meetings. Include attachments if files are needed to review.

CONSIDER A SHARED CALENDAR: Consider a family or a team calendar to help with keeping track of more than one person's schedule. If you have administrative support, make sure they are able to access your calendar to schedule meetings. Do a regular check-in with your administrative support to review your calendar preferences. Clarify your preferences e.g. "Please make Zoom appointments for 30 minutes and allow 15 minutes in between meetings." Also, if you share your calendar with others (your team, admin staff, partners, children) audit what people are able to see (e.g. doctors' appointments, haircut, meetings with lawyers.)

USE AWAY MESSAGES: Part of being deliberate about your calendar is blocking out time when you are away or out of the office. When on vacation, protect time to write, mark all of it on your calendar.

THE MICROSKILL:

9. SET LIMITS ON TIME SPENT IN MEETINGS

WHAT IS THE ACTUAL SKILL?

Create boundaries and clarify the need for meetings.

ADAIRA

For the longest time, I had no control over the number of meetings on my calendar. There were just too many. And while I respect my colleagues, some meetings objectively felt unproductive: no decisions made, no agenda, too much or not enough time allotted. In fairness, I led suboptimal meetings in the past. It happens to all of us. Over time, I learned to appreciate productive meetings and started to create boundaries around all meetings. Now I ask what the meeting is about and consider if it could become an email instead. I block out windows for certain types of meetings: for instance, Friday mornings are blocked for advising and mentoring meetings. And on Friday afternoons, I have a very high threshold to add any meeting at all. That 1:00 and 5:00 p.m. Friday period is my time to finish up outstanding tasks from the week—or to rest, if I am all caught up.

WHY DO WE NEED THIS SKILL?

Meetings seem to be the default mode of communication in the workplace. They dominate our calendars and our energy. Without question, they help establish trust and psychological safety as well as build community in remote and hybrid workplaces. They may be necessary for consensus building and for decision making. But in our opinion, they are often given too much weight and credit. Too many meetings and ineffective meetings prevent deep work and drain energy. One study found that decreasing meetings by 40% increased productivity by 71%.[45]

WHY IS THIS SKILL HARD TO ACHIEVE?

- Restricting meetings can feel countercultural, rude, or disruptive to the work and the team.
- You have to be organized and skilled at communicating outside of meetings.
- Your team is not interested in alternative means of communication.

WHAT ARE THE CRITICAL ACTIONS FOR THIS MICROSKILL?

RAISE THE THRESHOLD FOR MEETINGS AND WORK EVENTS: Meetings which drain you, which do not require your attendance, and which disrupt your deep work—trim or drop those. Restrict the number of events that are work-adjacent and optional, e.g., workshops, networking socials, and even mentorship meetings. These events, while helpful for connecting with the team, can deplete the few, free hours available.

SET WINDOWS FOR MEETINGS: Select windows each week where you hold meetings. Once the slots are filled, that's it. For instance, Adaira holds two meetings a month for mentees in college. So when she gets a request for a meeting, she looks at just that window and, if full, offers the next available slot. If it is truly urgent, it's no problem to adjust the calendar. Yet, many are not urgent and need not happen right away.

TRIM MEETING LENGTHS: Most meetings do not need to be as long as scheduled. Push back politely on the time allotment. Play with cutting down to give yourself time. Sixty-minute meetings often work as thirty-minute meetings; thirty as twenty, and so on. Ask, "Do you think we can get through this agenda in twenty minutes?"

STREAMLINE SCHEDULING: If resources are available, you can use scheduling software, like Calendly, or an administrative assistant. There is no one way to do this. Just pick a strategy which fits your workflow and can take away some of the hassle of scheduling a meeting. And make this practice a habit.

MEET ASYNCHRONOUSLY: Much work can get accomplished without a meeting. Consider email, communication platforms that build community, virtual documents, audio texting. We wrote our articles and this book with few meetings in favor of cloud-sharing documents, texting, and asynchronous voice messages.

USE VIRTUAL COMMUNICATION PLATFORMS: There are pros and cons to platforms like Slack and Microsoft Teams. They can allow efficient and continuous conversations. They are also a distraction culprit. Using these, however, may avoid meetings that require blocks of undivided time and allow you to multitask.

CONCLUSION:

You are the best person to protect and advocate for yourself.	When you are suffering, consider opting out of a task and seeking alternatives for your self-care	Recognize the value and limited availability of your time and protect it.

SUPPLEMENTAL RESOURCES:

Healthier Relationships

Real self-care takes real systemic change

There's No "Right" Way to Do Self-Care

2

MICROSKILLS TO MANAGE A TASK LIST

ADAIRA

In college I worked for the UC Berkeley food-service office. I delivered birthday cakes that parents ordered for their children at school. In the beginning I had no system to organize the purchase orders. I'd get cake orders emailed to my work address. Some came to my supervisor's email address. Some came by phone call. My setup was decentralized, and dropped cake orders were just waiting to happen. At first, I tried to keep a mental note of all of these orders. I used a few Post-its here and there. Ultimately, I lost track and forgot a few. Or...maybe more than a few. I was embarrassed when my supervisor Kim LaPean said, "These orders are very important. We need to find a way to avoid errors." But better, she helped me develop a task tracking system. "Every morning you can come in and get all of the new orders and then put them in a spreadsheet to track." I had never done that before. This one experience helped me become intentional with organizing my tasks. Since then, I've thought about what needs to be done and in what order.

Going through your to-do list can be daunting if you don't know where to start. The sense of intimidation or defeat can cause us to stall or power through without a plan. We want you to consider three concepts as you approach any task list: an order of operations, the economy of time, and your return on investment.

In the emergency department we prioritize our patient list based on how sick the person is. A patient with sudden abdominal pain and vomiting is higher acuity—sicker and less stable—than a patient with two weeks of wrist pain after playing a lot of tennis. Some patient related tasks should come first and take priority. Others can be deferred. While your workplace to-do list may not carry the type of stress as patient care, the truth remains: you need to understand and develop an order of operations. There are so many variables to consider when arranging your list: your supervisor's priorities, your priorities, your professional passions, the complexity of a task, timelines, team dynamics, and so on. And sometimes as we putter along we forget to pause and ask, *does this order make sense?*

Of course, the order of operations isn't everything. You also need to understand the economy of time. How we allocate our time on any particular task directly impacts the outcome of a day's work. And this rule scales up. How we spend the day, week, and year affects what we accomplish on a larger scale. And here is a key game rule: you can't spend the same amount of time on every task. You need to be able to ration your calendar strategically. This requires having a good understanding of anticipated time needed to complete the task and the amount of time available on the calendar.

We often hear the phrase "time is money" in conversations about efficiency and productivity. A bit of caution—we don't want you to think of time only in terms of money. According to time-management experts, when people strictly think of time in terms of money, "they become more agitated, less happy, always in a rush. And importantly, they get greedy. They become less likely to help people out."[46] Yes, money can make life easier and more luxurious; however money will not solve all of your problems—your interpersonal problems, your health problems, your insecurities, your communication problems, and your desire to simply be a good person. Design your work life to be passion driven—focused on bringing good into the world. Recognize the harms of centering your life around money.

One last concept: with literally any task, we ask you to consider the return on investment (ROI). ROI is the reward, the outcome, the product, the result you get in exchange for putting effort into a task. ROIs vary—it may be a sense of accomplishment, a promotion, skill development, networking, satisfaction in helping people, creating a legacy, or building a more efficient team. It can be your health, your sleep, or time with your loved ones. In many instances, the bigger the ROI, the more fulfilled your experience.[47] But even tasks like sending emails for your supervisor or scheduling meetings for the team can have a measurable ROI—you gain a reputation as a communicative, organized, and reliable colleague. If a task lacks measurable ROI: no obvious impact, the work is extraneous and goes unnoticed, then perhaps you need to spend less energy on making it perfect—just get it done. Or skip it altogether.

You'll notice we aren't advocating for some new software app that will magically help with task management. What we suggest is to focus on the mental exercise of prioritizing your work. This is a task for you, not technology. Because machine learning will not replace you—the human—who comprehends the order of operations, the economy of time, and the return on investment.

Here we share seven MicroSkills that will help you understand the value of being thoughtful with your task list.

MICROSKILLS TO MANAGE A TASK LIST:

1. Learn what your supervisors expect of you.
2. Determine the priority of a task.
3. Assess the resources needed to complete a task.
4. Set realistic timelines for any task.
5. Adjust due dates accordingly and tell others early.
6. Select tasks to take off your plate.
7. Design meetings to have a clear purpose.

THE MICROSKILL:

1. LEARN WHAT YOUR SUPERVISORS EXPECT OF YOU

WHAT IS THE ACTUAL SKILL?

Understand what tasks your supervisor wants you to focus on.

ADAIRA

I will never forget the seminar I attended on navigating the workplace. The speaker shared a story that taught me an invaluable lesson. He and a colleague were the two graduate students responsible for organizing a weekly workshop. They alternated who was in charge each week. His colleague went above and beyond for tasks, such as creating very designed and stylish invitations, writing a detailed agenda, ordering artisanal food, and making an extra effort to email personal invitations. The speaker shared that, in contrast, he spent much less time on those tasks. He sent a basic group email. The email message had no special formatting or font. He ordered food that was not fancy: pizza, soda, and bottled water. Where he did focus his time was on tasks he knew to be important and valuable to their supervisor: conducting research, giving lectures, and actively growing his own and the department's network. Ultimately, he was recruited for a faculty position over his colleague. He concluded the story by highlighting that his colleague was highly competent, yet she had not identified and focused on their supervisor's priorities. I walked away from that lecture understanding that just because I care about a task doesn't mean my supervisor does.

WHY DO WE NEED THIS SKILL?

The tasks your supervisors find important translate to the tasks they expect of you. By understanding what your leadership wants and expects from you, you are best positioned to move the needle in the workplace. We do not wish to stifle your thirst for creativity and exploration. Of course you can go above and beyond, as time permits, and do personalized work that fulfills you. However, you are hired for a reason and to do a specific job. And at bare minimum, you need to execute it. Additionally, you should know what you should not spend time on. When we work a shift in the emergency department, our supervisors want us to take the best care of patients and prioritize the sicker patients. We are not expected to be giving lectures or running meetings during down time in between patients.

WHY IS THIS SKILL HARD TO ACHIEVE?

- Without a job description, it's hard to know what is expected of you.
- You feel you should inherently know what is expected of you without asking.
- You worry that a request for clarification may not be received well.
- You lack people or network to give you the inside scoop.

WHAT ARE THE CRITICAL ACTIONS FOR THIS MICROSKILL?

READ THE COMPANY WEBSITE: Navigate the website and learn the mission statement, vision, or values of your workplace. This will help you identify the overarching priorities of the organization and its leadership.

OBTAIN YOUR JOB DESCRIPTION: Review the role and responsibilities for which you were hired. If you did not receive a job description, ask for it. If there isn't one, ask if you can draft it and work on it together with your supervisor. This is especially critical if you have that *I don't know what I should be doing* feeling.

SCHEDULE A CHECK-IN: Ask yourself, your supervisor, and the team: "Am I on track?" There is more risk than reward from powering through the work if you are struggling or confused. One time Adaira was preparing a ten-minute lecture on the anatomy of the human eye. She was not sure where to start so she was reading large textbooks and doing a deep dive into comparative animal anatomy. When she checked in with her professor, she got just the focus and re-direction she needed, "Just draw two eyeballs on the white board, and tell people two to three things about how each eye muscle works." Bottomline: clarifying expectations made Adaira's prep work much more manageable and on track.

SOLICIT TARGETED FEEDBACK: Learn to ask questions of the people you trust. You will get better input on the information you seek. Be specific with your questions. And be emotionally prepared for a report of strengths as well as areas for improvement.

	LESS CLEAR	MORE CLEAR	
Before they might just say "Survey looked good."	How does the survey look?	Are the survey questions clear? Did the survey take too long to complete?	*"Yes, the survey will give us valuable information. It took a while to complete. Suggest shaving off five questions."*
Before they might just say "Nice job."	How did I run that meeting?	Was the meeting organized? Were the action items and assignments clear?	*"I did not get an agenda ahead of time; that would have been helpful. I know my assignment, and the to-dos were clear."*

Learn to ask questions of the people you trust. You will get better input on the information you seek. Be specific with your questions and be emotionally prepared for a report of strengths as well as areas for improvement.

THE MICROSKILL:

2. DETERMINE THE PRIORITY OF A TASK

WHAT IS THE ACTUAL SKILL?

Evaluating a task as something to do now, later, or never.

RESA

In the emergency department, there is a priority for when tasks need to get done. The primary focus is to make sure the sick patients get the care they need with little delay. I remember an elderly patient brought in by ambulance after collapsing at home. He was unstable with low blood pressure. Turns out he was having a stomachache for a week. The team wanted to rush him to the CT scanner outside the emergency department, I knew this was not the right next step. It was dangerous for him to leave the trauma room with his blood pressure low. I squeezed ultrasound gel onto his belly, put a probe on his abdomen and looked at the ultrasound screen. I immediately saw something very wrong. His aorta—the large artery that delivers blood from the heart to the internal organs and the legs—was double the normal size. And he grimaced in pain exactly where the ultrasound probe touched over that area. This was a life threatening abdominal aortic aneurysm that was leaking blood. When they are as large as his was they rupture. And almost 100% of patients with this problem die. So I re-prioritized the order of care: first I told the team that the patient was not going to the CT scan. Then I called the surgeon and described the ultrasound and the critically unstable patient. Next I called the operating room coordinator and the anesthesiologist to book an OR. When the surgeon arrived, he asked me to show him the aneurysm and when he saw it on the screen he said "Let's go." The patient went directly to the operating room and walked out of the hospital a few days later. Not all cases are this extreme. Yet, it's clear that the emergency medicine profession taught me about timeliness, prioritizing, and selecting when to push a timeline and when to let it rest.

WHY DO WE NEED THIS SKILL?

You can't always do tasks in the order they appear on your desk. For most of us, that would cause a backlog and missed due dates. To stay on top of tasks, you must determine their priority. Prioritizing tasks is a skill which may decrease overwhelm and burnout. The goal is theoretically simple: identify the tasks that need to be done now, later, or never. Priorities are informed by supervisors, timelines, customers or clients, the time a task takes, the amount of time you have available, etc. So, it's probably best to say the actual act of prioritizing tasks is practically complex. This is why no single chart, pyramid, or two-by-two matrix can capture the rationale required to declare the priority of a task. This is not a plug-and-play exercise—which is why is it so hard for you. You need to develop a mindset that makes you stop and deeply explore the various reasons a task would be important to complete now, or not.

WHY IS THIS SKILL HARD TO ACHIEVE?

- A panel of tasks can be overwhelming. Especially if you have competing teams and supervisors vying for their priorities.
- You were not taught a logical way of thinking about the tasks on your plate.

- You don't believe that you need a strategy.
- Distractions and lack of interest veer you off track.

WHAT ARE THE CRITICAL ACTIONS OF THIS MICROSKILL?

WRITE A TASK LIST: A list can be hardcopy or digital—don't try to commit it to memory. We know there is a bit of variety in how people write their lists. Some do a general list of tasks ("apply for promotion"), others a detailed list of tasks ("update resume, ask for 2 letters of recommendation, finish personal statement, submit promotion packet"). The length and detail of the list should be adjusted to how much support and guidance you need to complete any task.

GENERAL LIST	DETAILED LIST
Give presentation 3/12	Pick topic for presentation
	Draft outline
	Create skeleton slides
	Show content to supervisor and edit
	Finalize slides and polish
	Practice presentation to colleagues and friends
	Give presentation 3/12

Write a task list, either digitally or on pen and paper. Adjust the amount of detail to your taste. The more you break down the task into smaller fragments, the better you are able to track your progress.

ATTEMPT TO ORDER THE LIST: After you have your list jotted down, double check the order of operations—which tasks will go now, later, and maybe never. Ask yourself questions to get to a list that feels strategic.

WAYS TO DETERMINE ORDER	QUESTIONS TO CONSIDER
By priority	Have any of these been communicated as higher priority?
By date	Do any of these projects have a due date that is approaching?
By motivation	Which tasks are you motivated to complete?
By team members	Who is affected if I accelerate or defer this project?
By impact	Which tasks will help build my credibility, expertise, and network as a professional?
By importance	Can any of these be taken off my plate completely?
By bandwidth	When will I have the time on my calendar to invest in this task?

UPDATE AND REORDER WORK: In the emergency department, new patients come and go at different rates. Tasks shift up and down a list all the time on any shift. You can similarly triage and reorder your task list, especially as new information arrives about any existing item on your task list. The less critical project can be moved down by the mandatory, emergent task that just arrived on your desk.

SEEK GUIDANCE: Seek feedback with the team, such as your supervisor, on how you prioritize tasks. Ask *why* when you are given advice. "Why do you think I should focus on this task now?" The why is so key because you need to understand the thought process behind a decision, not just the answer.

THE MICROSKILL:

3. ASSESS THE RESOURCES NEEDED TO COMPLETE A TASK.

WHAT IS THE ACTUAL SKILL?

Determine what it will take to make a task feasible.

ADAIRA

Years ago, I cocreated a podcast. We *pitched it to NPR*. (Yes, those were our exact words.) However, I had no experience recording podcasts. That being said, we went full in: bought equipment, assembled speakers, watched YouTube videos. The recordings featured emergency-medicine doctors who spoke openly about traumatic and powerful content: gun violence, racism, and dying by suicide. The conversations themselves were beautiful and heartfelt. My job was to edit the audio. But I didn't realize early enough the steps for producing good audio quality. I didn't understand the amount of time it took to edit a podcast. I didn't understand how pitching or selling a podcast worked. I had no understanding that I needed to assess up front if the project was even feasible. It would have been a different project and outcome if we had assessed necessary people and resources, including an audio expert. Needless to say, NPR never responded to our emails.

WHY IS THIS SKILL NEEDED?

Brainstorming fosters creativity and innovation while exploring a question or idea.[48] Yes, we love creating and approaching questions or problems with colorful Post-its. But generating ideas may be the easier steps. Projects often fail if you have not worked through the obstacles. Projects are feasible when pitfalls are anticipated and remedies are iterated expeditiously. We want you to have ambitious goals, but we also want you to understand the value of assessing a task's feasibility early on.

WHY IS THIS SKILL HARD TO ACHIEVE?

- Pausing and reflecting about the reality of a project takes time, and can feel discouraging as obstacles are identified.
- Identifying weak spots or shortcomings is humbling and makes you defensive. It can be easier to ignore finding obstacles.
- You may miss obstacles by focusing too heavily on potential success.
- You may not know enough to realize the resources and skills you need.

WHAT ARE THE CRITICAL ACTIONS OF THIS MICROSKILL?

ADJUST THE SCALE OF A PROJECT: At some point it is important to assess the feasibility of the project—and feasibility is often based on the scale of the project. Scale down if your resources are tight: if you have limited skills, if you lack admin support, if you have limited time, if your budget is small. Scale up if you have both the resources and motivation to do so. Remember, a bigger project means bigger stress and time commitment. Request more resources, if needed. Sometimes the size of the team can make a task overwhelming. When appropriate kindly scale down the team, which can help with efficiency.

SMALL SCALE PROJECT	BIG SCALE PROJECT
I want to start a fundraiser to raise $5,000 to donate socks and shoes to a local shelter for the upcoming holiday.	I want to start a nonprofit and raise $500,000 to continuously donate socks and shoes to a local shelter on a regular basis.

CREATE A LIST OF NEEDS: Spend time thinking about every possible need you have for a project. You want a comprehensive and accurate list. Run the list past people who have done similar work or might benefit or use the project or product you are working on. Ask them if there are holes you have yet to discover.

COMPARE NEEDS TO RESOURCES: Spend time thinking about what time you actually have available. Compare this to your list of needs. If you estimated ten hours of protected time to complete the task, but you only have two available, that is a problem. If your budget is $15,000 but your supervisor can only give you $2,000, this can be a major roadblock. We do not aim to discourage you, we just want you preemptively informed.

WELCOME FAILING FAST: Some ideas are truly great as an idea but fizzle when carried out. This could be due to a range of reasons—lack of resources, needs, interest, or skills—so the work stalls. Don't let ineffective projects carry on for too long. Speak with the team. Get their input and share your concerns. "I'm afraid this project isn't going at the speed we initially predicted."

THE MICROSKILL:

4. SET REALISTIC TIMELINES FOR ANY TASK

WHAT IS THE ACTUAL SKILL?

Plan a series of steps that will help you complete an individual task.

ADAIRA

I gave a national lecture for a women's leadership course led by Dr. Julie Silver at Harvard Medical School. The lecture was on writing op-eds and perspective articles for the lay press. She invited me about one year ahead of the conference. The planning was very organized. In our first meeting, we discussed the high-level concept of the talk. Then I sent her an outline, and we edited it and went back and forth on the structure. Next, I prepared skeleton slides and submitted them. After that step and review, we designed the slides. Then it was time to practice. The timeline and steps to this process were clearly communicated. I knew about it all in advance with adequate time to prepare for each step. This is one of my most successful examples of how an effective timeline looks.

WHY DO WE NEED THIS SKILL?

Okay, we admit it, we like structure. Or at least, we are accustomed to it. To push through college, medical school, residency, and fellowship takes respecting structured timelines. Whether you realize it or not, a timeline—especially with group work—allows everyone to organize and know the expectations. And we want to be clear about word choice: a timeline is a chronological set of events with a clear start and clear end. It should help you and your team be more efficient and keep everyone on task.[49] A due date is the end date and time for a project or activity.

One word of caution: studies show that when we have a task to complete, we focus on how much time we have available, rather than how much time is necessary. This is called Parkinson's Law: work will expand to fill the time we have available to complete the task.[50] This is why when you have a simple task to do, such as sending an email in the next hour, you can spend the full hour drafting and editing before you press send. Whereas if you gave yourself 15 minutes, per Parkinson's Law, you'd tighten your timeline to a smaller window based on how much time you actually need. Why is this important? Because it's easy to procrastinate, dwell, stall—and when it comes to staying on track with a timeline you should be aware of how easy it is to give yourself too much time to finish a task.

It is important to have a map of what might be next and when are you hoping to have it completed. This keeps the project on track and allows everyone to trail the progress.

WHY IS THIS SKILL HARD TO ACHIEVE?

- You need to estimate your time on a task and how many steps it will take to get to the finish line.
- Lists and structure can feel restrictive.
- Organization requires more upfront work and energy compared to pushing forward without a plan.

WHAT ARE THE CRITICAL ACTIONS FOR THIS MICROSKILL?

HAVE A GLOBAL DUE DATE: This is when overall work is due. And it should be clear. It may be set by you or someone else. If you do not know a due date, ask the supervisor or decision maker for the project, "When is this due?"

ESTIMATE TIME ON A TASK: The first attempt you make to estimate time on a task may be the hardest. You may prefer to work through it with someone who has done it before. If that is not an option, do your best. Put anything down. If you have completed similar work, then look back to see how accurate your estimates were before. Adjust up or down or keep the determination, depending on how accurate you were.

LESS GRANULAR TIMELINE	MORE GRANULAR TIMELINE
Email the project budget by the end of the week.	**Monday:** Draft a list of items and the cost estimates. Email a draft to teammates. Request input by Wednesday. **Tuesday:** Confirm a cost basis for each product/service. **Wednesday:** Review the input of teammates and integrate their feedback. **Thursday:** Email the near final budget.

A larger goal is broken down into smaller pieces. Each task is assigned to a specific day. The sequential days keep momentum.

Creating a task list can help determine pain points, potential obstacles, and the timeline.

SCHEDULE YOUR TIMELINE: Create a reminder on the calendar for yourself and the team. This creates a paper trail everyone can follow. For example, when writing this book, we put weekly meetings on the calendar and objectives in the meeting description. This declaration of "what is next?" helped us meet larger requirements to ultimately complete this book. Without that direction we would have been disorganized and would have missed goals.

CHECK IN WITH THE TEAM: If you are leading a team, send group reminders and individual check-ins. Don't publicly embarrass people who are not meeting their goals. Instead privately, explore the holdups and help troubleshoot. Keep it easy, and use a template so you don't have to rewrite an email each time. Even if you are not leading the team, consider asking others for updates on their status.

FROM:	
TO:	
CC:	
BCC:	
SUBJECT:	
MESSAGE:	Hello Team, This is a check-in with your progress on _____. During our last meeting on _____, we decided the next milestone for you was to finish up _____. Can you please let me know your progress by the end of business day. Thanks, Adaira

The goal of an email check-in is to assess how others are handling their workload. The goal is not to embarrass or punish others. Falling behind is common, which is why you want to discover when it is occurring early.

If you are not leading a team and still want to update others on your status, you can still send out an update.

FROM:

TO:

CC:

BCC:

SUBJECT:

MESSAGE:

Hello Team,

I finished my assignment for the project. All of the speakers confirmed participation, and they signed and emailed their conflict-of-interest forms to the administrator in the office.

Thanks,
Resa

Send the team updates in a way that is objective.
Be sure not to boast about the speed of completing work.

THE MICROSKILL:

5. ADJUST DUE DATES ACCORDINGLY AND TELL OTHERS EARLY

WHAT IS THE ACTUAL SKILL?

Be honest with yourself regarding how much time you have available for more tasks.

RESA

As a self-described rule follower, it's not a stretch to say that I always try to meet due dates. And we have plenty of them to meet along the way to becoming a physician, e.g. exams and application forms to fill out. These all have a firm date by which they need to be completed. These kinds of dates are absolute and essentially unmovable. However, there are other dates, which are moveable—ones where it's okay to request a change or extension. The due date for a job offer is one of those moveable dates. In my experience applying for jobs, the offer email or letter always has a "respond by" date. Typically the offer states the position and conditions of the offer, and the benefits of the position. At the end, there is always a "Please let us know within one week" or other designated time period. The stress this caused was real. Because often, I was juggling a few interviews and even a few offers. In speaking with experienced professionals, I learned that you can ask for more time. When I first made the ask, it felt risky and uncomfortable. "I won't be able to make a decision by the time requested. Might I respond in 3 weeks when I will have completed all of my interviews?" I wondered if they would withdraw the offer. Then I realized that if I asked for more time and they said no, then at least I would never regret not asking. Bottom line: I knew I needed more time and I asked for it.

WHY IS THIS SKILL NEEDED?

When it comes to the calendar its easy to be ambitious: pack it with work, meetings, etc. The risk? Life happens and we are all at risk of falling behind. Nobody wants to miss a due date. Yet, it occurs frequently. One study showed 76% of founders miss the deadline for product features.[51] We suspect this isn't because everyone is on extended vacation. It is more reasonable to assume that the initial timeline wasn't realistic for the work or the team (specifically the individuals carrying out the tasks). Even in supportive and compassionate environments, delays can be a nuisance and cause conflict with the team, customers, and supervisor.

WHY IS THIS SKILL HARD TO ACHIEVE?

- It's hard to predict how much time it's going to take to complete a task.
- It takes discipline to stop and audit your calendar for conflicts.
- Collaborating with a team adds complexity meeting the date.

WHAT ARE THE CRITICAL ACTIONS OF THIS MICROSKILL?

REFLECT ON YOUR OWN RELATIONSHIP TO TIME MANAGEMENT: Do you often miss due dates? Do you find yourself worried about getting work in on time? Do you find yourself finishing up work last minute? We have all been there. Here are four reasons why you might struggle with time management:

REASON FOR MISSED DUE DATES	SOLUTIONS
Too much on your plate	Avoid saying yes impulsively—give yourself at least one to two days to think over an opportunity. Identify tasks you can dismiss, defer, or delegate.

You procrastinate	Instead of constant all-nighters you may chip away at a project in small bits intermittently. The more you pace yourself and start early, the faster you are able to explore bottlenecks.
Accepting tasks that are outside your skill set	Challenge yourself with learning new skills. Remember, when working out of your comfort zone and learning new skills, you should budget extra time to get to completion.
The due date is not reasonable	State upfront to others your competing demands. Ask if there is flexibility. Break a big task down into smaller tasks and ask if a part can be delivered now and a part later. Ask if you can have support (such as admin or funding) to help you make the due date more realistic.

REVIEW YOUR CALENDAR: Pause before you confirm a due date. Take a look at your schedule and literally assess in detail, hour by hour or day by day, your open time slots. Avoid the double- or triple-book. Instead, look for chunks of open time where you will be able to focus and do meaningful work.

COMMUNICATE UP FRONT: If your supervisor says, "I need you to file the report by end of day," that might be difficult if you have a packed calendar. This is a great opportunity to let the person know as soon as possible. "Unfortunately, I'm fully booked. Is the timeline flexible?" Yes, all due dates should be respected, but many are not rigid and can be changed.

PROTECT YOUR HEALTH: In many cases, you are not being paid to do work outside of business hours. Working during the hours of sleep or meals is not optimal. We understand that not all workplace cultures adhere to standard hours. Emergencies occur and exceptions must sometimes be made. But over the long haul, avoid exploiting your health to meet a due date.

DELEGATE: If you are not going to meet a due date, divide work into pieces and ask for help. This can feel difficult. Believe us, we get it. But vulnerability is a strength—and it is often strategic to ask for and accept help.

THE MICROSKILL:

6. SELECT TASKS TO TAKE OFF YOUR PLATE

WHAT IS THE ACTUAL SKILL?

Recognize that not all tasks are worth your time and energy.

RESA

Quitting things used to be hard for me. Early in my professional career, I had never thought about quitting anything. Older physician faculty advised, "Say yes to everything." So I did. My plate was overfilled with writing projects, speaking gigs, emergency department shifts, meetings all days of the week, and international travel for medical education workshops. My focus was broad and I felt like I should always be working. As I approached midcareer, people advised me, "Say *no* except to projects and tasks that really speak to you or further your goals." Initially it felt uncomfortable and then it became habit forming. Quitting things and keeping fewer items on my to-do list allowed more deliberate rest, focus, and a deeper dive into developing expertise. This also allowed more creativity and joy in my work. And out of this came a podcast, papers published in non-medical outlets, and this book!

WHY IS THIS SKILL NEEDED?

To be clear, this MicroSkill is talking about quitting projects —large or small, titles, or positions you neither desire nor need. You volunteer to run late night socials but now you cannot? Quit. You hold a position that you dread? Quit. Quitting responsibilities that you no longer desire takes loads of work off your plate and gives you space to reflect on what is important to you and time for self-care.[52] It can also get you away from the team or the work that is not supportive, productive or aligned in interests. This also allows opportunities to open for other people.

WHY IS THIS SKILL HARD TO ACHIEVE?

- FOMO and no longer being tapped for opportunities.
- A sense of failure or letting yourself and others down.
- You worry the task you relinquish might be your big break.
- For financial or other reasons, you cannot quit.
- You fear losing your job or value in the workplace.

WHAT ARE THE CRITICAL ACTIONS OF THIS MICROSKILL?

WEIGH THE RISKS/BENEFITS OF DOING THE WORK: Before you quit a project or obligation, no matter how big or how small, think of the effects of this decision. How will this free time now help you? How will the lack of this experience hurt you? Will you be able to grow more and faster without a title or responsibility? Will you be seen as unreliable or uncommitted? Try to be as objective as you can so that you do not hurt yourself or your career. You need to be strategic about what you take off your plate. You likely cannot quit everything and still keep your job.

SPEAK WITH OTHERS ABOUT THE POSITIVES AND NEGATIVES: Go to your personal board of directors. Ask, "I am thinking about this responsibility that I have on my plate, and I'm unsure if I should remain or if I should drop it. Can I get your input?"

RECOGNIZE IF GUILT IS KEEPING YOU THERE: We do not recommend you stay on a job or role for an extended period out of guilt—guilt that quitting may hurt the team or the work. Remember what we said earlier, your industry company job will never love you back. The people may care about you. And you may care about them. But that "care for each other" is not enough reason to stay in a position if you are unhappy.

REDUCE YOUR FEAR OF MISSING OUT: FOMO, the fear of missing out. We want you to beware of how FOMO can knock you off balance. Know that this comes from a scarcity mentality rather than abundance. The truth is that there will always be more work and more projects and opportunities. Trust yourself and your decision to take items off your plate.

CELEBRATE THE JOY OF MISSING OUT: JOMO, the joy of missing out. Allow yourself to be happy to not be involved. To not have your name mentioned, to get less emails, to not be part of debates and controversy. You will be more focused and deliberate and intentional. As you take things off your plate, recognize your JOMO.[53]

CONTROL THE NARRATIVE: When quitting something, think carefully about the messaging. Find a good time to exit that feels authentic and not unfair to others—and quit. Don't blindside the people in charge; let them know privately that you have made a decision you'd like to discuss. As necessary, hold one-on-one conversations to alert key stakeholders before sharing anything by email to larger groups. This is not an exercise to burn bridges—be strategic and compassionate. Make the "why" clear (e.g. you are stepping down from a position to focus your attention on ….).

THE MICROSKILL:

7. DESIGN MEETINGS TO HAVE A CLEAR PURPOSE

WHAT IS THE ACTUAL SKILL?

Recognize when a meeting lacks purpose—attempt to make it useful or know when to cancel.

RESA

At one of my jobs, the supervisor asked for recurring monthly meetings. She offered to provide me with professional development and mentorship. The meeting was always unstructured without an agenda and after the meeting I did not walk away with any action items or solutions to my questions. She spent a lot of time gossiping. Over time, I saw little change and the conversations were repetitive. The one hour felt like a heavy time investment for little return. Initially, it felt tricky to opt out of a requested meeting with a supervisor. Over time though, I stopped scheduling them altogether. I tried to really turn this into a learning experience. My top three lessons: 1. When I have a regularly scheduled meeting, I try to be sure the agenda is clear. 2. I try to keep the discussion to the topic at hand, to leave with action items for everyone, and to match the length of the meeting time to meet its goals and objectives. 3. I remind myself of power dynamics in the workplace and keep the conversations away from office gossip.

WHY IS THIS SKILL NEEDED?

No matter your career stage, you will eventually be responsible for leading a meeting. And we want you to lead effectively.[54] So often, mentees and peers tell us they have no clue what's going on with a project. Or they aren't sure what they should be doing. When we probe deeper, we discover the core deficit: meetings with the team are not very helpful or productive. The goal of leading a meeting is straightforward—after a safe and productive discussion, attendees should leave with clear action items. But this goal can fall short if the meeting is not organized and supportive.

WHY IS THIS SKILL HARD TO ACHIEVE?

- No one has taught you or demonstrated how to run a productive meeting.
- You don't know the benefit of an agenda and clear task assignments.
- You do not feel empowered to speak up and control a crowd (i.e. too many tangents, unable to assign tasks, inability to control the room, meeting lacks focus).
- You do not know how to be decisive and move a meeting forward.

WHAT ARE THE CRITICAL ACTIONS OF THIS SKILL?

WRITE AN AGENDA: This need not be overly detailed, but having a list of topics to be addressed clarifies the meeting purpose. If shared early to a wider group, it also informs people of their relative need to attend, as well as what they should prepare. Ideally, you send it out ahead of time—or just include it on the calendar invite.

ASSIGN A NOTETAKER: If a meeting is more than a one on one, then ideally someone will take notes. Generally speaking, the meeting leader should not be the note taker. If there is not an administrative assistant designated for this role, then an attendee should be the designated notetaker. This office housework should not fall disproportionately to women; this can especially happen if volunteers are solicited. One study found that women were 48% more likely to volunteer for tasks that don't lead to promotion.[55] Also in the time of virtual meetings, be sure to ask if the meeting can be recorded and then the audio can be transcribed using commerical software.

REVIEW NEXT STEPS: Meetings should end with clarifying and reviewing next steps. This includes assignments and timelines. We want to normalize clarifying your own task list, "My understanding is that you want me to [insert expected duties]. And the timeline is [insert unit of time]."

CALENDAR THE NEXT MEETING: It is worth the extra effort to clarify who is needed in the following meeting. If feasible take a few moments to set up time to schedule the next meeting. This will avoid scheduling via email later. Say up front, "Let's take a moment to schedule our next meeting." Keep that attendee list as short as possible. Or task someone with the responsibility to set up the meeting later.

SEND A SUMMARY EMAIL: Write a brief email that summarizes the meeting. Or be sure to read the summary notes email that you receive. This is for clear communication, an update for those who could not attend, record keeping accountability, and keeping the to-do list on everyone's radar.

INVITE WAYS TO IMPROVE MEETINGS: If you are the meeting leader, welcome suggestions to improve meetings. Break the ice by offering the first suggestion, "I had a few ideas to get the group more engaged during a meeting." Or, "I think these meetings could be more productive and efficient. Let's keep them to 45 minutes rather than 60 and give 15 minutes of the day back to everyone."

CONCLUSION:

Order and complete tasks by priority. Review and re-order as needed.	Be kind to yourself and others with tasks. Keep FOMO in check. Embrace JOMO.	Understand the return on investment for any task.

SUPPLEMENTAL RESOURCES:

Time Management

Do Checklists Make People Stupid?

Tame the To-Do List

3

MICROSKILLS FOR POLISHED COMMUNICATION

ADAIRA

A few years ago a colleague, Dr. Tracy Sanson, gave a virtual lecture I will never forget. She discussed safe ways to care for patients who were agitated to the point of being a danger to themselves or other people in the emergency department. When the talk began her presentation froze on the introduction slide. While we struggled with the technology, Dr. Sanson started speaking. She did not let the frozen slides interrupt the lecture. She seamlessly told stories, integrated effective body language communication, paused, changed her intonation, and varied her word choice. The audience remained completely engaged with her content. None of us needed the slides to understand the message she was making. After watching her speak, I told myself, "Wow, now I know what they mean when they say 'a polished speaker can give a talk without slides.'"

What makes someone a polished communicator? The ability to deliver an engaging and effective message in a way that allows the audience to extract critical information. Good communication is intentional and compassionate. It demonstrates mindfulness of words, physical expression, timing, cultural competence, and more. Good communication is not just about being charming or funny or about avoiding "um" and "like" and "you know." Polished conversation can positively affect the workplace culture: it can lessen conflict and improve the morale and relationships on the team.[56]

Poor communication, on the other hand, creates work. Damage control may be needed to clarify, debrief, apologize, or remind. Ultimately, this distracts from the goal of working well together. It can also lead to conflict and confusion. In fact, we've seen the drama play out as emergency physicians on shift. While our day-to-day life isn't like the television shows *Scrubs*, *ER*, and *Grey's Anatomy*, we do juggle interacting with many personalities and communication styles in high-stakes and stressful environments. Strained communication makes our jobs more challenging.

Why put energy into being a polished communicator? Because success is not just about filling a role or assuming responsibility. Much of success is wrapped around understanding the power of words: volume, timing, intonation, and context, for instance. Importantly, communication calls upon us to intently listen and observe—the physical actions and emotional responses of others. It's about being self-aware of the power of body language. Though debated, experts state that communication is up to 90% nonverbal.[57]

OVER TEXT:

(Person 1) How are you?

(Person 2) I'm fine.

IN PERSON:

(Person 1) How are you?

(Person 2) I'm fine.

Understanding body language is crucial.
Information can be lost if we just rely on words alone

While the exact percentage doesn't matter, please do not underestimate the role facial expressions, hand gestures, body position and posture, and other bodily movements play.

So why aren't we all better communicators? Outside of an egregious communication error, we don't often receive deliberate feedback—someone to sit us down and tell us how to communicate better. We're somehow supposed to know how, and we end up taking a lot of our cues from other people. But if those people aren't skilled either?

Luckily, we are here to share ten MicroSkills to improve your communication.

MICROSKILLS FOR POLISHED COMMUNICATION:

1. Understand your body language, and read that of others.
2. Recognize language barriers and communication disabilities.
3. Cut to the chase; do not bury the point.
4. Use storytelling strategically.
5. Speak less, listen more, and share the stage.
6. Leverage asynchronous messaging.
7. Write emails that people will actually read.
8. Learn and use email tools: the CC, BCC, and Reply All.
9. Use caution when communicating negative emotions.
10. Schedule and send emails during working hours.

THE MICROSKILL:

1. UNDERSTAND YOUR BODY LANGUAGE, AND READ THAT OF OTHERS

WHAT IS THE ACTUAL SKILL?

Recognize how body language affects the meaning of a message.

ADAIRA

In the emergency department, patients are usually unhappy for good reason: long wait times, pain, nausea, fear, and anxiety. One time, a patient had been in the waiting room for five hours. Finally they got a room inside the emergency department. As I entered the patient's room, they sighed, rolled their eyes, avoided eye contact, and gave curt one-word answers. All of those cues were red flags to me. They were angry. Time for damage control. I sat down, unfolded my arms, and intentionally looked them in the eyes and made my body language read *I get your frustration.* I apologized and explained that I was with a very sick patient. We can never really go into details about what were were doing before entering the room. In this situation, I couldn't talk about the other patient, who was bleeding into their brain and needed multiple medications, imaging and emergent consultation with neurosurgeons to prevent the brain from swelling in the skull. Yet, I wanted to get across an overarching point that this patient equally mattered to me. I learned early on that the ability to read the patient's body language and adjust mine accordingly can really help avoid confrontation—which in the long run makes my job easier and less stressful. Often the simple act of sitting down next to the person and being eye to eye can really change the energy of the conversation without saying a word.

WHY DO WE NEED THIS SKILL?

Emotionally intelligent people commonly have a command of their own body language and can read that of other people. This is not true of everyone. People with certain developmental syndromes and disorders, such as Aspergers and Autism, may find challenges with socializing, such as interpreting body language. According to Daniel Goleman, emotional intelligence (EI) is based on four domains: self-awareness, self-management, social awareness, and relationship management.[58] EI can be simplified by respecting that the recognition of behavioral patterns—of the self and the team—can make us better communicators. Folding arms, turning your back to someone, nodding hello, raising eyebrows and smiling are not just movements, they are forms of communication.

WHAT IS HARD ABOUT THIS SKILL?

- Reading body language requires attention to subtleties that are integrated into a whole interaction.
- Cultural differences can make it hard to confirm if you are misinterpreting someone else's body language.
- Communication via text, phone calls, or video conferencing removes or alters body language as a clue to help you interpret words.

WHAT ARE THE CRITICAL ACTIONS FOR THIS SKILL?

PAY ATTENTION TO YOUR BODY: Do your arms, back, legs, hands, fingers, and neck feel relaxed, or stiff because you are stressed? Are you sitting straight up in a chair because you are engaged in the moment, interested, or attentive? Look in the mirror. Get to know how you stand, use or avoid eye contact, your facial expressions, posture and hand gestures. If you get recurrent feedback about your body language (e.g. if you often hear, "Are you okay? You look upset?") invest the time in becoming more self-aware. Work on reading how you are feeling and how that translates into your body language.

GET FEEDBACK FROM PEOPLE: Ask your personal board of directors, "Have you noticed anything about my body language when you are with me?" or "Have you found it hard to tell when I am happy, sad, upset, or stressed?" Get specific feedback. You want the details.

DO YOUR EYEBROWS FURROW WHEN YOU ARE CASUALLY THINKING, BUT IN A WAY THAT MAKES YOU SEEM UPSET?

DO YOU CROSS YOUR ARMS FIRMLY OR TAP YOUR FEET, WHICH MIGHT MAKE YOU APPEAR IMPATIENT?

DO YOU ROLL YOUR EYES IN AN OBVIOUS MANNER SO PEOPLE CAN TELL YOU ARE ANNOYED OR DISAGREE? DO YOU SIGH LOUDLY WHEN YOU'RE UPSET OR DISAPPOINTED?

DO YOU DROP YOUR JAW OR RAISE YOUR EYES WHEN YOU ARE SURPRISED?

DO YOU WALK AWAY FROM PEOPLE MID-CONVERSATION?

DO YOU POINT YOUR FINGER AT OTHERS WHEN YOU ARE UPSET?

DO YOU THROW YOUR ARMS UP WHEN YOU ARE FRUSTRATED?

DO YOU SLOUCH WHEN YOU ARE SAD OR FEELING UNDERAPPRECIATED?

Get specific feedback from your personal board of directors about your body language.

OBSERVE OTHERS: Pay particular attention to body movements of others. Watch people, e.g. at a coffee shop, on the subway, at the beach, on TV. Hold conversations with friends and family, and ask them if you are reading how they are feeling at specific moments. For example, "You seem stressed. Am I reading you right?" is enough to start gauging how others are feeling related to how they are moving and positioning their body.

CONNECT WITH YOUR BODY: You can learn your body language. Movement of your physical body can help you connect your body's outward expression, postures, and stance with your inner feelings. Get to know your body through activities such as stretching, sports including martial arts, yoga, meditation and other forms of body work. Getting to know and read the self will better position you to read the team.

THE MICROSKILL:

2. RECOGNIZE LANGUAGE BARRIERS AND COMMUNICATION DISABILITIES

WHAT IS THE ACTUAL SKILL?

Recognize that others might need assistance to communicate.

ADAIRA

Working in the emergency department means we are moving quickly. Efficiency becomes a challenge when patients and the hospital team speak different languages. Occasionally providers who are slightly familiar with a language, (e.g. Spanish) will attempt to communicate with patients who primarily speak Spanish. This is done to save time and the reality is: this is never a good idea. It's tempting though: there are so many patients so and we need to move, move, move. I recently had a patient who came in with dizziness. Dizziness is a very challenging symptom because the word "dizzy" means different things to different people. Therefore, a thorough history is important. A medical student interviewed the patient without using an interpreter. The student was familiar with Spanish, but not fluent.

He told me what was going on with the patient but there were many gaps. "When did it start? How long has it lasted?" The student had asked but wasn't sure of what the patient said back. So, I asked our in-person interpreter to join—I have learned many lessons from my past mistakes—and we obtained a much more thorough and nuanced history. Ultimately we diagnosed the patient with a stroke.

WHY DO WE NEED THIS SKILL?

We need to be able to understand each other. And sometimes we are able to use our native or acquired language and communicate directly with another person. However, we all have different abilities, and sometimes one party may need accommodations to best allow them to communicate. It is important that we do not try to push through any struggle and instead take the time to allow others to use their best vehicle for communication. It might be spoken words, a pen and a pad, or sign language.

WHY IS THIS SKILL HARD?

- It is awkward or uncomfortable to ask someone if they can understand you or about their abilities or disabilities.
- You don't know that resources, such as language interpreters, are available.
- You are unknowingly or intentionally insensitive to people with disabilities, or whose language is not your own.

- You have to restrain your frustration if someone is taking more time to communicate, e.g. someone who stutters.

WHAT ARE THE CRITICAL ACTIONS FOR THIS MICROSKILL?

AVOID ASSUMING EVERYONE IS FULLY ABLE-BODIED: Don't work from an assumption that everyone has the same abilities you have. Have a curious, open, and inclusive approach to communication, and know that a disability may not be immediately obvious. We often ask our patients (at the bedside) or the team (e.g. on Zoom), "Let me know if you are having a hard time understanding me."

ERR ON THE SIDE OF BEING SUPPORTIVE AND INCLUSIVE: People with disabilities can tell you what works for them. Ask what term(s) and/or communication mediums they would like you to use. For instance, there are video conferencing options that you can explore, e.g. Zoom has captions available to subscribers. Or, you may offer to discuss via email instead of voice call to people with hearing disabilities. You can adapt the slide color design (avoid red on green slides or yellow on white slides) if people are color blind.

BE PATIENT: Try to stop the impulse to speed people up. People with learning or physical disabilities or language barriers might need extra time to process and express their thoughts, concerns, or questions. No matter the location—in the office, with a study group, or at a conference—give others the time and space to communicate at their own pace.

LOCATE RESOURCES: In some emergency departments there are tablets with software that allows us interpretation services in essentially all languages, and video for sign language interpretation. Ask the team what services and resources are available to help support others. Remember the phrase, "There is probably an app for that." Many apps exist to help with communication.

THE MICROSKILL:

3. CUT TO THE CHASE. DO NOT BURY THE POINT.

WHAT IS THE ACTUAL SKILL?

State your point clearly and up front. Do not hide it within a message.

RESA

I remember the first time I had a patient who came to the hospital with "dead gut," also called ischemic bowel. This emergent condition happens when the patient's blood supply to the intestine is cut off. Patients are very sick and often die. At the time, I was a medical student. Up to that point, I had not witnessed a patient in such a horrible amount of pain: he was actually pleading "Take me to the OR (operating room). Take me to the OR." Oddly, he had no medical background or experience with the OR. Years later, I was working in the emergency department and a patient came in with similarly horrible abdominal pain. He was vomiting nonstop and thought it was food poisoning. He could not stay still on the bed due to pain and no amount of pain medicine helped him. I flashed back to medical school. I knew that a direct call to the general surgeon was in order. I did not waver. There was no small talk. "I am worried the patient has ischemic bowel and he needs to go to OR." The surgeon cancelled his clinic, took the patient to the OR, the diagnosis was correct, and the patient lived. When we call specialty doctors to consult on a patient in the emergency department, we really need to be focused. It could be that emergency doctors have an unfair advantage in learning how to get to the point and not bury the lede. This is crucial to our effectiveness as communicators. And it is definitely a learned skill.

WHY DO WE NEED THIS SKILL?

Burying the point occurs when we pad our primary message and use circuitous or ambiguous language to soften the impact. Or we go on and on without realizing we lack clarity and focus. The message is then unclear or hidden so deeply that it's hard to find. This behavior, deliberate or not, confuses the audience. Listeners might draw their own conclusions, ignore the comment altogether, probe further, or even look to other sources for their expertise. That form of miscommunication can lead to error or mistrust. Regardless of tone, mistrust develops when we dance around an issue. We wonder if there is something they are not telling us. We like the commonly used phrase "Clear is kind, unclear is unkind."[59] By the way, delivering a point directly doesn't require confrontation or aggression or a raised voice. Clarity still deserves respectful and polite language.

WHY IS THIS SKILL HARD TO ACHIEVE?

- Your point is underdeveloped, as you haven't enough time or expertise to solidify it.

- You know your point but do not feel comfortable and empowered to share aloud.
- You lack the emotional intelligence or cultural understanding to share with sensitivity.
- Speaking directly makes you worried about reception of information and your reputation.

WHAT ARE THE CRITICAL ACTIONS FOR THIS MICROSKILL?

KNOW THE AUDIENCE: Think before you speak. Who is in the room, on the email thread, or the text chain? Are they a high-positioned stakeholder, a customer, or a peer? Do you trust them if what you are sharing is confidential? Can you give an informal initial impression, or does your audience require a formal, and finalized response?

DECIDE YOUR POINT: Before starting to communicate, decide on your stance and how to convey that clearly. Ask yourself, "What message am I trying to deliver right now?" It's best to ask yourself this before you engage. Even when you are "speaking from the heart" you can still pause a moment to gather your thoughts. That pause is a nice place to prepare your words—versus thinking midsentence and fumbling.

TAKE YOUR TIME: Before speaking or firing off that email—pause, do not pass go. The angry 3 am email that is five paragraphs long explaining your side of the story is never a good look. Allow yourself to become informed: ask questions, assess all sides, and then take a position. Impulsivity has many downsides such as convoluted messages, overly long emails, coming across as abrasive, being incorrect and uninformed, etc. So if your response is not time sensitive, err on the side of preparing your thoughts.

START BY DELIVERING THE POINT: Yes, you can start any communication with "Hello," "Thank you," and "How are you?" You can even briefly summarize your understanding of the situation. Then you can get to the point. Be clear, in a respectful way.

LESS CLEAR	MORE CLEAR	
Can we meet to discuss something?	I'd like to schedule a meeting for next week. I am hoping we can discuss my salary and the number of shifts I am working per month.	— *Try to give people a heads up on meetings so that they understand the purpose ahead of time.*
I think I understand what you are saying but I'm struggling a bit with some things.	I follow the first point in your email. However, points two and three are confusing. Can you clarify as I don't follow the argument.	— *Let people know the specific issues that need clarification.*
I'm not so sure we should do that.	Your idea and plan for rollout doesn't seem feasible due to our restricted budget. Let's meet and brainstorm options to iron out the obstacles I see.	— *Express your concerns directly.*

SUPPORT YOUR ASSERTION WITH EVIDENCE: You don't need to brag. You don't need to get defensive; however, you can take a moment to explain your rationale. Put forth your expertise in a kind manner: share your logic and reasoning.

LESS CLEAR	MORE CLEAR
Can we meet to discuss something?	My recent patient reviews and 360 evaluation were positive and I exceeded the department metrics. Can we discuss my salary and if there is room to increase?
I think I understand what you are saying but I'm struggling a bit with some things.	Your second point is not evidenced based. In last month's survey, we saw the opposite data trend to what you wrote.
I'm not so sure we should do that.	This plan requires $15,000 in funding and we have $2,000. We don't have the admin staff to help with operational work so we need to figure out how to close the gap.

KEEP THE CONVERSATION GOING: Welcome questions, request feedback, keep doors open to more discussion. "How did my request sit with you? Any thoughts?" Or, "Did that make sense?"

THE MICROSKILL:

4. USE STORYTELLING STRATEGICALLY

WHAT IS THE ACTUAL SKILL?

Use personal stories to illustrate your message and connect with your audience.

RESA

My talks used to be pretty standard and bland. Lots of bullet points and references to the medical literature. Few if any personal experiences. And also very little about patients or scenes from the emergency department. I changed my approach thanks to a team storyteller and a few speaking coaches. I was preparing a TEDMed talk in 2014. The team suggested I illustrate with specific, personal, and real patient stories from the emergency department (with identifying details changed, of course). I felt uncomfortable as this was a completely new approach for me. Although a bit uncomfortable sharing personal stories, I went for it. I included the story of a patient—she was screaming in pain from the far corner room in the emergency department. Her tubal pregnancy had burst, and she was bleeding into her abdomen. Ultrasound made the diagnosis. She went directly to the OR and did well. Now, I wouldn't give a talk without including stories. As a speaker, I can actually see the moments when audience members get drawn in—when they emotionally connect and start identifying with my experience and with me.[60] I am a complete believer in the power of stories.

WHY DO WE NEED THIS SKILL?

We connect with stories. Stories motivate and help an audience understand you as a speaker.[61] They emotionally engage audiences and demonstrate the applicability of a concept or theme. Compared to tables, bullet points, and outlines, stories allow the audience to see themselves in the situation. When you are trying to convince a customer, a client, a supervisor, or an investor, a story draws them in and allows you to connect with them in a deeper, more impactful way. This is one of the reasons we share our stories with you in this book.

WHY IS THIS SKILL HARD TO ACHIEVE?

- You think you don't have any stories or that you aren't good or skilled at telling them.
- You worry stories may backfire, blur the message, slow the argument, distract, or be overdone.
- Sharing personal stories feels uncomfortable and vulnerable.

WHAT ARE THE CRITICAL ACTIONS FOR THIS MICROSKILL?

DECIDE IF IT'S TIME FOR A STORY: Stories can be as short as one minute or as long as a full-length feature film. Ask yourself: *Is this the time to share a story?* Read the room, e.g. if people are packing up or signing off then a story could engage them. If people are appearing bored or disengaged, then a story could reel them back in. If people are packing up or signing off, then hold the story for another time.

IDENTIFY THE STORY'S FOCUS: You need to decide which story to share. The best stories have a point. As obvious as this sounds, we don't want you to look like you are rambling or directionless. Finding the point allows you to tailor the details and connect it to the why. *Why am I telling this story? Why would they care to hear it?* It can take quite a few drafts and redrafts to get it down to the clarity and focus you seek.

LESS CLEAR	MORE CLEAR
I am going to tell you a story. It's about how one company kept having people leave. Especially people who felt they did not belong.	At one of my jobs, fourteen team members left over a year and a half time period. Twelve of them were women. Some without another job lined up. Every time an email announcement hit our inbox our morale took a hit too. Why were the women leaving?

MAKE IT ORGANIC: Make it a real and authentic share. Tell a story that that is relatable and conversational. Don't force it. The absence of story is better than sharing an obviously fictitious or hyperbolic story. Think of a real example from your life or one that affected someone you know. Tell the story that led you to making the point you want to make.

GIVE CREDIT AND GET PERMISSIONS: If you heard a story and want to reshare, give credit to the source person. If you are using identifying details, then ask the person, "Can I tell the story you shared with me?" Be open to changing details or anonymize the story while maintaining its purpose, if identifying details are of concern.

LOWER THE STAKES: When we say *storytelling*, we mean integrating a story into a conversation or presentation to prove a point. All of us have stories to share. And you don't have to be a award winning storyteller to do so. Stories can be brief. The goal is to connect with your audience and to convey a message or illustrate a point.

THE MICROSKILL:

5. SPEAK LESS, LISTEN MORE, AND SHARE THE STAGE

WHAT IS THE ACTUAL SKILL?

Practice radical listening. Make space for other people.

RESA

It took me years to find the language—both in words and in body—to react in the moments of witnessed disrespect at work. Once, I was running a meeting, and each person was taking a turn giving the group a general reminder of their current project and then the specific updates since the last meeting. One of my teammates—an early career woman of color—started her update. She was known to have expertise and a skill set few others held. Almost immediately her supervisor started speaking over her, correcting what she said, taking credit for her work, and silencing her. Unfortunately, this predictable behavior happened at virtually every meeting. For a moment the room fell silent as he spoke on and on. I decided to act. I politely put my hand up signaling him to stop. I simply said, "I'm sorry." I turned back to the younger colleague, and asked "Were you finished?" At which point, she smiled and continued her update. It's the system which allows disrespectful communication like this. It happens more commonly to junior teammates, to women, and to people of color.[62] Polished communication is about speaking less, listening more, and sharing the stage.

WHY DO WE NEED THIS SKILL?

Listening—deep listening—is important. The impulse to share our perspective and add to the conversation is strong. There is a balance, because your voice does have value. And if you value your voice, others can too. But everyone has important things to say. It is possible that by hearing the thoughts of others and building upon them, your contribution will be more informed and better timed.

WHY IS THIS SKILL HARD TO ACHIEVE?

- Silence provokes anxiety: You have a strong pull to fill time and space with words.
- You fear appearing disengaged, non-participatory, or incompetent if you remain silent.
- You talk too much and lack insight into the disproportionately large space you take up.

WHAT ARE THE CRITICAL ACTIONS FOR THIS MICROSKILL?

GET COMFORTABLE WITH SILENCE: Silence is important in communication. It allows space for you to think. It allows space for the other person/s to speak and think. Polished communication is a quality over quantity situation. Every moment need not be filled with talk.

MAKE YOURSELF A RADICAL LISTENER: Pause. Allow others to speak: try waiting until one or two other comments have been offered. No need to be first to answer when a question or comment is raised in your inbox, during a meeting, or on a panel.

USE NONVERBAL COMMUNICATION: Commenting with nonverbal cues such as a head nod, thumbs-up sign, or clapping can signify agreement. Raising a hand or a finger to demonstrate interest can add us to the queue without purposely taking the space or priority of others. This doesn't need to be every single time. But it should be noticeable to others that you are open to and welcoming of their comments.

AVOID MANSPLAINING, MANTERRUPTING, AND BROPRIATING: Bias in the workplace is real. One of the ways to avoid being that team member is to educate yourself and learn about how bias can show up when it comes to communication.[63] The data is compelling on how unfortunate workplace dynamics can especially silence women and people of color. Men play an important and powerful role in how they can show up as allies.[64]

TERM	DEFINITION	EXAMPLE
Mansplaining[65]	A man explaining something, typically to a woman, in a condescending or patronizing tone.	**Man:** "Let me tell you the best way to get the project done. What you want to do…" **Woman:** Has run similar projects at two other companies.
Manterrupting[66]	A type of gendered bullying where a man unnecessarily interrupts a woman, often repeatedly, as a means of silencing her or taking away her agency.	**Woman:** Sharing a group project update at a weekly meeting. "We…" **Man:** "Before you continue. I want to share the progress…"
Bropriating[67]	When a man proposes what is considered a good idea soon after a woman has proposed the same thing but was met with silence.	**Woman:** Suggests that the next meeting be an on-site in person visit. **Man:** Just after she makes her suggestion, "My idea is that we do an on-site visit in person to see their new department."

THE MICROSKILL:

6. LEVERAGE ASYNCHRONOUS MESSAGING

WHAT IS THE ACTUAL SKILL?

Learn more than one communication tool to allow you both synchronous and asynchronous connections.

RESA

In the emergency department, we have to communicate in all different ways. It's something you learn over time and it's a situational awareness nuance I try to teach trainees. For example:

EMAIL: I want to tell a primary care doctor their patient was in the ED, tests were normal, and they went home.

IN-PERSON CONVERSATION: Walk to the patient and tell them they have a fracture on their x-ray.

TELEPHONE CALL: A patient died and you need to alert their family who is not in the emergency department.

TEXT MESSAGE: While on shift, my faculty colleague texts a question about a lecture next week. I text back.

PAGING SYSTEM: A patient with abdominal pain has appendicitis and they need to go to the OR. I page the surgeon.

DIRECT CONNECTION VIA A HOSPITAL OPERATOR: I work in the emergency department and I call the operator to connect me to the intensive care unit nursing station.

OVERHEAD PAGE: A patient is having a heart attack and we need the cardiology team in the Emergency department STAT. The hospital operator will announce, via speakers, a hospital wide page to relay the message to the cardiology team.

WHY DO WE NEED THIS SKILL?

Everyone benefits by having more than one communication tool in the toolbox. The positive of asynchronous messaging is the ability to not respond immediately and then take the time to do so later, when convenient (during business hours). Asynchronous message provides a freedom we all need. By eliminating the need to have real-time conversation we are able to communicate when it is safe (not driving), convenient, and we can be thoughtful. This delay facilitates your ability to focus on deep work, avoid distraction, and increase productivity.[68]

WHAT IS HARD ABOUT THIS SKILL?

- Learning technology can be overwhelming and intimidating.
- You might feel vulnerable recording your voice or having your face on a call.
- You might prefer the comfort of real-time conversation.

WHAT ARE THE CRITICAL ACTIONS FOR THIS SKILL?

CHOOSE AN APP AND PRACTICE: While you could use multiple apps for different people and groups, we recommend starting with one to get used to the process. For instance, if you want to send voice memos. Use the text app that is preloaded on your phone or one everyone at work seems to use. Ask a friend if you can practice with them. Hold down the microphone icon, speak, and then send a voice text. Ask them to send one back. Practice recording, listening, deleting, and saving.

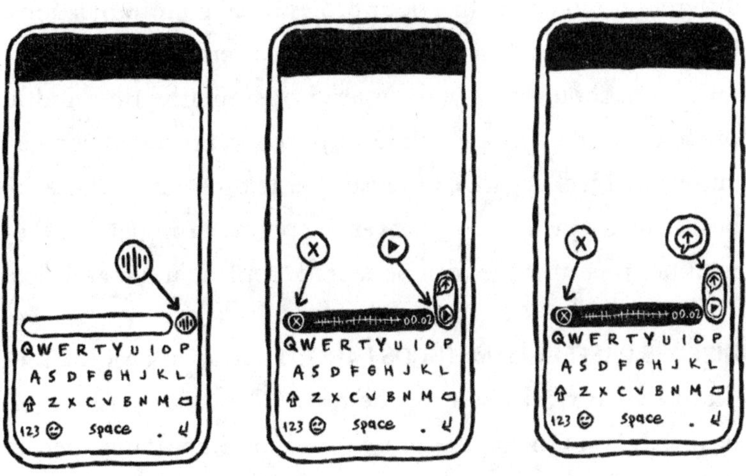

Leverage asynchronous messaging. For example, if you want to send a voice memo, use different phone applications, and practice recording, listening, deleting, and saving them with a friend.

MATCH THE COMMUNICATION TOOL WITH THE PERSON AND SITUATION: Texting is more casual, personal, and can keep the email inbox clean. Email is more formal and professional. Audio messages add more emotion and personality via tone and enunciation. Video messages also allow you to see and hear the person. However, we don't recommend recorded audio or video texting your supervisor unless you have the appropriate type of relationship Video, text, and audio messages are all less of a commitment than a phone call or meeting, which requires coordination and planning. Do not assume that just because someone is your age range or on the team that they want to text at all hours with you.

MIND THE CONTENT: Your personal conversations should have different boundaries than your professional communications. Just because you text a college friend in a certain way does not mean you should text your supervisor similarly. Be mindful of security when discussing sensitive content. Avoid conversations that feel negative or tense over text or email: those are best as real-time discussion over the phone or in person. Remember that messages can be shared, copied, and forwarded.

DISCUSS PREFERRED METHODS EARLY: You can ask for the medium which works best for the team. Generously ask others how they want to communicate. The most important aspect of polished communication is that parties agree on the medium and the boundaries (e.g. less communication late at night or over the weekend or no video preferred).

THE MICROSKILL:

7. WRITE EMAILS THAT PEOPLE ACTUALLY READ

WHAT IS THE ACTUAL SKILL?

Send emails that will be read and not ignored or deleted.

> **ADAIRA**
> I had drafted one of my first emails for a leadership program I co-founded. Before sending it, I asked my mentor Michelle Lin, MD, a really effective communicator, to read it. I sent her the email: four long paragraphs that extended to over a page. Her response was kind, clear, and direct. "People aren't going to read all of that." She attached an edited draft composed of three crisp, well-written paragraphs—and one only two sentences long. I laughed at the contrast in our two versions. She removed the sentences that brought no value, such as "I hope this is clear," or "I'm going to explain everything in this email." Her advice was priceless. No matter how well you write it, long emails run the risk of not being read at all.

WHY DO WE NEED THIS SKILL?

We must write readable emails. By *readable* we mean *shorter,* as people spend about eight to twelve seconds on an email.[69] And also, reportedly, sixty-five percent of email messages are ignored.[70] We also mean *clearer*: in organization, in providing key information, in not burying important details in long paragraphs. A lengthy email might be ok if it saves people more meetings on the calendar. And no matter what, we want you to write emails that keep that commitment to polished communication.

WHY IS THIS SKILL HARD?

- Writing a clear concise email including spelling and grammar checks takes time and effort.

- You have not had good modeling from supervisors.
- The team and the work cultures do not value optimized email communication.
- You assume everyone wants lengthy and detailed messages over a real time meeting.

WHAT ARE THE CRITICAL ACTIONS FOR THIS SKILL?

TITLE THE MESSAGE THOUGHTFULLY: A brief, high-level purpose should be in the subject line, e.g. Meeting Summary Notes: Nov 29.

CONSIDER A GREETING: This need not be long or extensive. Be yourself and be authentic, e.g. "I hope you had a nice weekend" or "Happy New Year." Even "Hello!" Be considerate and thoughtful and not performative. Acknowledge if you know someone is truly struggling is going through a rough period. Instead, "I hope all are safe and healthy" or, "I have been thinking about you and your family."

STRUCTURE THE BODY: Keep it basic and clean. Routine emails need not be overly structured. Key points can be highlighted as a mini paragraph or a bulleted list. Be careful with abbreviations and acronyms—in a global world and across industries, it might not be clear what you mean. If unfamiliar to the audience, write out the full name the first time you use it before abbreviating, e.g. "In the emergency department (ED), we…"[71] If you notice the email is lengthy consider: breaking big paragraphs into smaller ones, trimming all extraneous words (i.e. as matter of fact, it just so happens) or picking up the phone.

PROVIDE A SUMMARY: This can be a sentence. Make an email summary especially if the email is lengthy. Include any necessary contact information, attachments, and links. Offer dates and times for meetings. Make key details discoverable: bold, italicize, underline, or color very critical information. Don't overdo aesthetic with font choice and color. We stick with black sans serif fonts (i.e. Arial or Helvetica) or simple serif fonts (i.e. Times New Roman). We also like summaries at the top of the email.

MESSAGE:

Hello Resa,

I hope your holiday was great. — Start by addressing the group or individual. It is optional to add a short pleasantry such as "I hope your weekend went well" or, "Hope your day is going smoothly."

Were you able to meet with Sara about our upcoming fundraiser? — State the purpose of the email. I wanted to circle back to see if you and your supervisor picked a date for the workshop. We would like to finalize this by **Monday**. — Make key details discoverable: bold, italicize, underline, or color very critical information.

I'm free today from 4-5pm EST to discuss. — Avoid "When are you free?" and instead give them options to work with.

Thank you,
Adaira

555-555-5555

Emails need not be lengthy or complex.
Normalize sending essential information only and highlighting critical information so it will be discovered by the reader.

DOUBLE-CHECK DETAILS: Errors are bound to occur—especially with autocorrect functionality. It is worth the extra few minutes to check dates, times, locations, hyperlinks, spelling of names etc.

TRIM EXTRANEOUS INFORMATION: Read the email again to remove extraneous and distracting information.

REMEMBER TONE: By nature of the medium, a lot of emotion is stripped out of emails. Therefore, be wary of sounding abrupt or cold. Be careful with overdoing exclamation points, all caps, or question marks. Consider refraining from using words like <*sigh*> or <*gasp*> to show your frustration. Emoticons and emojis, punctuation, and GIFs can help convey emotion but also make the email casual. Expressing oneself with these accessories, especially exclamation points, is often gendered, i.e. women do it more than men.[72] There should be no pressure for women or people of color to conform to sounding excited or apologetic. Be authentic. We want to normalize feeling neutral, unbothered, indifferent. We encourage you to relay a direct message without worrying about being seen as bubbly or animated. If you need to deliver a message, do not feel pressured to soften the blow by adding "haha, lol, or tee hee hee." Just get the message delivered in a polite and clear manner.

SIGNATURE LINE: Make a default signature line under email preferences in the software program so that it auto populates your messages. Adjust the details to your comfort. The goal is to help people identify who you are and to provide access to further information to get to know and follow you.

SIMPLE	MORE DETAILED	
Adaira Landry 555-555-5555	Adaira Landry, MD, MEd Assistant Professor, Harvard Medical School Co-founder, Writing in Color Twitter: @AdairaLandryMD 555-555-5555 (work)	*List full name, credentials, key titles, and company/ institution*
Resa Lewiss	Resa E. Lewiss, MD Professor of Emergency Medicine She/Her/Hers Website | Instagram | LinkedIn	*Provide contact information according to your comfort. Use hyperlinks for websites or online contacts*

Consider listing your full name in your signature, as well as your credentials, key titles, and company/institutions that you belong to. Provide contact information and use hyperlinks for any websites. Provide your pronouns, if comfortable.

THE MICROSKILL:

8. LEARN AND USE EMAIL TOOLS: THE CC, BCC, AND REPLY ALL

WHAT IS THE ACTUAL SKILL?

Use CC and BCC deliberately, and limit use of Reply All.

RESA

I love the occasion when someone *e*-introduces me and I can reply "Thanks for the introduction and moving you to BCC to save your inbox." The BCC is underappreciated; I love it because it is a kind way to avoid Reply All and provides the option to maintain the privacy of recipients. It's a great tool, which is generous and respectful of someone's time and inbox. I had not fully understood its benefits and had seen it used in retaliatory ways to create a paper trail.

WHY DO WE NEED THIS SKILL?

Hopefully, we have established by now that thoughtful emailing is good for polished communication. So to that end, you need to learn the tools and accessories to emailing. Thoughtful emailing can help us decrease the reportedly five hours we spend a day reading emails.[73] We wrote about a *compassionate email culture*, where we all take care of our colleagues' inboxes.[74] By creating a culture that is thoughtful of your peers' workload, you help them, and they, practicing the same behavior, help you.

WHAT IS HARD ABOUT THIS SKILL?

- You don't know the difference between all the email options.
- Your supervisors and peers have different email preferences when it comes to communication—"CC me on everything," versus "CC me only when necessary."
- You are hesitant to change previously established email patterns.
- You believe Reply All is always helpful the team.
- You believe BCC should be used for stealth communication (i.e. adding a recipient to the BCC without informing others they are reading the email).

WHAT ARE THE CRITICAL ACTIONS FOR THIS SKILL?

FROM:	Chris Hoffman
TO:	primary.recipient@example.com, another.primary.recipient@example.com
CC:	for.your.information@example.com, also.fyi@example.com
BCC:	secret.person@example.com
SUBJECT:	This is an email
MESSAGE:	Here are the contents of this email:

USE THE TO LINE: Everyone on this line should be considered directly relevant to the conversation. People in this line are visible by all recipients of the email. They can see who is on the CC (Carbon Copy) line. They cannot see who is on the BCC (Blind Carbon Copy) line. When a recipient in the TO line presses the REPLY ALL button that email will go to everyone (except people BCC'd).

USE THE CC: The CC is great for keeping someone informed. Typically if we're asking something directly of someone or telling them key information, we might CC another party who would benefit from being involved. Consider this the "FYI" line, included for informational purposes. In general, no direct action is required of them. The person on the CC line is not private. Like those on the To line, those on the CC line are visible to all recipients of the email.

USE THE BCC LINE: The biggest value for BCC is that it eliminates the risk of Reply All responses that quickly clutter everyone's inboxes. How is that possible? Because each recipient in the BCC are unable to reply all to other BCC recipients—they are all hidden from each other. So if you want to email 20, 50, or 100 people, put them all in the BCC to avoid the Reply All chaos. The second value of the BCC is that you can hide the identity of recipients who collectively need to hear the same sensitive information. (e.g. A portion of the project team is behind on their task. You can send one message and not publicly call out individuals.)

ADDRESS THE RECIPIENT LIST IN THE SALUTATION: Remember, people who are receiving the email in the BCC line cannot be seen by anyone other than the sender. For communication transparency, clarify in the email greeting all who are receiving the email—the To: line and the BCC: line. When Adaira emails her 40 students, she puts them all in the BCC line and starts the email with, "Hello Students,"

USE REPLY ALL CAREFULLY: Be careful with the Reply All, especially on emails with long recipient lists. Pause and ask: *Is my response critical or necessary for everyone?* You can always reply to the sender directly and they can forward more broadly at their discretion.

THE MICROSKILL:

9. USE CAUTION WHEN COMMUNICATING NEGATIVE EMOTIONS

WHAT IS THE ACTUAL SKILL?

If you have negative feelings toward or about someone or a situation, pause before sharing anything.

> **ADAIRA**
>
> During my fourth year in emergency-medicine training, I was selected as a chief resident. One of the responsibilities of the role was for chief residents to create the shift schedules for all residents for the year. Another part of the job was fielding comments and feed back about the schedule. Some of the emails were pretty harsh. We were told that our ability to create a schedule was flawed. This is a bit of a paraphrase but I remember being told effectively "you guys suck at your job." The other chiefs and I made a rule: No responding when sent harsh and unprofessional comments. We developed a process: one chief drafted a polite response to the angry email; another chief had to read the response before sending. Then, all emails needed a twenty-four-hour wait period followed by a second proofread. This prevented a negatively toned email reply on our end.

WHY DO WE NEED THIS SKILL?

Part of being a polished communicator is pausing and being careful before sending an angry email or a text full of content that could backfire. Our immediate reactions and emotions are often raw and most authentic. These feelings need to be processed. However, that doesn't mean they need to be expressed in the workplace. Yes, you are allowed to be angry, tired, frustrated, jealous. This is normal. Yet, strategy is required in how and when and to whom you reveal those feelings. Remember messages can get forwarded, edited, and misinterpreted. If your emotions are raw and heated, then your practical points can be lost, and the emotions themselves can become amplified. We want you to be strategic. Be in control of what you say and write.

WHAT IS HARD ABOUT THIS SKILL?

- It's hard not to react, defend yourself, or explain your perspective.
- We may think it will be productive or therapeutic to the self and the team if you demonstrate strong emotions.
- You may not want to restrain your voice nor change what you truly believe about the workplace.

WHAT ARE THE CRITICAL ACTIONS FOR THIS SKILL?

GET DELIBERATE REST: A stressful encounter on top of baseline fatigue makes this MicroSkill challenging. When you are rested, you can better control knee-jerk responses and reactions. Sleep deprivation is related to more difficulty controlling emotions, including anger and aggression.[75]

PAUSE BEFORE YOU REPLY: When upset, frustrated, annoyed, practice breath work (i.e. slow, deep inhalations and exhalations). Step away: go for a walk, go to the bathroom. Just give yourself a minute. Physically stepping away from a situation that's causing you stress is going to help your body as well as the situation. Eat something if you are hungry.

PHONE A FRIEND: Run your thoughts by someone you trust, ideally someone removed from the situation. Ask if there is any content that is unclear, exaggerated, or reflects poorly on you.

WRITE A DRAFT: Get it out and write it down. Even if you plan to have a call and have no intention of emailing anything emotional, drafting your thoughts ahead of time will help with clarity and healing. Draft your thoughts on note paper, or Google docs, or Word. Avoid writing controversial thoughts in your work email inbox. It's easy to accidentally press send.

REVISIT THE COMMUNICATION: Unless it's time-sensitive, wait until the next day to review what you write. Give yourself time so that you feel less triggered. Edit for clarity, brevity and objectivity. Cut out the anger, frustration, resentment. Why? Because we don't want your emotional response to distract from the change or advocacy you are trying to create.

BE CURIOUS: To keep the conversation open, try to be curious about their perspective. Do not steep the conversation in your assumptions and projections. You can explain your perspective and accept that you may not know the whole story.

MAKE A PLAN: Ultimately, you must decide—when you are calm, cool, and the initial emotions have passed—if you want to send the message, schedule a meeting, or move on.

THE MICROSKILL:

10. SCHEDULE AND SEND EMAILS DURING WORKING HOURS

WHAT IS THE ACTUAL SKILL?

Keep emails to your work hours, not your leisure time.

ADAIRA

A few years ago a doctor colleague sent me an email to complete a research survey at 9:00 p.m. on a Friday night. It seemed nonurgent. I told myself, *I'll do this on Monday.* On Sunday night the colleague sent another email: *Hey, just checking in to see if you got my email?* Then on Monday at 7:00 a.m. there was another nudge: a text message asking if I could fill out the survey that day. It was a lot of messages outside of standard business hours. To be fair however, when I was more junior like my colleague sending these messages, I also crossed after-hours boundaries. I remember asking a colleague the same question over a short period of time. So, many of us have been there. But in fact, many items are not that urgent, and it's healthier to respect people's time off work.

WHY DO WE NEED THIS SKILL?

Working hours vary (especially in a hybrid or international or shift work environment). Decide with the team what you consider the default working hours. We understand that some companies are open 24/7 and that communication needs to occur frequently. However, even within that culture there can be boundaries. In our article "What a Compassionate Email

Culture Looks Like," we intentionally talk about off-hour correspondence: that it unfairly brings the recipient back to thinking about work.[76] As emergency doctors, we also understand that we are often working when others are home or asleep. However, we recommend thinking of the email recipient and their schedule. Off-hours generally means nights, weekends, vacations, leaves, and holidays. Being kind to the team means not sending during these times; otherwise, many feel compelled to reply in the moment or to work during their time off. And they need time not working.

WHAT IS HARD ABOUT THIS SKILL?

- You are driven to get tasks off your desk, especially quick items.
- It is hard to not respond when an email arrives to the inbox.
- You believe that your team expects an immediate response.
- Your workplace has an unhealthy email communication culture with few personal boundaries.

WHAT ARE THE CRITICAL ACTIONS FOR THIS MICROSKILL?

MIND THE TIME: Check in with the team and ask "Is there a way we can optimize the timing of the emails that are shared?" The Athena Swan Charter, which provides guidelines for gender equality in higher education and research, advises it is generally safe to assume that working hours are 10:00 a.m. to 4:00 p.m., Monday through Friday.[77] However, if you work with team members across the globe, you may provide alternatives to these windows to help others.

DRAFT IT AND SCHEDULE SEND: Draft the email outside of working hours and schedule it to deploy whenever suitable. If you don't already know how to schedule send, go to your web browser and type in the search bar *how to schedule an email in Gmail* (or Outlook, etc.). Gmail and Microsoft Outlook have built-in features whereas other systems may require you to download a browser plug-in, such as Boomerang, to schedule your emails.

ADD A LINE TO YOUR SIGNATURE: Add a line at the bottom of your email signature, e.g. *I work M–F 9am–5pm and may not respond outside of those times*, or *I may not respond on nights, weekends, and holidays.*

SELECT ANOTHER COMMUNICATION MEDIUM: If something is urgent and cannot wait, consider if email is the best medium to use. Will a single email lead to multiple back and forth messages? It might be easier to discuss over a brief 5-minute phone call and resolve the issue.

CONCLUSION:

Aim to use clear and concise language when communicating.	Recognize that your body language plays a critical role in communication.	Not everyone communicates the way you do; be curious, open, patient, and welcoming.

SUPPLEMENTAL RESOURCES:

Effective Communication

Think Fast, Talk Smart

Write Better Emails

4

MICROSKILLS TO BUILD AND MAINTAIN YOUR REPUTATION

ADAIRA

I knew a surgeon with a bad reputation. One day, he entered the emergency department and walked over to the computer workstation. I saw a few of my coworkers grow tense. One nurse looked away as he walked by. No hellos were exchanged. I saw the technician performing the EKG on a patient with chest pain roll her eyes as he passed by. I asked the nurse next to me if everything was okay, and she told me that surgeon had yelled multiple times at people, and nobody wanted to interact with him because he spoke rudely and talked down to them. They considered him a bully. Consequently, she preferred to not interact with him. I never asked him directly though I wondered, *Does he know he comes across as disrespectful and difficult to work with?* and *Does he care that this is his reputation?*

Like it or not, we are all known for something: aspects of our character, such as being hardworking, friendly, ambitious, or lazy. We have behaviors and ways of speaking which feed how we are perceived and how people describe us. The wild thing is that the bulk of our reputation is derived from subjective criteria.

A good reputation takes a long time to build because it requires repetitive examples and exposures over time. Consistency is key. In contrast, a bad reputation takes moments to create and requires many fewer instances. And it's hard to shed a bad reputation once established. We have been told many times, "don't worry about what people think of you." And for the most part, we agree: take care of the self and conserve your energy—don't worry about things you cannot control. But the workplace is not that cut and dry—you shouldn't just focus only on the self. Certain outcomes—a salary increase, a promotion, a new team assignment or responsibility—are not always up to you. In fact, what happens with your career—if you work for an organization, company, hospital, or institution—is largely based on how others view you. And if they want to work with you.

This ties into your reputation. Data shows that people will rely more on reputation than their own first impression. For instance, 90% of online customers will read and trust a review before visiting a business for themselves.[78] And we can't argue against the convenience of crowdsourcing impressions, even at the individual level. We should only focus on aspects of you that are great and positive so they can be further nurtured. We want you to discover if you are dependable, warm, decisive, creative, and curious. It is equally important to self-reflect and consider your less positive attributes. For example, are you often moody, prone to outbursts, unpredictable, or late all the time?

There is an unfortunate issue we must address. Although

your physical and demographic attributes, such as height, age, biology, gender and sexual orientation, and skin color should not influence reputation in the workplace, they do. These traits should be disconnected from your reputation; however, not everyone shares our philosophy. Success and acceptance in the workplace are related to who we are and what we look like.[79] We want to be clear. We can only focus on aspects of our reputation that are within our control. And yet, how others perceive your personal attributes might make building your reputation a challenge. This chapter should be a reflection to see where you can and want genuinely to grow. We are not asking you to be a fraud or inauthentic. We are not suggesting you should change who you are, what you look like, or how your personality presents to fit in.

In this chapter we discuss nine strategies to build a positive reputation, steps to maintain it, and how to employ damage control when your reputation becomes tarnished.

MICROSKILLS TO BUILD AND MAINTAIN YOUR REPUTATION:

1. Respect due dates and communicate with the team.
2. Complain carefully.
3. Share your failures to normalize your humanness.
4. Understand the impact of a lie.
5. Understand how your engagement is perceived and valued.
6. Nurture your local reputation.
7. Be careful about gossip.
8. Mind your ego.
9. Practice damage control in the setting of a bad reputation.
10. Apologize thoughtfully, and explain your mistakes.

THE MICROSKILL:

1. RESPECT DUE DATES AND COMMUNICATE WITH THE TEAM.

RESA

The first time I was on a team with a teammate who did not meet due dates, I felt the effect it had on everyone including me. It was hard because they would say they were working on their piece of the project at every check-in; yet, each time a target date came, there was nothing. No slides for the workshop. No paragraph draft for the manuscript. No email response to the poll, which specifically requested everyone's input. It took a toll on the team. First, there was the stress of anticipation: Would they follow through? Second, there was disappointment that they were holding up the progress of the project. Third, there was resentment that other people had to pick up the slack. I saw the team's morale drop and frustration build. No matter how nice and friendly they were when they greeted people, they had the reputation of being unreliable and full of excuses. And it stuck. Few people wanted to work with them as a result. Conversations and check-ins ultimately had no impact. I learned a lot from this experience: when I am that person to miss the due date, I own it, and update the team so they know what to expect next.

WHAT IS THE ACTUAL SKILL?

Communicate with the team to let them know where you are with your piece of the work.

WHY DO WE NEED THIS SKILL?

Ghosting, meaning silence with no updates, should never

be the default option. This is bad. People will notice. Your reputation will take a hit. Sometimes it is just not possible to complete a task, based on interest, competing demands, skill set, or other limited resources. Sometimes it's a sudden personal crisis that needs your attention. If delays are not typical, people will get that you are human and sometimes life happens. And even if you predict they will not be understanding, you should let them know.

WHY IS THIS SKILL HARD?

- Time management is a challenge for you.
- You assume due dates and timeline don't matter to the team.
- You don't want to let people down so you avoid communicating.
- Providing updates is less of a priority for you than doing the work.

WHAT ARE THE CRITICAL ACTIONS?

SHARE COMPETING DEMANDS UP FRONT: Let the team know your assessment of the project and anything competing for your attention. If everything looks good and you agree with the work, email a simple confirmation and plan, such as, "Hello, this plan works. Will share by Friday." If you anticipate a need or you want a different plan, offer, "I can complete this task if we can move the due date to one day later?" Or, "I have a large presentation due the day before." Or, "My other supervisor asked me to prioritize our annual report ahead of this. Is that okay?"

SEND AN UPDATE: Send a brief progress note. *I completed the budget estimate* or *The room is booked. And the speaker is confirmed for the workshop. I should finish the rest of the details by the end of the week.* Updates can be a request for help, *I'm struggling on this last step. Can we schedule a meeting to work through the roadblocks?*

OFFER ANOTHER OPTION OR TIMELINE: If something arises and you won't make a timeline, send an update, briefly explain, and offer another option. *I'm so sorry. I'm running behind and request one more day.* On time is the best update, but sending out a delay message is better than no message at all.

UNDERPROMISE AND OVERDELIVER: We do like the under promise—overdeliver concept. Try to complete tasks and, if feasible, submit ahead of schedule. Avoid promising to be ahead of the timeline. And avoid pushing yourself to burnout to beat a due date. However, if your goal becomes realized, being ahead of schedule can only help your reputation.

THE MICROSKILL:

2. COMPLAIN CAREFULLY

WHAT IS THE ACTUAL SKILL?

Express negative or criticizing opinions thoughtfully.

ADAIRA

I was leading a multidisciplinary team of engineers, marketing sales reps, and clinical experts. We were designing a medical education tool. Overall, the team dynamics were productive and healthy. However, every once in a while, one team member would complain. "We are moving too slowly. We need to catch up to the bigger competitors." Technically, he was right. We were not as advanced and developed. However, the complaining felt disparaging and disruptive. There was also no clear point or solution offered; just a reminder that we were behind. The timing often occurred as people were giving status updates, so it felt personal to the individual who just spoke. Many of his complaints were valid—and yet, from an emotional standpoint they didn't seem thoughtful to the ego's of others in the room. And because of that morale dropped. At first, I didn't know how to channel that complaint from a rant to a productive solution. I just felt bad. Then I spoke with him directly and reframed his complaints into something more productive, "What could we change to make this issue easier for the team?" That direction helped shape how and when he brought up his concerns.

WHY DO WE NEED THIS SKILL?

It's common to remark on and object to the things that are dysfunctional in the workplace. Reportedly, people spend between ten and twenty hours per month complaining at work.[80] We can complain; however, we need to do this strategically. Too much negative commentary can bring down your energy and that of the team. Also, venting to the wrong person and in a damaging way can harm your reputation—or your position. Strategic unloading is good: it can happen in a safe place to vent and may even lead to change. The hard part is finding the right intensity, audience, means, and purpose for the issues you raise.

WHY IS THIS SKILL HARD TO ACHIEVE?

- It's hard to be solutions-oriented when you are focused on the negative.
- The complaint is recognized by many, however you fear being identified as the whistleblower or instigator.
- If you complain you will be tasked to find, fix, or lead the solutions.
- You dont realize you are complaining to the wrong person or too much.

WHAT ARE THE CRITICAL ACTIONS FOR THIS SKILL?

THINK BEFORE YOU SPEAK: Take a few breaths before you complain. Take a walk. Exercise. Make sure you have eaten. Calm your body and nerves. Find a trusted colleague, friend, or family member and start there—allow them to help you pause and cool down.

NAME YOUR EMOTIONS: Understand your current emotional state before you make a formal complaint. Are you calm? Have you reflected enough? Are you still angry with a lot of tension in your muscles? Rage and lack of control are major red flags that you are not ready to enter a state of complaining. Do not pass go. Process more. In general, its a risk to go to the team, like a supervisor, with raw, negative emotions.

FIELD TEST YOUR COMPLAINT: Remember your personal board of directors, the table full of peers, colleagues, friends? Start there. Share your complaint and ask, "Do you think this is an issue worth raising? If so, this is how I was planning to handle it? How would you handle it?"

PREPARE TO BE SINGLED OUT: This might not happen, but you should emotionally prepare yourself to be identified as the person "raising the issue" even if it affects everyone. Even if everyone speaks about it behind closed doors. The moment you raise a complaint, be aware that is the moment you accept possible repercussions.

OFFER SOLUTIONS: One way to turn the complaint into something productive is to offer solutions. It's a great skill and complaints are likely better received. Offering solutions shows a vested interest in the issue. We must normalize one point—you can bring up an issue even if you lack a solution. In fact, there is significant and reasonable pushback towards expecting employees to be problem solvers—the biggest reason is that it can be intimidating and foster a culture of fear.[81]

THE MICROSKILL:

3. SHARE YOUR FAILURES TO NORMALIZE YOUR HUMANNESS

WHAT IS THE ACTUAL SKILL?

Share failures to demonstrate and normalize the human experience.

ADAIRA

In hospitals, departments commonly hold a weekly conference called "M&M," aka morbidity and mortality. It's a medico-legally protected meeting where patient cases are independently reviewed by a team of doctors and then discussed to identify the root cause of the error. The discussion focuses on systems issues and patient safety; however, often it feels very personal for the doctors involved in the case. I had a patient case selected for M&M early in my career. The patient was very volatile from recreational drugs and threatened physical violence. He said he would punch staff. It did not work when I tried to calmly speak with him and deescalate his behavior with verbal redirection. When he punched the security officer, I made the decision to sedate the patient by injecting medications. This intervention often works to relax patients. Sleep and time allow recreational drugs e.g. cocaine, alcohol to metabolize and the volatile behavior usually resolves. During the M&M discussion of my patient case, in front of a packed classroom, the doctor panel reviewed the case and solicited the audiences' opinion. The decision was that I had managed the case incorrectly—I should have given less sedation. Ooof. It was embarrassing and my confidence took a hit. Now, I'm glad it happened because I know M&Ms happen to everyone. It's one of the more humbling parts of the job—to say yes, I'm a doctor, and I'm a human who makes mistakes.

WHY IS THIS SKILL NEEDED?

Everyone experiences failure. And no matter the profession, mistakes happen. In medicine, errors can mean patients dying or being permanently injured. We are now seeing failures and subsequent shame discussed a bit more openly in medicine.[82] We believe that sharing mistakes makes you more credible, relatable, and approachable. However, the overriding culture of most workplaces is to show and discuss the wins. Rarely are the losses published or discussed.

WHY IS THIS SKILL HARD TO ACHIEVE?

- Discussing failure makes you self-conscious, uncomfortable, and vulnerable.
- You fear that revealing a flaw or failure could be leveraged against you.
- Modeling failure is hard if you don't see leaders or the team doing the same.

WHAT ARE THE CRITICAL ACTIONS OF THIS SKILL?

DECIDE WHAT YOU ARE COMFORTABLE SHARING: Adjust the content to your comfort level. This is your choice, and you are in charge. You may feel comfortable sharing that a pitch or new idea was rejected or about a unfavorable client review. You may feel less comfortable sharing that you are having partner problems at home and this is affecting your mood at work.

SHARE WITH OTHERS: Test drive and start off small. Practice sharing something. You can talk to your closest coworker—a relationship that feels relaxed and familiar. Or you could share it with an individual who needs to understand that you are human too—perhaps a mentee who is going through their own episode of failure. If you are looking for guidance and emotional recovery from a mistake or rejection, talk to a friend or board of director member first. Then decide if you want to share beyond your immediate trust circle.

MAKE IT TEACHABLE: Take your lesson and make it teachable. People will appreciate your honesty and the share. What did you learn and how are you a better person? "I was not granted the promotion I applied for. I asked for feedback and learned three things you need to do before going up for promotion…"

THE MICROSKILL:

4. UNDERSTAND THE IMPACT OF A LIE

WHAT IS THE ACTUAL SKILL?

Be honest about yourself and your work.

RESA

When I have a patient come to the emergency department complaining of bleeding from the rectum, I am sure to examine the area to see how serious the bleeding is. The challenge is that the emergency department is crowded, chaotic, and without a lot of privacy for physical examinations. We teach residents to be honest. If they forget to examine a part of the body or to ask a question, they can always go back to the patient. Yet for some reason—shame, ego, other—this is one of those situations where I have seen them lie.

ME: What did the rectal exam show?

THEM: It was normal.

ME (TO THE PATIENT): So the resident did a rectal exam and there is no internal bleeding.

PATIENT: They did not do a rectal exam.

ME: They told me he did a rectal exam.

PATIENT: I am telling you, I would remember if the doctor put a finger in my bottom.

A difficult and important conversation with the resident follows. We cover topics of honesty, professionalism and safe patient care.

WHY IS THIS SKILL NEEDED?

Simple lies are easy to forgive and forget: "I'm almost there" when you haven't left home yet, or "Oh yes, that makes sense" when you have no clue what they are talking about. However, the effects of a significant lie can last for decades. For example, it's hard to recover from a lie where you list an MBA on your resume—and never got one. We lie by commission, omission, or embellishment. And no matter the style of lying, there could be big consequences including job termination and in irrecoverable loss of reputation.

On an individual level, we have seen how trust is lost when someone lies about an important matter. Sometimes a relationship is impossible to repair.

WHY IS THIS SKILL HARD TO ACHIEVE?

- You are insecure about yourself and your skills. You feel unsafe being honest.
- You are a people-pleaser and cannot resist impressing others.
- You are afraid of losing your job or getting a bad evaluation.
- You think what you are doing is mild "stretching" of the truth.

WHAT ARE THE CRITICAL ACTIONS OF THE SKILL?

DRAFT A STOCK RECOVERY PHRASE: Having a stock phrase for a situation where you may be tempted to lie helps. Take a deep breath and say, "I'm sorry, I wasn't able to get to that task" or "Unfortunately, I wasn't able to get to that task, I apologize" or "I feel terrible saying this, but I was the one who caused the error" or "This is not easy to confess, but I lied about what I said earlier."

EXPLAIN THE SITUATION: After the apology, you can offer a brief explanation. Don't belabor the details. "I let the pressure to meet a deadline make me take short cuts in my work." Or "I did not want to let you down so I felt pressured to…" Or "I got distracted due to a personal situation."

WEIGH THE RISKS: What is the risk of the lie? People, accounts, products can be harmed, and your reputation could be tarnished. You could lose a client or get a bad customer review. In the emergency department, patients could die. Of course, not all lies are destructive; Adaira tells her children that Santa Claus exists and brings gifts every Christmas. Telling this lie allows her children to have so much joy. But in the workplace, there is rarely an upset to lying.

CONSIDER THERAPY: If you feel the need to habitually lie or impress and are concerned that you have a hard time being honest, consider seeing a therapist. We want you to value your mental health. If you prefer, start by talking with someone you trust (a friend or a relative) about your compulsion. However, if that doesn't work, consider seeking professional support.

THE MICROSKILL:

5. UNDERSTAND HOW YOUR ENGAGEMENT IS PERCEIVED AND VALUED

WHAT IS THE ACTUAL SKILL?

Pause to assess your level of engagement and decide if you'd like to change it.

ADAIRA

My first job out of college was restocking shelves at a grocery store. I'd grab groceries from the checkout counter and return them to their designated shelf. I'd repeat that about two million times per shift. After completing a molecular cell biology major and applying to medical school, I was less than inspired. The store manager said, "Adaira, if you seemed interested, I could promote you to bagging groceries." It made me think about everything: my body language, facial expression, talkativeness, and demeanor. Even though I felt like I was doing exactly the tasks asked of me, I had missed that there was a level of connectedness people have when engaged with work. The next day I showed up and greeted my peers and engaged everyone in sincere, friendly talk. I did that for each shift, and soon I was bagging groceries. This was a standout lesson. Engagement was not just doing the mechanical work, it was how I interacted with people and the entire workplace culture.

WHY IS THIS SKILL NEEDED?

Successful people do boring work as well as exciting work. We know that boring work can make it hard to engage. So can challenging work or work that brings no purpose. So it's easy to zone out, tune out, and close off. However, people will notice if you are checked out. How? They will notice if your audio is always muted on a video call or if you don't go into the office; if you sit in the corner on your smartphone; if you never respond to emails; if you never raise your hand or contribute questions in the virtual chat; if you give one word answers when people ask you about your weekend. And if you get feedback that you seem disengaged or checked-out, you must ask yourself, *Do I care that they notice I am not engaged at work?*

WHY IS THIS SKILL HARD TO ACHIEVE?

- You are burnt out, emotionally or physically fatigued.
- You feel that you do not belong, are disrespected, unwelcomed, or unappreciated.
- Work is a means of income and not your passion.
- Your personality does not match the generally accepted rules of engagement.
- You prefer not to smile or make eye contact.

WHAT ARE THE CRITICAL ACTIONS OF THE SKILL?

DECIPHER IF BURNOUT OR DEPRESSION ARE PLAYING A ROLE: It can be hard to decipher these two. Meet with a mental health specialist to help. Burnout is a physical psychological or emotional manifestation of being overworked or stressed from the work environment. If you think it's burnout, rest and time away from work (e.g. PTO or a sabbatical) will help. If this is depression, persistent sadness and loss of interest, then professional help with therapy or medications may be needed. Start by running your feelings and symptoms by your personal board of directors—ask them if they feel you need additional help, if HR and your supervisor need to be looped in, if they have any specific suggestions for you.

REMOVE DISTRACTIONS: Be mindful of your cell phone use. Don't be on email when in a one-on-one meeting. Be in the moment. We won't tell you to store away your phone all shift—

that'd be impossible for most of us. But most of us aren't hired to scroll on our personal social media accounts so we need to be mindful of how much that is being done while on the clock.

GET INPUT AND FEEDBACK: Ask the team (including your supervisor) how you come across. Request specifics so you can learn what they see and perceive. Ask for suggestions on concrete behavior changes you can adopt.

SHOW INTEREST: Have an (un)scheduled check-in with the team. Ask the team what they are up to and if there is anything you can help them with. It's better to show your interest in learning than it is to sit quietly and not let people know that you are interested progressing and contributing.

SELECT YOUR WORKAROUNDS FOR SOCIALIZING: To be clear, we are not asking you to go to socials or mixers if that is anxiety provoking for you. However, we do encourage you to find a comfortable route to demonstrate your interest in the team. Pick the action that matches your comfort level, e.g. make eye contact, smile, wave hello, nod, start light conversation.

SHARE PROGRESS AND OUTCOMES: You may show engagement by telling people what you have done. A nice tactic is to circle back with your team, like your supervisor, and let them know what you have checked off the list. Email updates keep them posted and share progress you are making on a task or goal. This could be as simple as letting them know that you had the meeting with the client or sent the email you promised.

THE MICROSKILL:

6. NURTURE YOUR LOCAL REPUTATION

WHAT IS THE ACTUAL SKILL?

Nurture your local day-to-day relationships and reputation at work.

> **ADAIRA**
> I worked for a company where the CEO was a serial entrepreneur and had started other companies with major acquisitions. In the field he was seen as a trailblazer. People trusted his opinion, and he was always speaking internationally about his philosophy of leading companies. "That man is a genius!" was the type of language I heard at conferences. Plus he was widely respected for making lucrative deals and recruiting top talent. However, on the day-to-day, inside the company, he was seen as disorganized and unaware of the inner happenings of the organization. People feared his reactions to negative customer reviews. "This customer hated the product, don't let him know otherwise he's going to blame us for a product we didn't make." The national reputation didn't align with his local reputation across the teams.

WHY IS THIS SKILL NEEDED?

Your reputation starts locally in the workplace. As you grow your reach and reputation, especially at the hands of social media, make sure you take care and pay attention to your work home base. It's important to invest in being a good citizen and contribute to your organization's mission, priorities, and responsibilities. Local connections are important. Neglecting your local duties for wider fame or other positions can hurt others on the team. People talk and word will get around.[83]

WHY IS THIS SKILL HARD TO ACHIEVE?

- It is easy to take the local work and the local team for granted.
- You want your work to be seen and acknowledged by a larger audience.

WHAT ARE THE CRITICAL ACTIONS OF THIS MICROSKILL?

MAINTAIN YOUR DAY-TO-DAY RESPONSIBILITIES: You should make sure that you are not neglecting the work and the team. Respect due dates. If you are overwhelmed with new and growing responsibilities, speak to your local team about adjustments.

NURTURE RELATIONSHIPS: Make time to check in with the team and see how they are doing. Is there anything that you can help with? Offering to be a source of support, especially to those who are junior to you, positively contributes to the culture of your workplace.

SHARE TO TEACH: Share your accomplishments in a way that allows others to learn your approach. Don't gatekeep the strategies for success. We are particularly aware that underprivileged and underrepresented groups may not be a part of the conversations which share how to access opportunities.[84] So instead of saying, "Oh, yeah, I spoke in Paris. It was fun," try,

"I had no idea how to access international speaking opportunities until someone told me about the 'call for speakers' on most conference websites. Apply when you see the open call on the website I forwarded."

THE MICROSKILL:

7. BE CAREFUL ABOUT GOSSIP

WHAT IS THE ACTUAL SKILL?

Understand the role, the risks, and the consequences of gossip at work.

RESA

People at work talk. Even when the discussion is cloaked as confidential. And even when they give you their word. At one job, I told my supervisor that I was interviewing for positions at other hospitals. I sought their support. They looked me in the eye. "I won't tell anyone. This will stay between us until you tell me otherwise." I actually naïvely believed them. Soon thereafter, I was in a meeting, and out of nowhere a colleague said, "Oh, come on, Resa, everyone knows." My stomach dropped. I was shocked, felt manipulated, and I lost complete trust in the supervisor. In retrospect, there is no question this was an incredible learning experience. When mentoring and coaching colleagues, I share this story and advise them that as soon as they share any news, they should assume it is public knowledge. Many have circled back to thank me as this proved to be true in their experience. Confidential information is definitely not always kept secret.

WHY IS THIS SKILL NEEDED?

It is human nature to talk about and be interested in other people. However, we want you to be smart with workplace gossip. Gossiping doesn't just harm the people you are speaking about, it is actually a reflection on you and how trustworthy you are with confidential and private information. As you gossip or even listen to gossip, other parties wonder, *What do they say about me when I'm not around?* Or *I wonder if they tell my business so easily as well.* Yup, when that occurs we want you to ask yourself, *What benefit does sharing this information give me or the people I am discussing?* If there is no benefit, pass.

WHY IS THIS SKILL HARD TO ACHIEVE?

- You don't know how to shut down gossip as it is unfolding in front of you.
- You don't like the person at the center of the gossip and there's something satisfying or validating about hearing their information spread.
- Gossiping seems harmless and you see social gain for yourself.
- You feel cornered into sharing information, despite knowing details shouldn't be shared.

WHAT ARE THE CRITICAL ACTIONS OF THE SKILL?

DISCUSS IDEAS: Keep your conversations high level. We respect the quote, "Great minds discuss ideas; average minds discuss events; small minds discuss people." We are talking about reputation here, and we don't want the first thing people think of you is as a *gossiper.*

TAKE THE GOSSIP ELSEWHERE: We understand the impulse to share, debrief, and reflect on work news with another person. If you must, share your gossip with trusted contacts outside work.

WALK AWAY: If you are uncomfortable with the content and don't want to be associated with gossip, walk away. You can do this silently or say "I'll be right back." Or, "This feels like personal information we shouldn't be sharing so openly."

SHARE CAREFULLY: As stated above, we understand the itch to share news. Processing information aloud can feel therapeutic—especially for complex information that you have personally been told or witnessed. Focus on being safe with what you talk about, whom you talk to, and where you exchange this information. Remember, people who are very loosely connected to you might share that you are their source of information. So please, if you must, do it with very trusted friends and colleagues.

THE MICROSKILL:

8. MIND YOUR EGO

WHAT IS THE ACTUAL SKILL?

Understand how your confidence level appears to others.

RESA

Doctors can have big egos. This probably comes from a few places: Medicine has a vertical and hierarchical leadership structure. There are a lot of sacrifices made to get through the training, and some people place doctors on a pedestal. The "G-d complex" is real. At one of my hospital jobs, I met regularly with a senior health care executive, who held expertise in leadership and in finance. Although many of their board members and meetings were with physicians, they were not a physician. I remember them saying something that I think about often. It reminds me to keep my ego in check. They said "You know Resa: doctors do often think they are the smartest people in the room (and they often are), but they fail to recognize and appreciate the benefit of the presence of many other equally smart and accomplished people who have just chosen a different path than medicine."

WHY DO WE NEED THIS SKILL?

You should seek competence and a healthy amount of confidence. In that vein, it's important to understand how your level of confidence comes across. When it comes to reputation, overconfidence is more likely to get us into trouble. Scientists David Dunning and Justin Kruger warn us of the Dunning-Kruger effect: low performers overestimate their abilities. High performers underestimate their abilities.[85] What is the translation? Some people who know very little do not know how little they don't know. There can be a gendered aspect to this. Tomas Chamurro-Premuzic in his book *Why Do So Many Incompetent Men Become Leaders and How to Fix It* asserts that in many industries the majority of leaders are men. Yet women leaders outperform men in terms of competence. And many workplaces promote people who are overconfident and narcissistic, falsely thinking these are markers of competent leadership.[86]

WHY IS THIS SKILL HARD TO ACHIEVE?

- You don't realize your overconfidence if you lack insight into yourself and your abilities.
- You boast about yourself due to a feeling of insecurity or inadequacy.
- You lack feedback on how you are perceived.

WHAT ARE THE CRITICAL ACTIONS?

LISTEN: Don't underestimate the power of listening. In fact, listening may be more valuable than speaking. Of course, we don't want you to remain silent all the time. You can and should speak up and contribute. But we are saying don't prematurely tout your knowledge. Demonstrate your competence and hard work through the quality you deliver: let the presentation you give, policy you draft, sale you bring, deal you close speak for itself.

STAY HUMBLE: When you are learning, building your subject-matter expertise, keep a healthy sense of humility. Ask yourself, *Am I making others feel small or less than? Am I truly overly confident, or am I actually insecure and overcompensating? What might I be missing?* Or, *Where are my deficiencies? How can I be and do better?*

VALUE MENIAL TASKS TOO: There might be some tasks that seem menial and just need to get done. For those jobs, try to take pride in executing them. For example, in the emergency department, we are glad to get blankets when patients are cold, and help with bedpans when asked. Eliminate the "I'm above that type of work" mindset. That attitude can be seen as arrogant and can really hurt your work, the team, and your reputation.

SEE CONFIDENCE AS A PRIVILEGE: Workplace confidence and competence are judged differently for different people. For example, for women and people of color, demonstrating confidence is not universally rewarded; however, men are more consistently allowed to be confident, even when incompetent.[87] Women and people of color further struggle, as a lack of confidence is often cited as a barrier to promotion.[88]

REQUEST FEEDBACK: You may be completely unaware you are coming off as overconfident. It can honestly be a shock when you find out. Get ahead of this by asking the team at the next check-in. Give them a heads-up: "In our upcoming meeting, can we discuss my confidence and competence: do they match? Is there a correlation to my performance at work?"

THE MICROSKILL:

9. PRACTICE DAMAGE CONTROL IN THE SETTING OF A BAD REPUTATION

WHAT IS THE ACTUAL SKILL?

Actively work on your bad reputation, if you have one.

RESA

Years ago, I had a colleague who spent a lot of time trying to leave shifts early. People thought they were not serious about being an emergency doctor. They talked a lot about parties and about their dating life at work. While we think it's important to have a life outside of work, it's strategic to be careful when discussing everything and sharing with people who are colleagues and not friends. Things changed. By the time they were a senior resident, they developed a more serious demeanor and grew into a more focused doctor. They were helpful to teammates, and stayed late after shifts to finish their work. I would definitely have let them care for me or any family member. However, they carried remnants of that negative reputation throughout all of the training years. I was surprised at how hard it was for them to shake it.

WHY IS THIS SKILL NEEDED?

A good reputation is a slow and steady build. A bad reputation takes no time. It's easy and quick to develop a negative reputation even if inaccurate and unfair. The person with the bad reputation is faced with what to do and how to act when this happens. A bad reputation is thought to stem from one of the following transgressions: bad attitude or bad behavior.[89] If you find yourself in a situation such as this, there are positive things you can do to turn negative views around.

WHY IS THIS SKILL HARD TO ACHIEVE?

- You are not aware of your reputation.
- It takes work, attention, and energy to course-correct and make changes.
- Words and behaviors cannot be taken back, and your apology and corrective behaviors may not work.
- Damage control has never been modeled for you.

WHAT ARE THE CRITICAL ACTIONS OF THIS MICROSKILL?

DO RESEARCH ON YOUR REPUTATION: Ask trusted teammates,

your supervisor, or even friends outside of work about your professional reputation. Send a message ahead of time asking, *I'm curious if you have time to meet for feedback on how I am perceived?* This gives them time to collect their thoughts and perhaps get input from others. It's likely that you already know and just need specifics pointed out to you.

DEMONSTRATE CHANGED BEHAVIOR: Just talking about changed behavior does not go far. You need to actually demonstrate a change. And it takes a commitment to show the long-term, not a one-and-done effort. People will see through performative actions. They need to see it as real and lasting, with no going back.

SEEK ASSISTANCE: There are some problems you can solve alone, and some that require help. If you feel the issues harming your reputation are recurrent or hard to change, a therapist, a coach, or educational materials may be warranted. Whatever it is you need, be proactive in obtaining the help, review, or skills you need.

BE PATIENT: Change is slow when it comes to eradicating a negative reputation. Extend yourself grace and allow time to heal situations and to show your amended behavior.

THE MICROSKILL:

10. APOLOGIZE THOUGHTFULLY, AND EXPLAIN YOUR MISTAKES

WHAT IS THE ACTUAL SKILL?

Recognize when you need to apologize—and do it authentically.

ADAIRA

As a mentor I support students and residents along their paths. A few years ago, before I really even started writing myself, a young college student asked me to read an essay they had written. It was incredibly personal and heartfelt. I also saw many places where the writing could have been clearer and briefer. So I immediately jumped into the areas where the writing could be stronger. My rationale was *this feedback will make their essay better.* I spent an hour editing and revising, assuming I was helping. In truth, I had no experience giving feedback on personal writing. My unfiltered feedback was received as harsh and blunt. I found out via another peer that my "comments were a bit too granular and perhaps made them feel like they hadn't done a good job." I felt horrible. I reached out immediately and apologized. I explained but did not overexplain my thought process and shared how I had reflected on my errors. And I shared the places I planned to grow. I concluded by sharing how I plan to learn more about giving feedback.

WHY DO WE NEED THIS SKILL?

Apologizing marks the difference between someone who takes ownership of an error and someone who does not. As a disclaimer, we don't suggest you have such a low threshold that you are apologizing all day long. We've seen this happen with women in the workplace—a group that has been socialized to over apologize.[90] But we do want you to learn how to apologize and acknowledge that you genuinely made a mistake. We need to balance between our sense of self and our willingness to apologize. Refusing to apologize has been shown to boost self-esteem, value integrity, and create feelings of being in control.[91] On the other hand, apologizing makes us human, expressing empathy and understanding and acknowledging wrongdoing.[92]

WHY IS THIS SKILL HARD TO ACHIEVE?

- Your ego prevents you from owning your words and actions.
- Guilt and shame are real emotions, and they can drive you to stay quiet or deflect blame.
- Your workplace culture does not model apologizing and instead hide and minimize mistakes.

WHAT ARE THE CRITICAL ACTIONS?

LISTEN AND DON'T DISMISS: If an error is brought to your attention, take it seriously. You may disagree and discover that you actually did not make a mistake. But in the initial window, stay open, receptive, and evaluate the situation before dismissing it. Depending on the scale of the error, you may want to discuss with your personal board first before making the apology.

ASSESS YOUR FEELINGS: Check in with yourself. How do you feel about the mistake? How do you think it happened? What might you do differently next time? Allow yourself a bit of time to find answers. Discuss it with someone kind, empathetic, and trustworthy.

SELECT AN APPROPRIATE MEDIUM TO APOLOGIZE: The medium that you choose should be proportional to the seriousness of the error. Forgot to respond to an email and no measurable harm? A simple *I am sorry* email will work. You make a bookkeeping error that cost your company tens of thousands of dollars? Consider an in-person or virtual meeting. Apologies in-person allow others to hear your authentic voice, read your body language, and have the ability to respond in real time.

APOLOGIZE IN A TIMELY MANNER: The best apologies happen around the time of the event—we're talking within hours or one or two days, not months or years later. That being said, an apology that is delayed, authentic, and reflective is better than one that is quick and superficial or never given at all.

CREATE A SIMPLE STRUCTURE: We love to rehearse difficult conversations. It just helps temper the emotions. With practice, you are more at ease and gain clarity on what you wish to get across. Here is a framework for approaching an apology.

GOAL	OBJECTIVE
Express self-reflection and regret	**Try:** "I'm sorry for being late. I need to better prioritize being on time." **Avoid**: "Everyone is late. It's not a big deal." **Avoid:** "I am sorry I was late. I was grabbing the folders you asked me to pick up. That caused my delay."

Avoid being defensive or normalizing behavior that is unprofessional. Avoid retelling in a way that gaslights or minimizes the experience of the other person.

Convey empathy	**Try:** "I'm sorry I hurt your feelings with my joke." **Avoid:** "It was just a joke. Don't take things so seriously."	— *Apologize, acknowledge, take responsibility, and at the same time show empathy.*
Delineate what you learned	**Try**: "Going forward, I won't rush my email response. I am going to respond more thoughtfully and wait until I've processed my emotions." **Avoid:** "Oh, just ignore my response. You know I didn't mean it."	— *Share how you have learned and how going forward you will act differently. Include preventative measures you might take to avoid it from happening again.*
Don't steal the spotlight	**Try:** "I'm sorry I disappointed you and the team. I get why this went over poorly." **Avoid:** "This entire incident made me feel terrible. I haven't been able to sleep. The timeline was virtually impossible."	— *The goal of the apology is to hold space for the other person. Acknowledge yourself and also don't make it all about yourself to deflect responsibility.*
Be open to a response and conversation	**Try:** "I'm happy to hear your thoughts." **Avoid:** "Actually, that's technically not what happened. I think you are over analyzing."	— *Let your colleague speak without interrupting. Do not talk over them, minimize, or explain away their experience.*

It's important to rehearse difficult conversations in order to help temper emotions.

CONCLUSION:

What you say and write, how you behave and engage all influence your reputation.	Be yourself. And also, apologize for mistakes.	Take care of relationships around you. Help others, and appreciate how they help you.

SUPPLEMENTAL RESOURCES:

TED Talk

Complaining Productively

Forbes

5

MICROSKILLS FOR BECOMING A SUBJECT-MATTER EXPERT

ADAIRA

In 2021, I stepped down from two separate positions where I functioned as a mentor and advisor for physicians. This transition opened up much more time on my professional calendar. I decided that I wanted to write a book—it had been a personal goal for years. So I spent time learning as much as I could about writing. I explored children's books, romance novels, everything. I read, watched, and listened to experts discuss the process of book writing. I spent weeks, actually months, reading blogs and books about writing. I joined online and in-person writing communities. When I felt sure that writing a book seemed possible, I pitched the idea to Resa to write one together. And thankfully, she was in. And we learned even more together. After weeks of discussions and writing a book proposal, we felt confident and knowledgeable enough to seek out a literary agent and publisher as co-authors.

Expertise often comes from formally obtaining a degree or a certificate—like college, or a doctorate program. It is also compounded by reading books, gaining work experience, and collaborating with experts. For some jobs, structured education is necessary: to be a neurosurgeon you do need to go to medical school and do specialty training. To be a pilot for an airline, you need to complete training, put in your flight hours, and gain credentialing.

Luckily for all of us, the internet has changed the expertise game. With its wide reach, content, software, and human capital are accessible and create two key changes in how fast and easily you may build your expertise. First, you can learn faster. Videos and podcasts can be listened to at double speed at any time of the day. You may join lectures without traveling, work with tutors across the world, write papers using artificial intelligence, earn degrees from home, and collaborate via email and video calls. If you don't have a talent or skill, you can find an app or even outsource someone else to complete the task. Second, you can reach a broad audience. Social media, newsletters, podcasts, websites, and blogs all augment the process of spreading a message and sharing content with the click of a few buttons. With wide reach you can create massive influence faster.

A word of caution: expertise is not guaranteed when a person has degrees or high profile position or titles. In fact, there are loud voices with large platforms, who are controversial for sharing misinformation. So, it's worth saying that having followers or a platform does not make someone a reliable, ethical, or widely accepted expert. Expertise is not just having a strong opinion; it is having informed and accurate knowledge.

We also want to push back against the idea that anyone can be seen as an expert. In fact, expertise is recognized and comes more easily to certain demographics—such as older white men. In one medical patient survey, 32% of patients assumed their woman physician was a nurse. And 75% of men were correctly identified as physicians.[93] It's not that nurses are not highly skilled and trained—they are in fact professionals with expertise. It is the bias that women are not seen as physicians, even when they do the extensive training and meet the credentials. While we cannot change the biases you may be up against, we can equip you with skills to push forward. In this chapter, we cover 10 MicroSkills to help you develop subject matter expertise.

MICROSKILLS FOR BECOMING A SUBJECT-MATTER EXPERT:

1. Brainstorm the expertise you would like to develop.
2. Take a multimedia approach to learning the topic.
3. Test ideas with your network.
4. Set measurable benchmarks, and move toward them.
5. Collaborate with others to deepen your skills and establish credibility.
6. Deliberately practice new skills as often as possible.
7. Create a social-media presence.
8. Gauge leadership roles related to expertise.
9. Apply for awards and honors in your expertise.
10. Learn to grow and evolve your expertise.

THE MICROSKILL:

1. BRAINSTORM THE EXPERTISE YOU WOULD LIKE TO DEVELOP

WHAT IS THE ACTUAL SKILL?

Create a list of ideas without any fear of judgment or need to commit.

RESA

Women and, more so, women with intersectional identities are paid less for doing the same work as men. This is certainly true for women physicians. Fewer rise to leadership positions, fewer receive keynote-speaker invitations, and fewer are asked to be the subject-matter experts in the room or in a public forum. Women are less visible and their voices are less heard. During the COVID-19 pandemic, I had more time at home. So I thought about creative ways to share information and dive deeper into amplifying the stories of inequity in the workplace. I thought about how I wanted to share the information, the data, and the personal narratives. Ultimately, I launched a podcast, and it took brainstorming to settle on a name. Visible, Invisible. Voices, Faces, People. I played with the words and phrases and then started bouncing word combinations off people—close friends, acquaintances, colleagues. Ultimately, I landed on a name that shared the message and mission of the show: *The Visible Voices Podcast*. We aim to amplify the voices of people, both known and unknown, covering topics of health care, equity, and current trends.

WHY DO WE NEED THIS SKILL?

It's common to stick with one idea because it's the first one, not because it's the best one. It's also normal to want to be safe and follow the path someone may have created for us. Brainstorming challenges the idea that what is obvious and in front of us is the only way. Brainstorming is an exercise in creativity. It pushes us to extend our boundaries to iterate and find the ideas yet to be uncovered and waiting to be discovered. It's okay if your list is long...or short. This exercise isn't about immediately identifying what is a good or bad idea. It's about thinking outside the box, coming up with ideas you would never have considered. What really matters is the time you put into creating the list. You want to embrace the thought process behind saying, "Yes, that could work because..." and "No, that wouldn't work because..." A good list feels free, unrealistic, daring, and creative.

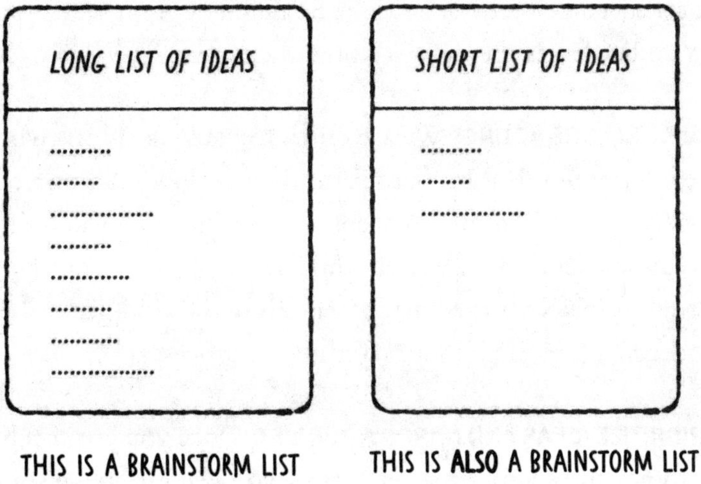

LONG LIST OF IDEAS

SHORT LIST OF IDEAS

THIS IS A BRAINSTORM LIST

THIS IS **ALSO** A BRAINSTORM LIST

Brainstorming is an exercise in creativity. Create a list of ideas without any fear of judgment or need to commit.

WHY IS THIS SKILL HARD TO ACHIEVE?

- You have no experience with brainstorming.
- You feel uncomfortable thinking outside the box.
- You feel self-conscious to share your ideas with others.
- Your list of ideas overwhelms you.

WHAT ARE THE CRITICAL ACTIONS OF THIS MICROSKILL?

CREATE A LIST: Create a list of topics about which you want to be an expert. The topics should interest you and be useful to others. Talk to a lot of people so you can expose yourself to what you have not yet considered. Trust us, there is always something you haven't considered. Adaira's five-year-old daughter, Nova, often shares what she wants to be when she grows up. "A doctor!" because that's all she knows. She's never met an *architect* or a *lawyer.* So neither option would end up on her list as she doesn't know they exist.

PAUSE BEFORE ACTING: We are quick to make decisions when we are excited. But be mindful and settle down. Sit on your list before you commit too deeply (e.g. making company-wide announcements, buying website domains, moving your family across the country.) Smart decisions in the workplace often undergo a logical and rational thought process.

PRIORITIZE IDEAS AND NARROW THE LIST: Once you create a list of topics and spend time reflecting, you need to make some decisions. There are only twenty-four hours in the day, so filter out the options that are not right or not right for right now. Select for the now. Defer the rest for later or may be for never. Look at what remains on the list, and select your top choices. Narrow the list by asking:

1. Does this topic bring me energy, excitement and joy? Does it feel sustainable?

2. Is this topic unique? Will I be entering a space that is overrun with experts? If it is crowded, do I have a unique spin, delivery, or voice?

3. Who is the audience for this topic? Is that audience too narrow? Or too wide and nonspecific?

4. Will this topic have a measurable impact? Will it enable me to grow and gain new skills in ways that feel important to me?

EXPLORE A TOPIC: Now is the time to poke holes in the idea. Read more on the topic. See what exists. Look for gaps. For instance, if you want to be an expert in artificial intelligence, you may find that the field became popular and crowded fast. However, consider using artificial intelligence for a yet explored topic such as mentorship. At this stage you should be energized—it's new, it's exciting, and it could lead to more opportunities. The best thing you can do is listen to your gut—and keep researching.

START SMALL AND GRANULAR: We love ambition, and we recognize that when it comes to developing expertise, small, slow, and steady is better. Seek granularity. For example, if you want to be a manager, you could generically develop your leadership skills. However that is not as unique and compelling as developing management of early career graduates. Get specific and concrete and go deep.

THE MICROSKILL:

2. TAKE A MULTIMEDIA APPROACH TO LEARNING THE TOPIC

WHAT IS THE ACTUAL SKILL?

Access a variety of resources when informing yourself on any topic.

ADAIRA

I had decided to improve my public-speaking skills and establish expertise as a lecturer. I started with a storytelling course with Marianne Neuwirth at Stanford University. She taught me the art of telling short, emotional stories. She also taught me how to use hand gestures to convey ideas and emotions. After the course, I read a few books on speaking. I used educational funds to hire a speaking coach for a single two-hour, one-on-one session. Also, I watched online videos, even though this is not my preferred learning style. However, the online tutorials on slide design using various software platforms were useful. In the end, no single resource was enough to teach me the finer skills of public speaking, but together they helped me reach my goal.

WHY DO WE NEED THIS SKILL?

There are an incredible number of resources available at any time on almost every topic. Relying solely on on-the-job learning is neither smart nor efficient. Videos, podcasts, books, smartphone apps, blogs, conferences and lectures all deepen our expertise. Even local or national meetings remain a great way to connect with people and learn from experts in real time.

WHY IS THIS SKILL HARD TO ACHIEVE?

- The wealth of information is overwhelming.
- It's hard to figure out which references are good and trustworthy and worth your time and money.
- Learning takes effort and time outside of working hours.

WHAT ARE THE CRITICAL ACTIONS OF THIS MICROSKILL?

IDENTIFY A PLACE TO START: Find a singular reference that will be your starting point, and branch out to others. This can be an online video, a newsletter, a podcast, or a person. You can even start learning via social media by following experts. Adaira does this often: she finds an expert on social media for a particular topic and then checks who they follow and then gradually follows some of those people.

CREATE AN OUTLINE OR PLAN OF STUDYING MATERIAL: You don't need to learn everything all at once. And this need not be formal. But the order of content you learn should feel organized and intentional. When we were learning about the book writing process we started by learning about agents, then later we learned everything about publishers. We didn't try to learn about marketing before we even had a book deal.

STREAMLINE LEARNING TO DECREASE COMMITMENT: An efficient work hack is to incorporate an educational experience into your commute or daily run and listen to a podcast or audiobook then. You can also use learning opportunities such as attending workshops or webinars as an opportunity to network and meet other experts as well as learn.

THE MICROSKILL:

3. TEST IDEAS WITH YOUR NETWORK

WHAT IS THE ACTUAL SKILL?

Run ideas in progress past the people in your network.

ADAIRA

I've always wanted to start a nonprofit that was focused on two of my passions: mentoring and writing. I did a deep dive researching existing nonprofits and organizations. I learned it was a lot of work. Essentially, setting up the paperwork, trying to fundraise, building a website, and then hosting programs and projects would consume all of my time. I spoke with an amazing colleague, Dr. Farah Dadabhoy. We had a track record of working well together. It seemed like a natural fit to develop subject-matter expertise on nonprofits together. After reading and learning as much as we can on our own, we then tested out our ideas with people in the nonprofit space. We also began pitching it to people familiar with leading teams and fundraising. Those conversations helped us to find our knowledge gaps and discover obstacles we hadn't considered. They were literally crucial to revealing our oversights.

WHY DO WE NEED THIS SKILL?

Sometimes we don't share ideas until we believe we have figured it all out. That's too late. Now you might be far down the road with your ideas. Or, too invested to pivot. Instead, we want you comfortable sharing and brainstorming unfinished ideas. When it feels too early to share, start pitching to others to get input. By doing so, we're able to get early outside perspective and better refine the original idea. We also are able to get validation that what we are thinking makes sense. Feedback, even if constructive, can create a sense of excitement and interest for all parties that an idea is now better shaped to move forward.

WHY IS THIS SKILL HARD TO ACHIEVE?

- You don't know the value of sharing your idea early.
- You feel vulnerable, uncomfortable and you don't know what to ask.
- You fear people only want a finished product before they talk to you.
- You fear sharing your idea will result in it being scooped by another person.

WHAT ARE THE CRITICAL ACTIONS OF THIS MICROSKILL?

CURATE A LIST OF PEOPLE: Consider this a dream list. If you are very early in your career, we know it can be intimidating to ask anyone for help. But we want to normalize meetings with select supervisors or mentors to get their opinions. We have even found valuable advice from our network outside of medicine. A focused list of relevant people you trust is better than a long list that might intimidate, confuse, or distract you from moving forward. Even one meeting can provide valuable reflection.

PITCH BEFORE ITS POLISHED: Do not wait for ideas to be perfectly bloomed. Yes, some people may want something in a final draft mode. No problem. Tell these individuals you will circle back with them soon. They are not your first round brainstorm people.

ASK HIGH LEVEL QUESTIONS: Early on, when you meet with people, you should ask high level questions. You want to know if your train is on the right track and going the right direction. Some starter questions:

What do you think of this idea?
What red flags do you see?
Do you see this as career advancing?
What can I do to prepare myself for this opportunity?
Is there a need for my expertise in this area?
What are obstacles you foresee?
Will I be able to stand out among a crowd of peers?

ADOPT AND BELIEVE THE ABUNDANCE MINDSET: Do not worry about an idea being scooped. Ideas are cheap and what really matters is the execution of an idea. If someone runs with your idea, consider it a compliment and nod to your creativity and innovation. And remember the same idea can be developed and executed in 10 million ways.

THE MICROSKILL:

4. SET MEASURABLE BENCHMARKS, AND MOVE TOWARD THEM

WHAT IS THE ACTUAL SKILL?

Create a way to track your progress toward expertise.

ADAIRA

In residency we must become proficient in a certain number of skills. As emergency medicine physicians the list is quite broad; we are responsible for a variety of emergencies. We must be able to deliver babies, reduce shoulder dislocations, manage severe respiratory distress, drain abscesses (Don't know what an abscess is? Google Dr. PimplePopper). Yet, my leadership team didn't just throw us into the ring and say, "learn it all." That'd make an already grueling residency even more chaotic. Instead, they checked my progress every year and helped me set goals. "Okay, next year I'd like you to have more lumbar punctures." That raised flag created an alert to seek out those procedures on shift, when indicated clinically. With out those checkpoints it would have been easy to wander aimlessly for 4 years and be told towards the end of graduation, "Why haven't you delivered those 10 babies?"

WHY DO WE NEED THIS SKILL?

We all need positive signs of movement and a way to track progress toward our goals. Tracking progress fosters excitement and validation; it also allows us to redirect how we spend our energy. The goal is to force yourself to answer, *Am I moving? Do I have signposts of success and progress?* Adopting a framework or cataloging system facilitates planning and operational structure. Remember if someone is openly and aggressively rude to you when you request their help—don't take it personally. That's a "them problem"—move on and consider yourself blessed that you didn't further engage before discovering who they truly are.

WHY IS THIS SKILL HARD?

- It is hard to quantitatively measure progress.
- It is demoralizing if you are stalled and unsure how to move forward.
- Measuring yourself against others is disheartening. You might lose sight of the big picture.

WHAT ARE THE CRITICAL ACTIONS OF THIS MICROSKILL?

CREATE OBJECTIVE MEASURES: Start by identifying your key objective to build expertise. Let's say you want to become an invited speaker at a national conference. Decide upon small discrete steps that you will learn about this goal: 1. Read one to two books on public speaking; 2. Watch YouTube videos of three notable talks; 3. Identify a few peer coaches or paid, professional coaches to improve your speaking skills; 4. Nominate yourself or ask someone to nominate you for open call speaker opportunities; and 5. Cold email or cold call people in your network to book a talk.

TRY A FRAMEWORK: One to try is the OKR or Objective and Key Results framework, which asks you to identify your main objective. Next, the framework asks you to execute very measurable and quantitative results that will help you get to your objective.[94] I want to become store manager (objective); I'm going to improve customer survey feedback by 15% (result), I am going to increase revenue by 10% (result), I am going to meet with the regional manager 2 times this year (result).

TRACK YOUR MOVEMENT: You can use a free digital spreadsheet or paid subscription services to track your tasks. Post-it notes or back-of-the-envelope lists if you want to be informal and casual. No matter what medium, make it readable and easy to access, otherwise you won't feel good about using it. Color-code, underline, bold text if you wish. You might have multiple tabs or rows for different goals. As you can see—style doesn't matter as much as keeping it clear and easy to access. Here's an example of how we track our writing programs.

TRACKING SHEET FOR WRITING ARTICLES ABOUT THE WORKPLACE

PUBLICATION OUTLET	TOPIC	STATUS
Harvard Business Review	Fuel-Efficient Mentoring	Submitted; awaiting editor response
Fast Company	Toxicity in the Workplace	No response; submit to a new outlet

CNBC	Healthy Eating on Shift	Accepted, publication pending
Nature	Early-Morning Meetings	Published
To be determined	Work-Life Balance	In process; writing first draft

Use a free digital spreadsheet or paid subscription service to track your movement on tasks.

SOLICIT FEEDBACK: Feedback helps improve your skills. Some people will volunteer feedback; mostly you need to seek it out. Thinking about becoming a national speaker, you might ask, "How was my talk? I tried to use more stories. What's one thing that worked? What's one thing you would have changed or liked less of?" The feedback will be qualitative and can shape how your progress is being perceived or interpreted.

ASK FOR HELP: You might not be able to reach all of your objectives on your own. Asking others to help you is a normal part of the process. Ask your network, "I'm really hoping to be a national speaker on this topic, can you keep me in mind for any opportunities that come your way that would be a good fit?"

GAUGE YOUR PROGRESS: We want to be clear: this is not a competition nor a race. But you can gain insight from observing the progress of other people. And asking them about their progress. For instance, think about a colleague who is at the same age yet seems further along in establishing expertise. Gently and respectfully probe them on what they did to gain expertise and opportunity. Try to get specifics. Hearing them say "I just worked hard" isn't very helpful. You want to know what buttons they pressed, who they called, and what emails they sent.

THE MICROSKILL:

5. COLLABORATE WITH OTHERS TO DEEPEN YOUR EXPERTISE AND ESTABLISH CREDIBILITY

WHAT IS THE ACTUAL SKILL?

Further your learning, teaching, and reputation through collaboration.

RESA

At my first emergency medicine job leading a section of clinical ultrasound, I noticed the impact of organizing a monthly educator series. It started as a fun way to invite friends to visit me in New York City. Win-win: I could amplify their expertise, they met my team who expanded their networks, and my friend could add a line item to their résumé. At the same time, the resident doctors and early-career learners gained small-group-style education and an audience with nationally known subject-matter experts. In reality, the series became so much more. The sessions were opportunities for collaboration I had not anticipated: research projects, group papers and publications, regional workshops, and speaking invitations that went both directions. Without realizing it, these collaborations helped me establish expertise in ways I never imagined. I have since continued the monthly series concept everywhere I have worked.

WHY DO WE NEED THE SKILL?

Working with other people unlocks new perspectives and

transforms less mature skills into stronger ones. Collaboration can help your reputation. It builds your network within your company and wider industry. And with the help of virtual platforms and social media, collaboration builds national and international networks. Collaborating allows established and new contacts to watch your journey to becoming an expert.

WHY IS THIS HARD TO ATTAIN?

- You have a limited network and you feel hesitant to ask people to collaborate.
- People are hard to access. Not everyone has publicly available contact information.
- The hierarchy precludes experienced people from working with young or inexperienced people.
- You are not interested in collaborations.

WHAT ARE THE CRITICAL ACTIONS FOR THIS MICROSKILL?

IDENTIFY THE OPPORTUNITIES: As you learn more about your field or industry, you will realize areas in need of development. As you attend lectures or listen to podcasts, find the holes in arguments. This means there is room for someone to investigate further or solve unanswered questions. Develop a working knowledge of what is already done and optimized, and make a list of where you see deficits. These are your opportunities. Before you reach out, its nice (though not mandatory) to do some homework. The most important question to ask is *What opportunity do you want this person to help you with?*

IDENTIFY A COLLABORATOR: Start with one person. Based on your gaps and needs, reach out to person with whom you wish to work. Email or social media or another professional channel, such as a list-serv or newsletter can work. If someone you know knows the person, then request an email introduction. Be careful, respectful, and intentional when you ask for this. Don't expect the same person to personally introduce you to everyone in their network. Then, be receptive to being the one to whom people later reach out.

FROM:	
TO:	
CC:	
BCC:	
SUBJECT:	
MESSAGE:	Hi Adaira, I am designing a podcast episode on health tech founders who are physicians. You mentioned someone on the phone when we spoke last week. Can you please introduce me to them by email? Resa

Identify a collaborator based on your gaps and needs. Email, social media, or another professional channel, such as a Listserv or newsletter, can work. If someone you're acquainted with knows the person, then request an email introduction. Be careful, respectful, and intentional when you ask for this.

FIND YOUR COMMUNITY OF PRACTICE: Communities of practices are informal, often voluntary, groups of people who gather to share knowledge about a particular topic. Depending on the area of interest, they may be easy to find. Search online for events in a particular area. Join social media groups. You want to be where similar experts are and, at the very least, observe the conversation. Adaira participates online with a few writing communities. Resa participates online with a few spoken and writing storytelling communities. You may want to engage by sending a request to connect or follow or a direct message or by responding to a discussion. Join or apply for training programs in your field or interest. All of this puts you closer to like-minded individuals and an opportunity to collaborate and share expertise.

THE MICROSKILL:

6. DELIBERATELY PRACTICE NEW SKILLS AS OFTEN AS POSSIBLE

WHAT IS THE ACTUAL SKILL?

Demonstrate your developing knowledge and growth to others.

RESA

I could not figure out why I was not getting speaking invitations. No keynotes. No grand rounds. No plenary sessions. No podcast guest invites. I thought I had followed all the steps to developing expertise in clinical ultrasound (publishing papers, leading organizations, teaching at workshops), but for a while it was crickets. So I spoke with an emergency-medicine friend who was the chairperson of her department.

RESA: I am trying to figure out why I am not getting invited to give grand rounds lectures.

FRIEND: Do you want to come give grand rounds here? I will have my administrative assistant reach out with dates.

And just like that, I became an invited grand rounds speaker at an academic emergency medicine department. In that conversation I realized that markers of expertise aren't everything. Sometimes opportunities happen through networking and simply by asking.

WHY DO WE NEED THIS SKILL?

Sharing your skill through speaking is one way to develop comfort with the material. Joining projects is another. No matter the opportunity type, putting your name in the hat and showing up to do the work is a great way to demonstrate your knowledge. You and others can see your strengths and the areas needing development. This helps build a name for yourself and demonstrate capabilities.

WHY IS THIS SKILL HARD TO ACHIEVE?

- You have anxiety or fear of being seen as an impostor.
- You don't feel ready and think you need experience, a certain position, age, advanced education—before you show what you know publicly.
- People tell you that you are not ready.

WHAT ARE THE CRITICAL ACTIONS OF THIS MICROSKILL?

UNDERSTANDING IMPOSTER SYNDROME: Imposter syndrome, is commonly described as feeling fraudulent about fitting in at work. We hear people self-diagnose often, "I have imposter syndrome." Yet rarely is this feeling caused by feeling deceitful or fraudulent within a workplace. Most often, imposter syndrome floats around as an idea because you lack the recognition and support you need. And that negative space makes you feel othered and doubtful of your potential. This lack of support is especially harmful for marginalized communities (e.g. women, people of color, people with disabilities).[95] We want to remind you—you have skills and you deserve opportunities to demonstrate them.

RECOGNIZE A GOOD OPPORTUNITY: As mentors and educators one issue we see with early career professionals is that they struggle to identify a good opportunity when its right there staring at them. And even if they recognize the opportunity, they don't know the next action to take. As you can see in the table below. No matter the opportunity the action to take starts with the self pushing forward.

OPPORTUNITY	GOAL	ACTION TO TAKE
A position opens to become director or manager of your specialty, niche, or group.	You want to work your way to executive-level leadership.	Speak with your supervisor and mentors about the opportunity. Ask "How can I best position myself for this opening?"

There is a call for speakers for the annual conference in your subject area.	You want to become a recognized speaker for a particular field or practice area.	Apply to speak. Submit a few ideas for workshops, lectures, panels. Invite colleagues to join.
At a networking dinner you sit next to someone who shares career paths and has your dream job.	You want to follow a similar trajectory and move into a similar job.	Let the person know about your shared interest. Ask about their journey. Ask for their contact information to continue the conversation.
You have an idea for an article you would like to write, and you see an open call for submissions.	You hope to write about the topic to grow your expertise as a writer.	Reach out to the editors and share an article draft with your pitch.

As mentors and educators, one challenge we see with early career professionals is that they struggle to seize a good opportunity when it's right there before them.

ASK AND ADVOCATE FOR YOURSELF: No one at work is losing sleep because you aren't getting opportunities. It's not that they don't care about you, it's that you need to care about you. How? Just like in Resa's story above, start asking and advocating. Think about friends from your training and schooling. Where are they working? What are they doing? See if they can help provide opportunities for you to develop the expertise. Normalize asking. You might have heard the message *ask them, the worst they can say is no.* But in fact, Adaira tells her mentees that the worst thing that can happen is that your contact would have said yes, but you never asked. Accept the no's. Never regret asking.

COMMUNICATE YOUR ABILITIES AND EXPERTISE: You have a few options here to share your expertise with others. Create and publish a personal website. Post on social media. Add a title line to your LinkedIn profile or a sentence in your email-signature line. Start putting your expertise out there.

TRUST AND LISTEN TO YOURSELF: If you are told you are too young or not ready, remember that you don't need to take this advice. Trust yourself. Ask for feedback from your personal board. Think big and never regret advocating for yourself.

THE MICROSKILL:

7. CREATE A SOCIAL-MEDIA PRESENCE

WHAT IS THE ACTUAL SKILL?

Take the time to create and maintain a social-media presence on a relevant platform.

RESA

When I started The Visible Voices Podcast, two friends I trust implicitly told me I had to get onto more social media platforms. I was really hesitant. I thought one was enough. I did not want more social media outlets. However these friends—one an educator with an MBA and the other a CEO with a law degree, angel investor, and serial entrepreneur—both advised the same thing independently of each other—join LinkedIn. They knew the importance of a professional network and the effectiveness of that outlet. They were spot-on. It's one of the easier ways to connect with people who are motivated to learn, share, discuss topics of mutual interest, and even form groups around an expertise area. On many occasions, this is how I met, connected with subject matter experts, and invited them as podcast guests.

WHY DO WE NEED THIS SKILL?

You can only build so many relationships in the workplace. After a while you need more. It's not just us advising this: the *New York Times* agrees that social media is good for business and your career.[96] Social media is a force multiplier. The medium allows you to have access to people and resources on a global scale. Access can mean active one-on-one communication with new people or passively interacting, such as observing what other experts write, say, and share without ever directly interacting or interfacing with them. The return on investment can be large in growing your expertise.

WHY IS THIS SKILL HARD TO ACHIEVE?

- Social media brings trolls and toxic, triggering people.
- It takes work to build a profile and learn the platform system approach and settings.
- Participating can be a large time investment and addictive.

WHAT ARE THE CRITICAL ACTIONS FOR THIS SKILL?

MIND HIGH-RISK TOPICS: We won't censor what you write. We want you to do that for yourself. Be mindful if you wish to dive into controversial social or political topics. Think twice about rants, complaints, or grievances about your company. Decide how much of your personal life you want to share: pictures of children, vacations, exterior/interior of your home.

PICK A PLATFORM: There are many social-media platforms. Find out where your target community participates. Ask the team and your personal board what they recommend. Focus on the ones that work for you.

BUILD A PROFILE: Observe other people's profiles, and note what you like and don't like. Model yours after the ones you think are most effective, look good, aligned with your interests, and read well. Remember: this is for professional purposes. Use the same name that you would use at work. We recommend using a professional photo that shows your face.

OBSERVE, DIRECT-MESSAGE, AND COMMENT PUBLICLY: Start by observing how others use the platform. Study the content. What gets attention? You can direct-message people as well to comment on their work and introduce yourself. If you feel comfortable, you may comment on posts and discussions publicly.

KNOW YOUR LIMITS: Always remember why and for whom you are engaging in social media. If this is to establish and grow your expertise, then that should be the center of your content generation. Trust your comfort level and respect your own boundaries on what you put out on social media. Be mindful of controversial or vulnerable topics.

THE MICROSKILL:

8. GAUGE LEADERSHIP ROLES RELATED TO EXPERTISE

WHAT IS THE ACTUAL SKILL?

Decide which expertise-related leadership roles are worthwhile.

ADAIRA

Prior to taking the role as Harvard medical school advisor to forty medical students, I thought about what was important to me. At the core, it was helping others develop their careers. My goal was to make sure I had a detailed understanding of the expectations of the role. Prior to applying, I spoke with my supervisor, who felt this to be a great leadership opportunity and steppingstone. I talked to people who previously and currently had the same position. The job description mentioned that I'd be responsible for monitoring students' progress through medical school. I found out that the role requires me to meet with students in the evenings and weekends. This detail was not clearly advertised on the flyer. It didn't deter me but it was a new data point I took into consideration. I also asked medical students about their perception of faculty in this role. The deep dive helped me see if the position would be worthwhile. I had a very clear understanding of the risks and benefits. And in the end, this leadership opportunity seemed perfectly aligned with my expertise goal.

WHY DO WE NEED THIS SKILL?

Many leadership opportunities will come along. Not all are worthwhile or high-yield for your growth. You should critically evaluate an opportunity and weigh the pros and cons. This includes salary, culture, job description, time commitment, need for travel, and more.[97] It's easy to sign up for a position thinking that it will help you grow, network, and establish credibility only to find out it's not true. You don't want to be bogged down by a leadership position which adds administrative work, takes up a lot of time, or drains your energy, all without guaranteed opportunity to be creative and independent and move you towards expertise.

WHY IS THIS SKILL HARD TO ACHIEVE?

- You fear asking too many detailed questions.
- You fear the honesty received, by doing your own background check, could discourage you from applying.
- You believe all leadership opportunities are a good investment.
- You cannot determine if and how declining an opportunity will affect your career.

WHAT ARE THE CRITICAL ACTIONS OF THIS MICROSKILL?

KNOW THE JOB DESCRIPTION: Learn all you possibly can before you take on a new leadership position. Read about the responsibilities. Learn the time commitment and off-hours expectations. Seek out the details that are not immediately shared.

TALK TO PEOPLE WHO HOLD OR HAVE HELD THE ROLE: It's helpful to explicitly ask why they left—if they did. Ask potentially uncomfortable questions ahead of taking the position. "How were you treated?" "Why did you leave?" "Did you feel appreciated?" "Did it help your career to take this role? If so, in what ways?"

FIND OUT WHERE PEOPLE GO NEXT: Assess where the role leads. Is this a terminal position, or is this one that will likely feed you into a larger and more impactful role? Understanding the trajectory will help you also focus on the skills and opportunities that you need to take for the best next step.

GAUGE THE AMOUNT OF SUPPORT AND RESOURCES: Do you have the proper administrative support, financial resources, and authority to carry out the tasks of the role? Will this be a position where you will be all on your own without structure and support? Ask specific questions to the person who is interviewing and hiring you about the responsibilities and resources provided.

ASSESS THE REACH AND IMPACT OF THE ROLE: You were likely considering taking on this role because you want experience as an expert. Are you impacting five people or five thousand? Are you going to be in someone else's shadow, or will you be a spokesperson for the work that you do? Will you have opportunities to demonstrate your work to the executive leadership of your company, industry, or field?

LEARN HOW TO PASS: Saying yes and saying no can be difficult. When opportunities comes along, it's tempting. *I'm finally get-*

ting noticed. Or, *This is my chance to shine.* Trust your gut. Do your research to really find out before saying yes. Remember the goal—you want a position that helps you become a subject matter expert. Here is standard phrasing for declining an offer: "Thank you for taking the time to consider me. After careful consideration and speaking with my mentors, I have decided to pass on this opportunity. Please keep me in mind for future endeavors."

THE MICROSKILL:

9. APPLY FOR AWARDS AND HONORS IN YOUR EXPERTISE

WHAT IS THE ACTUAL SKILL?

Self-advocate for recognition, awards, and honors.

ADAIRA

When I started my emergency medicine faculty job at the hospital, I noticed my colleagues were receiving awards. And the same people seemed to receive them over and over again. Years passed, and I was not receiving any recognitions. I thought maybe I was too junior and I hadn't done anything outstanding and "award-worthy." Then while congratulating a colleague, the playbook was revealed. I said, "Congrats on winning so many awards and honors. It's amazing you are being recognized for your expertise." He said, "Yup, I ask people to nominate me. Or, I have had people who want to nominate me, they just ask me to help put together the nomination packet." At that moment I realized that my peers had been active participants in their own award nominations. I was shocked because all along I thought I should just sit around waiting for someone else to help me get recognized. I couldn't believe that all of the upward movement I had been seeing wasn't by chance, it was by self-advocacy.

WHY DO WE NEED THIS SKILL?

It is a human need to be seen. To be heard. To be recognized for the work we do. As women, we particularly know that in academic institutions it is easy for our work to lack acknowledgment and recognition.[98] Worse, credit may be given to or taken by someone else. Awards and honors establish expertise and credibility. The key is knowing how to apply and how to be nominated. We too thought we would magically be recognized for our work.

WHY IS THIS SKILL HARD TO ACHIEVE?

- You believe others are going to knock on your door to nominate you.
- You have reservations about self-nomination due to discomfort or lack of knowledge.
- Culturally you think it's not okay to ask, assert yourself, or self-nominate.

WHAT ARE THE CRITICAL ACTIONS FOR THIS MICROSKILL?

STOP WAITING: Of course, you know stories of people who have endless amounts of support: mentors, sponsors, coaches, advisors. But that isn't everyone. Most of us ultimately find support because of proactive searching. We don't want you waiting for others to spontaneously and unsolicited ask you, "How can I help you get awards and gain expertise?"

EMBRACE DISCOMFORT: Come to peace with the discomfort. Ask the team and your personal board how they achieved awards and honors. See if there are practices to adopt. Practice asking. Become more comfortable asking. Try out a phrase such as "Would you be willing to nominate me for this award?"

KEEP A LIST OF OPPORTUNITIES: Recognize that there are many opportunities available. Ask people inside and outside the field: they can point you to awards, recognition, prizes, training, or development programs. Even if now is not the time to apply, create a spreadsheet and record the name of the opportunity, the requirements, the timeline, etc.

KEEP YOUR RÉSUMÉ AND CURRICULUM VITAE UPDATED: This one seems easy but can be very hard to sustain. Place a reminder on your calendar to do this monthly or quarterly or by some other timeline. Give a talk, add it to the résumé. Publish a piece, add it to the CV. Real time is a great way to do this. We both keep our resume updated, online and live, on Google Docs, so we can add and edit from any location at anytime.

DRAFT YOUR OWN LETTER OF RECOMMENDATION: Help the person submitting the nomination on your behalf. Write the first draft of your Letter of Recommendation.[99] Open the letter by writing the objective facts about the person submitting the nomination. Then spend two or three paragraphs writing objective facts about yourself that are nuanced. Double-check the work to make sure that the dates and names are spelled correctly. Send this letter to the nominator, who can finalize the letter. They can add all of the superlatives, such as *the best*, *the greatest*, or *the most innovative*. Caveat: if you sign a statement saying that you have not viewed the letter, don't draft it. Period.

THE MICROSKILL:

10. LEARN TO GROW AND EVOLVE YOUR EXPERTISE

WHAT IS THE ACTUAL SKILL?

Continue to deepen and broaden your skills and knowledge.

RESA

I have had an evolution of roles as an emergency medicine ultrasound educator. They built upon each other. Just. Like. MicroSkills. The small incremental steps actually illustrate the growth and development of subject matter expertise. Fellowship: First, I completed a one-year fellowship in ultrasound. Participant learner: Initially, I sat in the audience as the learner attending the ultrasound workshop. Speaker educator: In time, I soon stood on stage as a speaker invited to lecture on ultrasound and teach as a bedside educator. Workshop organizer: Later, I was in charge of organizing a two-day workshop and running the logistics and details. Coach mentor: Finally, I trained the trainer. I coached, mentored, and supported junior faculty, fellows, and junior doctors take charge and run the workshops. Storyteller: Interestingly, all of that experience teaching, learning, lecturing, and writing built up speaking, writing, listening, and storytelling skills. The path is not always linear, yet the evolution of roles shows a progression in expertise.

WHY DO WE NEED THIS SKILL?

Our curiosity and desire for learning should never be stagnant. You should hold a mindset of always trying to grow and to learn.[100] We know that sometimes fields, trends, or practices go extinct, but the skills and knowledge you acquire will always have value. Thinking about the ways you can adjust, expand, and pivot from one niche to the next is a skill.

WHY IS THIS SKILL HARD TO ACHIEVE?

- It is hard to have sustained motivation.
- Being proactive and intentional takes a lot of time.
- The team is stuck in a fixed mindset doing things the way they have always been done.

WHAT ARE THE CRITICAL ACTIONS FOR THIS MICROSKILL?

COLLABORATE WITH BOTH OLD AND NEW PEOPLE: It's easy to work with the same people over and over. Especially when trust is established and there is a good rapport and cadence. Seek new people to collaborate with. Add one person at a time, if you prefer. Cycle people in and out. Embrace new voices and new ideas with projects you take on. Be kind: don't drop people or make them feel cut off, e.g. "I really enjoyed working together. I hope we can collaborate again in the future."

READ AND LISTEN TO CURRENT EVENTS: Subscribe to news and social-media outlets that address your area of expertise. Remember, adjacent topics are useful so that you keep up-to-date and aware of complementary and opposing larger discussions happening outside of your immediate work group in your company.

ATTEND CONFERENCES AND WEBINARS TO NETWORK: When we attend conferences we go to some lectures but spend even more time in the halls or cafes meeting other attendees. The currency is education and the ability to connect with others in real time and in person. You don't want to miss that opportunity. If you see a friend sitting alone, ask to join them and see what they have been working on lately. Same with webinars, see who is attending, send them a private message and offer to meet further afterwards to debrief.

MEET WITH COLLEAGUES AND MENTORS: Share your work and seek input on what else you could be doing to expand your knowledge base and expertise. More experienced people may have a global picture of the landscape of your field and where it's going. Peers may be aware of the latest updates, and younger mentors can tell you what's new and what's outdated.

CONCLUSION:

Establishing expertise is a continuous build of concrete experiences.	You won't build your expertise alone. Work with people and ask them for help.	Don't stagnate or become rigid. Stay open and flexible to learning growth and opportunities.

SUPPLEMENTAL RESOURCES:

Malcolm Gladwell with Robert Krulwich: Science of Success

Freakonomics

Business Insider

6

MICROSKILLS TO LEARN YOUR WORKPLACE CULTURE

RESA

I was working in the emergency department one day. While I was speaking with the lab about a patient with a dangerously high potassium level, a medical student came to tell me about a new patient he had interviewed and examined. The student walked up, did not pause, and started presenting the patient to me while I was on the phone. He spoke louder than the person on the other end of the line so I pivoted my body on the swivel chair, smiled, motioned in the air with my finger to hold a minute and showed him the phone at my ear. I was not mad; I simply saw that he was not aware. Typically, a student would establish eye contact, wait, and be sure I was ready to give attention and listen. Very sick patients merit immediate interruption—but this was not the situation. The student also could have been nervous and unfamiliar with the culture, but this was also not so. We had worked a few shifts together and it was the end of his four weeks on the emergency department rotation. Despite experience and receiving feedback, he had not picked up on social cues, the way to present patients, or the flow of the workplace. I definitely don't pick up on all social cues and at the same time, this was an opportunity for him to learn situational awareness.

Your workplace is more like an emergency department than you may think. There is a culture, a workflow and a way of life that allows the team to interact with and complete the work. And you must be open, curious, and intentional in how you go about learning that culture. Generally speaking, a healthy workplace culture includes people acting with kindness, respect, support, communication, collaboration, and timeliness. Some would say that these characteristics make the environment "appropriate" and "professional."

Arguably though, these terms in relationship to workplace culture can be charged, subjective and biased in interpretation. What happens when what you consider professional and appropriate does not mesh with that of your team or supervisor?

As women, we have navigated a workplace that has a very gendered hierarchy: women make up over half of all medical students in the USA but only 23% of all department chairs.[101] In other words, we might be in the talent pool, but we aren't climbing the ladder to the top. Though we know it's not true of all industries, data suggests that the majority are led by men. A 2022 report gave a hat tip to increased diversity in C-suite leadership, yet still 89% of CEOs, CFOs, and COOs are white and 88% are men.[102] A 2021 report of Massachusetts K–12 educators showed that people of color makeup only 5% and women only 39% of superintendents.[103] Why bring up gender and race in a chapter about culture? We bring this up now to acknowledge that a workplace culture may not feel right or good if you do not belong to the majority group represented in the workplace. Gender concordance and race concordance affect how you feel. To be clear, a universal workplace culture does not exist—which is why we can't teach you *exactly* how to respond to a uniform manner. The unique nature of each workplace makes learning the culture feasible only through observing and the lived experience.

In this chapter we discuss eight MicroSkills to help understand the workplace culture.

MICROSKILLS TO LEARN YOUR WORKPLACE CULTURE:

1. Introduce yourself, and address people by their names.
2. Learn the communication style of others.
3. Understand your company reporting tree.
4. Read your contract, guides, handbooks, and HR policies.
5. Understand the value of self-monitoring.
6. Check your privilege.
7. Upstand for the self and the team.
8. Socialize carefully at work.
9. Notice how bad behavior is handled.

THE MICROSKILL:

1. INTRODUCE YOURSELF, AND ADDRESS PEOPLE BY THEIR NAMES

WHAT IS THE ACTUAL SKILL?

Ask, repeat, and remember people's names; share yours too.

ADAIRA

There are very few Black women physicians in medicine. We are truly unicorns. Because of our rarity, we stand out in nearly any room or meeting or shift. An uncomfortable byproduct of being a Black woman in predominately white spaces is that I am confused for other women of color very frequently despite differences in our height, weight, hair style, hair length, skin color—and the list goes on. Someone once asked me, "Did you cut your dreadlocks?" I have literally never had dreadlocks. It was another woman of color, who looks nothing like me. To a certain extent, names are easy to forget. There are so many people on an emergency department team: administrators, nurses, technicians, students, physician assistants, physicians—and many of these people rotate in and out of their roles. I've started to forgive myself and recognize that I cannot remember everyone's name. I apologize when I make a mistake. I do, however, ask them their name, ask how they'd prefer to be called, and try to remember it for the rest of the shift. It goes from an honest mistake to offensive when a person shows no interest in getting to know me, my name, or its pronunciation. I give people grace and remind them. But it's exhausting.

WHY DO WE NEED THIS SKILL?

First impressions are key to building trust with people in the workplace. As emergency doctors, we have a brief window to establish a rapport with the team and with each of our patients. So we practice building rapport multiple times a day. Introducing yourself is good for your sense of self, asserting your identity and integrating into a team.[104] And in kind, addressing people by their name helps them feel welcomed and respected. People should know your name and you should know theirs.

WHY IS THIS SKILL HARD?

- You don't feel a part of the team.
- You are embarrassed to ask a person their name, especially one you should know.
- You are unsure how to pronounce someone's name.

WHAT ARE THE CRITICAL ACTIONS OF THIS MICROSKILL?

SPEND TIME TEACHING OTHERS YOUR NAME: When you first meet someone make an effort to repeat your name a few times. Repetition helps the other person store the name. You can make an audio clip or write the phonetic spelling to include on social-media accounts or an email signature. Record your name (e.g., *https://cloud.name-coach.com* or *https://namedrop.io*). An example of what to say if someone mis-pronounces your name: "It's actually pronounced Resa with a long E like Reese's Peanut Butter Cups."

BE HONEST AND ASK FOR A REINTRODUCTION: It's simple. Be honest when you forget someone's name, and ask for a reintroduction. Offer your name as well. "I'm so sorry. Can you remind me how you like to be called? My name is [insert your name]."

ASK FOR PRONUNCIATIONS: Take the time to ask for pronunciation. Sometimes having them phonetically spell the name can help. If you leave the conversation very unsure how to pronounce their name, try again. You may say, "I want to pronounce your name correctly. Do you mind sharing again how to say your name?" It shows you care.

BE MINDFUL OF INDIVIDUALITY: Have you ever witnessed this situation at work? Someone from a marginalized community is confused with someone else—yet they have no physical resemblance except e.g. the color of their skin. When this happens repeatedly, it's dehumanizing and gives a message: you are all the same. Or, your name isn't worth learning. Accidents happen, yes. Apologize. If you make this error, own it. "I'm so sorry to mix you up with someone else. Can you please remind me of your name? I'll be sure to be more attentive."

AVOID UNTITILING: Untitling occurs when you remove someone's credentials or position. This practice unconsciously serves to disrespect someone's title and expertise.[105] An example: at a meeting with two guests with executive positions. "We welcome CEO Mark Jones and Anita to our meeting." At one of her jobs, Resa was the team leader and one of two physicians on the team of six. The project manager kept calling her "Resa" and called the male doctor Dr. XX.

THE MICROSKILL:

2. LEARN THE COMMUNICATION STYLES OF OTHERS

WHAT IS THE ACTUAL SKILL?

Recognize how communication varies depending on the scenario and setting.

RESA

Texting always seemed benign to me until a specific incident made me more careful. I text-messaged a colleague who was late on her chapter for a book I was editing. My coeditor and I were running our list of loose ends and missing items, and this author was weeks late. "Hi there. We are doing the weekly run of the list of pending items for the book. Do you have a sense of when you can send the final piece?" There was no intention of meanness, anger, or ill will. There was no disclosed emergency happening on her end. Yet, she texted my coeditor saying that I was bullying her. I was shocked. A few friends helped me realize that some people consider texting personal and more intrusive than a phone call or an email. Tone is lost, and texting can feel invasive and people can feel attacked. I am more careful and thoughtful now—especially with workplace related texts.

WHY DO WE NEED THIS SKILL?

Being a good communicator can really help you become an effective leader.[106] The challenge is that each person and place has specific communication styles and nuances. As a consequence, the rules of and strategy around communication become unpredictable. Also, the culture within the larger company could be totally different from that of your smaller team. Similarly, the current virtual workspace varies from the pre-pandemic in-office culture. And since most communication is nonverbal—connecting through communication platforms or conference calls is a challenge. Without hearing a voice, seeing facial expressions, or reading body language, the quality of communication suffers.[107]

WHY IS THIS SKILL HARD?

- Your communication style and preferences don't work effectively for the team and the work.
- You feel that being universally casual with communication is acceptable.
- Someone else's communication preferences make you uncomfortable.
- It takes time, energy, and attention to effectively communicate.

WHAT ARE THE CRITICAL ACTIONS OF THIS MICROSKILL?

OBSERVE THE BEHAVIOR OF OTHERS: Gain an understanding of how people communicate with each other at work. You don't have to be directly in a conversation or involved in an interaction or conflict to gain valuable information. Gather concrete practices such as the medium people use, the time of day they communicate, the level of politeness, etc.

WATCH FOR SOCIAL CUES: It's important to pay attention to the details. Is there a clear hierarchy and structure? Do people use the word *sir* or *ma'am* or *professor*? Do they interrupt others and walk in on meetings? Does everyone else respond to an email within twenty-four hours or forty-eight hours? Does the team prioritize apps, like Slack, or text message?

ERR ON THE SIDE OF BEING POLITE AND AVOID EXPLETIVES: Some of us prefer to be overdressed rather than underdressed when we don't know the dress code. When it comes to communication, err on the side of being polite and gracious. Avoid swearing: although you might see others doing it, this is one of those things that can garner negative attention and may unnecessarily offend people. Remember to protect your reputation. The team may not let you know in the moment that profanity offends them, but it may breed negative energy.

COMMUNICATE SENSITIVELY: We all have different proficiencies with speaking, listening, or writing. Accents and vocabulary change across regions and continents. Many might have difficulty with hearing or speaking loudly. Don't put people on the spot. Don't say, "I have a hard time understanding your accent." Be sensitive and patient. Send an email out ahead of the meeting, e.g. "Please email me directly if you require any communication accommodations."

BUILD EMPATHY: Imagine yourself in someone else's position. For instance, when you witness conflict or challenge, read the emotions in the room. Notice the behaviors in front of you that are harmful. Imagine how the situation could be improved. Think about what you would do if you were involved in the conflict. Reflect on times you have been in similar situations and the emotions you had. Label the emotions you are witnessing from others. This is a strategy to actively build empathy—a mix of observation and reflection.

CONSIDER THE CIRCUMSTANCE AND BE THOUGHTFUL ABOUT THE COMMUNICATION MEDIUM: You want to think twice about how you communicate based on the circumstance and the medium.

CIRCUMSTANCE	EXAMPLE	MEDIUM
Sensitive Information	• You need to check on a teammate who is not meeting deadlines. • You are planning to provide someone with feedback that they are not performing at the level you expect. • You need to discuss a racist joke your teammate made.	• For topics considered highly sensitive, seek a medium that allows you to take the time to see the person's facial expressions and body language and vice versa. Ensure that all parties feel safe and comfortable with this medium. Meet in person whenever possible. Zoom is less ideal but can suffice if video is on for all parties. While there are no hard rules, avoid email and text.

Urgency	• You need someone to cover your shift or project emergently. • A deadline has been moved to a much earlier time frame. • The technology that allows one to give a lecture is broken, and someone's talk must be given without slides.	• For time sensitive information, seek a medium that allows you to reach the person immediately and to confirm receipt. This is a phone call or texting situation.
Length/ Complexity	• You are asked to explain a situation at work that did not go as expected. • Someone wants your perspective on a workplace conflict. • You want to step down from a position.	• Long and complex emails and texts are often skimmed, at best. If you find yourself writing a long email, pause and rewrite it more concisely. Or speak by phone or in person.

Familiarity	• You are sending a meeting request to someone you don't know well. • You are checking in with a person whom you have met once.	• Consider the person you are speaking with and how comfortable you are with them and your relationship. Consider the chain of command as well between you and the other person(s). Email works well to initiate these conversations.

THE MICROSKILL:

3. UNDERSTAND YOUR COMPANY REPORTING TREE

WHAT IS THE ACTUAL SKILL?

Learn the hierarchy and reporting tree of your workplace.

RESA

I had just started at one hospital as the emergency-medicine ultrasound director. I was contacted by a physician from another department. He wanted me to help him develop an ultrasound program for his group and for his department at another hospital. He began emailing me for detailed updates. I had no clue who he was, so requested an in-person meeting. At the meeting he took a hierarchical tone. He ordered me to complete a list of tasks and to report my progress to him. He ended by reminding me of his hospital title. Something did not seem right. So I spoke to someone I knew for sure was my supervisor. She clarified the reporting structure, my role, and my responsibilities. Turns out, I had no obligations to him or to his department. She advised me to discontinue communications with him and to let her handle the situation going forward. I was glad I trusted my gut that something was off in the reporting structure.

WHY DO WE NEED THIS SKILL?

Most organizations have a graphical representation of the workplace structure called an organizational chart. They demonstrate the hierarchy, relationship, alignments, and management responsibilities within the institution.[108] The reporting structure and hierarchy can be vertical or more equitable and horizontal. At the end of the day, no matter the number or type of dotted-line relationships, someone has to be in charge to assume risk and responsibility. Which means at your job there is a chain of command you need to know. You should understand who is in charge, who are the middle managers, and who are your peers.

WHY IS THIS SKILL HARD TO ACHIEVE?

- There is no organization chart accessible to you.
- The organizational chart is old and not updated.
- You feel intimidated to ask to see the chart.

WHAT ARE THE CRITICAL ACTIONS OF THIS SKILL?

ASK TO SEE THE ORGANIZATION CHART: If not freely available on a website or in a handbook, ask your supervisor for a copy of the chart. If it's outdated or in draft mode, ask if you can get a copy of anything that is available. If you are told there is nothing formal, request a verbal discussion and take notes. Ask from a place of curiosity: "To better understand the company and where I fit, would you be able to share an organizational chart of the leadership structure?"

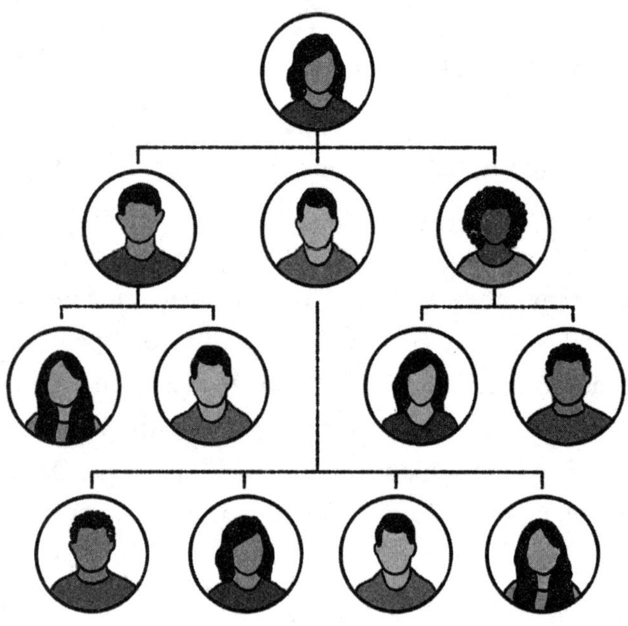

Ideally, at the start of joining a workplace or taking a new position, ask to see the organizational chart of the leadership structure.

IDENTIFY SOMEONE WHO UNDERSTANDS THE COMPANY STRUCTURE: Seek out people who have been with the organization for a long time—someone who has offered to help and seems professional and knowledgeable. Ask them to give you the lay of the land of the company structure. Open the conversation by asking, "Can you tell me about the leadership structure here?"

PAY ATTENTION TO WHO MAKES THE DECISIONS: When you are in meetings at work, take a look around and see who's leading those meetings. Notice who has the majority of input or whose comments are considered final answers. Those are the people in charge.

THE MICROSKILL:

4. READ YOUR CONTRACT, GUIDES, HANDBOOKS, AND HR POLICIES

WHAT IS THE ACTUAL SKILL?

Pay attention to the fine print in the written policies of your workplace.

ADAIRA

During residency, I spent a month on a surgical rotation. The first day of the month stands out the most. We had just finished rounds sitting around a table and discussing our patient roster and the to do list. We then all got up and walked to the elevator to do bedside rounds and speak with patients. I left the room first and reached the elevator door, ahead of the pack. I pressed the elevator button and when the doors opened, I walked in first. The team, who was previously talking, grew silent. Everyone literally stopped talking, I turned around and saw them staring at me. I continued watching them, draped in long white coats and folded arms, staring at me until the senior resident said, "You are standing in the wrong place. That is not where you stand." My facial expression must have said: You've got to be kidding me. It turns out there was some very fine print in the orientation manual. There were specific instructions on how and where we should be standing in the elevator. The most senior person on the team needed to walk in first and stand in front of the elevator buttons. This person was the one to decide which floor we visited. Therefore, they needed to comfortably be the one to press the button. After the faculty entered, the senior resident got on. Then the interns and then the students. Whether or not I agreed with this exercise and ritual, it was clearly a culture for the team and I missed that fine print.

WHY DO WE NEED THIS SKILL?

Day-to-day, you probably don't need to be familiar with the minutiae of your employee handbook. These days, most are online and easily accessible. However, when an issue arises—medical or parental leave, harassment, or discrimination—you need to be able to access the details. It's important to know what's covered with your benefits and, equally, what is not covered. Think of the employee handbook as a communication tool with lots of content, policies, and codes.[109]

WHY IS IT HARD TO ATTAIN THIS SKILL?

- Policy handbooks are onerous, detailed, and sometimes incomprehensible.
- Websites are poorly organized or outdated with information difficult to find.
- Colleagues don't know where to find the policies either.

- You are nervous to ask your supervisor or HR for the resource you need.

WHAT ARE THE CRITICAL ACTIONS OF THIS MICROSKILL?

ONBOARDING: Pay close attention during the orientation period for your job. Get to know how to contact HR—there may be a single person who is responsible for all or a part of HR. Gain familiarity with the forms and information you need. Honestly, sometimes critical information is not easily discoverable. The more you save and catalog earlier the better for later.

ASK YOUR COLLEAGUES ABOUT POLICIES: Identify people who have been at the company/organization/institution a long time. They are a good place to start. If you are not sure you want to reveal details of your situation, keep the question general. It's totally up to you if you want to ask vague versus specific questions.

VAGUE QUESTIONS	SPECIFIC QUESTIONS
"Where can I access the employee handbook with policies?"	"My partner is ill, and I need to take family leave. Where is the best place to learn about the company sick-leave policy?"
"Can you share the retirement plan and company matching policy for this company?"	"What happens to my retirement plan and company matching if I leave the company before being here a year?"

Identify colleagues who have been at your organization for a long time and ask about company policies.

ATTEND WORKSHOPS AND SEMINARS: There may be internal workshops or seminars that cover some of the fundamentals of insurance, retirement, or disability, for instance. It may be a one-hour investment and time well-spent. After the meeting, you can refer to any referenced materials or schedule a follow-up meeting. You can connect with your HR representative for a one-on-one meeting and review your benefits in full.

THE MICROSKILL:

5. UNDERSTAND THE VALUE OF SELF-MONITORING

WHAT IS THE ACTUAL SKILL?

Be accountable for your behaviors and productivity at work.

ADAIRA

I was a resident when I was listed on an all-department email intended to publicly name residents who had not finished their notes or completed their patient charts. I felt embarrassed every time the list came out. I'm not proud of my excuse, but I had just been selected as chief resident and I was planning a wedding—so I objectively didn't spend as much time on charts. I will never forget when a senior colleague said, "Adaira, I saw your name on the list. I have always imagined seeing your name on lists. But not these types on lists." On one hand I was grateful he highlighted the issue, as he offered strategies on how to chart more efficiently. On the other hand, I was also very surprised; I assumed other people didn't really notice my chart tardiness. That moment helped me understand that in the workplace people notice what you do. And people notice what you don't do.

WHY DO WE NEED THIS SKILL?

There is a sociological and psychological term called *self-monitoring*. This refers to modifying your behavior in response to workplace norms. If you are a low self-monitor, you tend to behave according to your internal feelings. If you are a high self-monitor, you will adjust based upon what the situation asks of you.[110] We subscribe to the importance of monitoring how you behave. We do not ascribe to the *any publicity is good publicity* adage. We also do not suggest you behave however you want all the time. In any workplace there is the self, the team, and the work. Being fully unhinged and ignoring the presence of others doesn't work for all. It might work for public figures, but it does not work for you in the workplace. In fact, we want you to have as little unwanted attention as possible.

WHY IS THIS SKILL HARD?

- You strongly object to being overly scrutinized and micromanaged.
- You think no one is paying attention to you at work.
- You do not have time to complete the tasks assigned. You do not have the energy to pay attention to how you are behaving at work.

- You are barely staying afloat. It's hard to self-monitor when you cannot be more productive.

WHAT ARE THE CRITICAL ACTIONS OF THIS MICROSKILL?

IDENTIFY WHAT IS EXPECTED: Pay attention in meetings, virtual discussion rooms (i.e. Slack) or in the hallways. Watch how the culture handles errors or delays. Is everything blown out of proportion or are people relaxed and supportive? Make note of tasks and accomplishments which get positive attention and prioritize these. Make note of people's words and actions which garner negative attention. All of this research allows you to understand how to self-monitor.

MEET DUE DATES: Outside of an emergency, as we know these happen, it is important to meet due dates and to show up on time. If you sign up, show up. If you are scheduled to work, arrive to the shift on time. Or inform the team if you are late. Remember that as you are building your career, you are building a reputation as reliable. If you are unable to meet a timeline—don't ghost. Call, email, text—inform key stakeholders.

KEEP EMOTIONS IN CHECK: Yes, you are entitled to have emotions. No, you should not shout at, demean, harass, undermine, belittle, or threaten others. Just because a workplace culture allows behaviors and emotions such as these, doesn't mean it's right. And you may not get the same "passes" as others do with bad behavior. If you have repetitive patterns of uncontrolled behavior you may ask yourself if you are in an environment that is allowing you to thrive. Or, if the environment is over amplifying negative feelings that you shouldn't feel forced to express regularly.

THE MICROSKILL:

6. CHECK YOUR PRIVILEGE

WHAT IS THE ACTUAL SKILL?

Understand that there are inherent aspects of your identity and background that affect your experience at work.

ADAIRA

Towards the end of my shift, a dangerously sick patient came in. My colleague later arrived to start his shift; he would assume care of the critically ill patient so that I could go home. He asked me to help close the loop on this patient's care. "Could you speak with the ICU team and get a bed arranged for the patient?" This was a fair request. I called the ICU faculty to ask if the patient may be admitted. The ICU doctor was unable to accept the patient—they were too busy at the moment with other patients. So I told my colleague and asked if he could call the doctor back in twenty minutes, when he would be less busy. My colleague volunteered, "I wouldn't have asked him to admit the patient. I would have told them to admit the patient now." He had a point—I could have been more definitive and made a demand. But I thought of all the times I had been called aggressive, threatening, and scary. I didn't want to be peer pressured into being tough, knowing how "tough" would be perceived coming from me. For a Black woman, authority can be easily viewed as aggressive. My colleague, a white man, felt that he could be assertive, direct, and clear at any point. The risk itself is a deterrent and the stress of ruminating on how I might be perceived is also exhausting. This was a time where my colleague didn't recognize his privilege.

WHY DO WE NEED THIS SKILL?

So much of how we succeed is tied to who we are. And what we look and sound like. This is why we couldn't separate out a chapter just on "identity" from the book. It's an issue woven throughout. Here's a simple example: if you showed up to a C-suite meeting in pajamas and slippers, you will be treated differently than if you wear a tailored business suit. Right or wrong, that is the truth. Being treated for what you wear is a more palatable example of privilege compared to some of the destructive reasons differential treatment occurs: age, race, physical ability, sexual orientation, socioeconomic status, pedigree. We want you to consider that your identity directly influences the opportunities you have. And whether you feel you belong or not. This is important because empathy directly impacts the culture of the workplace. If you recognize your privilege and use it to advocate for others, that creates a better workplace environment for all.

WHY IS THIS SKILL HARD TO ACHIEVE?

- You are focused on yourself and blinded by your own struggles.
- You believe if everyone works hard they can have what you have.
- You believe privilege doesn't exist and there is

no difference in treatment based on race, gender, age, etc.

WHAT ARE THE CRITICAL ACTIONS OF THIS MICROSKILL?

IDENTIFY YOUR PRIVILEGE: Do an inventory and ask yourself, what has made my life a bit easier? We are not asking you to be ashamed of this list. Just to recognize that privilege, for many, has existed in the background all along without ever being named.

OBSERVE WHAT GETS REWARDED: When you are in meetings or reading company newsletters, pay attention to what work and what efforts are awarded. Look at who is getting promoted and who is left out. Do they belong to the same groups? Are all people recognized equally?

OBSERVE WHO STRUGGLES WITH WORK: While there will be a group of employees getting praise and promotion, look at who is being asked to leave or passed over for promotions and opportunities. There is plenty of evidence that people of color, people with disabilities, and women struggle at work (e.g. are under mentored, over disciplined, more likely to leave the workplace).[111]

SHARE YOUR RESOURCES: If you find yourself well connected—able to access people, opportunities, funding—share. There is enough room at the top for multiple people to succeed. You will build a stronger reputation for yourself if you are authentically helpful to others.

THE MICROSKILL:

7. UPSTAND FOR THE SELF AND THE TEAM

WHAT IS THE ACTUAL SKILL?

Advocate respectfully by using your voice and influence.

> **RESA**
> I was leading a group of physicians on a writing project for an academic medical journal. I suggested assignments for each person, each person agreed, and we set a timeline. We were working off a shared Google document. One of the authors asked if his administrator could have access to the Google document offering that she was a good copyeditor. I was confused since we were writing the first draft and did not need copyediting. It became apparent that this author was having his administer write his part of the paper. I kindly suggested that we add the administrator as an author since she was doing the work. When the paper was published, both the physician and his administer were authors. Months later, I ran into the administrator at a work event. She pulled me aside and thanked me over and over.

WHY DO WE NEED THIS SKILL?

Allyship is an attitude that can be learned. It is a collection of values that we internalize that makes others feel safe. An upstander is a person who speaks up or acts in the moment. The behavior requires not just sympathy, empathy, but also courage—upstanding occurs when a person steps up in real intime, in front of others. It sets the tone that bad behavior is not welcome and fairness, safety, compassion is required. Men are needed to be allies and upstanders.[112] An upstander is different from a bystander—someone who notices a wrongdoing but does not intervene in real time. The world needs more upstanders than bystanders. We would never discourage you from speaking up against wrongdoings that disrupt safety, such as racism, sexism, ageism, ableism, homophobia, etc.

WHY IS THIS SKILL HARD?

- We remain quiet because we fear negative consequences or retaliation.
- When we hear of offensive behavior we are shocked, caught off guard and we do not have a response ready.
- No one has modeled advocacy; what to say, when to speak, and to whom we address the message.
- Upstanding is penalized.

WHAT ARE THE CRITICAL ACTIONS OF THIS SKILL?

COMMIT TO THE CONCEPT: Maybe you have been harassed and bullied. Maybe you have witnessed it. Maybe your friend, family or colleague has shared their experience. If you want to be an ally, if you want to create cultures of workplace safety, then commit to allyship and educating yourself on upstanding.

THE BYSTANDER	THE UPSTANDER
Pulling someone aside after the event: "Just so you know, I don't agree with what he said to you."	At the time of the event: "We don't do that here. Please don't use that language."

An upstander speaks up or acts in the moment. A bystander may notice a wrongdoing but does not intervene in real time.

PRACTICE SPEAKING UP FOR OTHERS: We are all caught off guard when these events happen. So practice and prepare for when you find yourself witnessing something. Work on becoming comfortable and sure of your actions and words. Think about a time in the past where you didn't stand up for others. What would you say now? Next time you watch a show or movie and there is conflict ask yourself what you would say to defend one of the characters. Spoiler alert: it need not be heavily crafted. Simply saying, "What you just said or did is not acceptable" is sufficient.

DEVELOP STOCK RESPONSES: Being an upstander is hard and a burden for us all to carry. If you have a few phrases stocked, then the job will be easier.

SCENARIO	UPSTANDING
A teammate is trying speak up and is being ignored	"Let's make sure everyone has the opportunity to speak." To the teammate: "What are your thoughts?"

The team leader is making fun of a teammate's accent	"I don't find that funny."
A supervisor is verbally bullying your teammate and steps into their personal space	"Please step away from her. I don't agree with the way you are speaking."
A teammate makes comments about another teammate's appearance each week, e.g. clothes, makeup, hairstyle. She is visibly uncomfortable.	"Your comments are inappropriate. After you apologize, can we keep this to talking about the work?"

TAKE CARE OF YOU FIRST: Upstanding may not feel safe or the right path. We get it. Upstanders can become the object of retaliation, bullying, etc The ultimate decision to upstand is a personal one.

ACT IN THE MOMENT: Focus on acting to stop the bad language and/or behavior. This can be speaking up. This can be body languages such as putting up a finger or your hand signaling the offender to stop. This can be putting yourself between the two people, and more.

SEEK SAFETY: Take care of your physical and emotional health; be mindful to stay out of harm's way. We have sadly seen many assaults in the workplace. In fact healthcare professionals have one of the highest rates of physical assault across all industries.[113] In general, we recommend always moving away from physical danger.

THE MICROSKILL:

8. SOCIALIZE CAREFULLY AT WORK

WHAT IS THE ACTUAL SKILL?

Note how socializing with colleagues is different than socializing off hours with friends.

RESA

One of of my doctor friends had worked the overnight shift. In the morning, the two overnight teams went out for breakfast. Everyone went to the local strip club for the "Legs and Eggs" special. I was surprised, yet curious to hear the thought process behind choosing that location. They told me, "Everyone does it. It's no big deal." Continued surprise. Continued curiosity: "What was the sex and gender make-up of the team?" They said, "Oh, the intern was a woman, and she thought it was great." I had so many thoughts running through my head. I share a few of many reasons why any of the teammates would not have thought it was great. Given the hierarchy of the team, any one of the trainees may not feel comfortable speaking up. The intern, as the most junior person on the team, probably feared a bad evaluation or even social isolation from the team. The conversation pretty much ended and thank goodness the team tradition eventually ended too.

WHY DO WE NEED THIS SKILL?

The culture around socializing at work varies from company to company and office to office. Of course, socializing is an important part of team building. The issue is being aware of the boundaries for social interactions. For example, the culture around drinking alcohol at work events varies tremendously. Individuals should abstain from drinking if they wish. However, employees may feel pressure to drink alcohol when the team drinks.[114] Dating culture in the workplace also varies—so don't make assumptions here, read the fine print of your workplace policies.[115] In medicine, faculty are generally not allowed to date residents due to risk of compromising power dynamics, evaluations, and disrupting team comfort. As mentors and members of many teams, when someone makes a mistake with socializing, the typical response is "I let things get out of hand." This is why we emphasize the importance of caution with the team.

WHY IS THIS SKILL HARD TO OBTAIN?

- You don't know workplace rules.
- There is social pressure to participate and conform to someone else's expectations.
- You don't feel comfortable self-advocating.
- You think your behavior is acceptable since "everyone else is doing it" or "no one has said anything yet."

WHAT ARE THE CRITICAL ACTIONS OF THIS SKILL?

THINK ABOUT ALCOHOL AND OTHER DRUG USE: The workplace is still where you want to protect your reputation. And on this issue, we know not everyone agrees. We do not recommend drinking alcohol in excess at work functions. We also want to normalize abstaining. People do not drink alcohol for a myriad of reasons: designated driver, pregnant, religious observance, history of addiction, Al-Anon member, unable to metabolize it, etc. Chances are, you aren't alone and your advocacy can help others. Overall, as physicians, we do not recommend illegal drug use. We also recommend keeping any other legal drug-use behavior separate from work.

RECONSIDER ROMANTIC RELATIONSHIPS AT WORK: This is one of those talk-to-HR-early-and-quickly topics to clarify what is permissible in your environment. For example, in medical training programs, supervising doctors are not allowed to date the people they supervise. There are power differentials that threaten consent and the ability to objectively evaluate the person in training. Do not assume consent, ever, and especially with workplace colleagues.

DO NOT EXPLOIT COLLEAGUES: Do not take pictures of your colleagues in compromising positions. And don't send these photos out or post them on social media. This is unkind and disrespectful, and reflects more on you than them.

AVOID OFFICE GOSSIP AND DRAMA: Advocating for what is right is not the same thing as involving yourself in office drama. Things to avoid: instigating or contributing to inflammatory conversations, spreading lies, or gossiping. Gossiping can be identified as the spread or request of information to parties who should not have access to it. Gossip can be used as social ammunition to tarnish someone's reputation. Be careful what you share and where you spread it.

THE MICROSKILL:

9. NOTICE HOW BAD BEHAVIOR IS HANDLED

WHAT IS THE ACTUAL SKILL?

Recognize what happens when unwanted behavior is reported to the appropriate supervisor.

RESA

Every time I met with my friend, she had another story about her supervisor. This time it was about the shift schedule. The shift assignments came out without much advanced notice. New physicians were assigned overnight shifts without the opportunity to get familiar with the department. Younger teammates were given a lot of "on-call" shifts while senior colleagues had few. (On-call shifts require you to be free and available, geographically close to the hospital for a 24-hour period in case a colleague calls in sick or has an emergency.) When she brought this up to her supervisor suggesting it contributed to decreased team morale, they lost their temper and berated her. They yelled, claiming that nobody had ever complained about the schedule and that she was the only person in their whole career who had a problem with it. (Many faculty complained about the schedule.) When it happened to her, she thought it was a one-off. When she heard this supervisor threw a tantrum at another colleague, we identified a cultural trend. It turns out this supervisor had a longstanding history of losing their temper and gaslighting. They held their leadership position for decades. Everyone knew about their behavior and people looked the other way. How an institution handles unprofessional behavior speaks to the workplace culture. It's worth noting when a system protects and prioritizes its leaders and their bad behaviors over the safety of its employees.

WHY DO WE NEED THIS SKILL?

Less than 25% of employees strongly agree that they feel connected to their company culture.[116] And a toxic work culture is ten times more likely to cause an employee to leave their current workplace than any other work-culture contribution.[117] We understand that everyone can have a bad day. But that shouldn't result in bullying, anger, or yelling. When it comes to learning about your workplace, we want you to notice not only how praise is shared but how bad behavior is addressed. Notice. Observe. Read what is being messaged. Observation is a powerful exercise that still delivers dividends. In fact, there is a technique called Visual Thinking Strategies (VTS) in the art industry that focuses on asking three questions when looking at a piece of art: What's going on here? What do you see that makes you say that? What more can we find? This develops skills of observing and critiquing by developing attention, curiosity, critical thinking, and respect.[118] This practice of watching and noticing will quickly let you know early on what type of workplace you are entering and help you decide your next steps: advocate for change, ignore and stay, or go elsewhere.

WHY IS THIS SKILL HARD?

- In the past your institution or company has minimized bad behavior or been hesitant to address it.

- You don't know that HR serves the institution and not the employee.
- You don't know how to seek help.
- You report a bad behavior and may not know what, if anything, is being done behind the scenes to address it.

WHAT ARE THE CRITICAL ACTIONS OF THIS SKILL?

RECOGNIZE PATTERNS: Inevitably in any workplace, even if slight and subtle, bad behavior occurs. Your goal is to notice and understand how behavior is handled. When harassment occurs, notice if anyone is asked to step down, leave the company, take professionalism courses. Does the company send an email with a stance? Is a town hall hosted amongst scandal? Or, is everything kept hush hush and swept under the rug? Don't gossip. Or spread rumors. Just observe and note patterns.

EDUCATE YOURSELF ON OPTIONS: Read, search the company website for resources. There may be an office of professionalism, support groups, HR, a Title IX office, and more. Consider if you wish to bring a situation to an official body, including a lawyer. Avoid documentation upfront, ask for meetings ideally in person.

FOLLOW UP: If an incident occurred with you or related to you ask your supervisor or HR about the resolution. A simple question, "I'm curious what occurred since I have reported the event to you?" They may not be able to tell you details. However, even a high-level answer to this question will inform a lot about your company culture.

CHOOSE YOURSELF: We would like to suggest strongly that if you feel that your workplace culture is toxic, abusive or otherwise not right for you, then leave. Try to secure another job first so your transition is easy and does not leave you without salary and benefits. We understand that circumstances make this easier said than done. But your health well-being and respectful treatment should be your first priority.

CONCLUSION:

Understanding workplace culture requires situational awareness.	Use your voice, and privilege when possible, to support other people.	Be intentional with your behavior and learn how bad behavior is handled in your workplace

SUPPLEMENTAL RESOURCES:

Culture, Candor and More

Check your privilege

Harvard Business Review Ascend

7

MICROSKILLS TO BE A TEAM PLAYER

ADAIRA

A really pale patient came to the emergency department. She had nausea and was vomiting. The patient's initial blood count from the lab was ok. The nurse found me and said, "She smells like blood." This stood out: if we had not had excellent team collaboration, the outcome would have been bad. Based on the nurse's comment we repeated her blood count and it was definitely dropping—a sign for internal bleeding. We ordered a stat CT scan of her abdomen and our concern proved to be true: she was bleeding in the stomach. The resident emergently called the gastroenterologist and interventional radiologist—specialists who stop the bleeding. All of a sudden, we heard her family member, "Someone please help her! NOW!!!" Our patient was vomiting frank blood with large grapefruit sized clots all over her gown and projected onto the floor. She kept vomiting blood. The team knew what to do and jumped in. A swarm of people arrived to the room. "How can I help?" was the question I heard over and over. I assigned roles in an organized fashion. It was phenomenal to see how everyone worked together for her care. I think of this case often—especially the trauma to her family and the team. This patient survived and without question it was due to the teamwork.

The work we do is rarely a one-person show. Functional workplaces are collaborative, respectful, organized and supportive. It is worth mentioning that collaboration is not just the mechanical click of buttons between different people. It's intentional conversation—sharing ideas, supporting, and being vulnerable. It's also the compassionate, nonverbal cues—a head nod, clapping, eye contact. It's making power dynamics horizontal rather than vertical so that everyone has a voice. And this interplay between the team sets the tone.

So where does collaboration fall apart? When we stop acting like team players. When we worry more about the self at the expense of the team. A solo mission centers on "my" work, "my" projects, "my" promotions—me. A collaborative mission centers on "our" work, "our" projects, "our" promotions—us. You may wonder: Can we support others while we support the self? 100% yes, and this is not a zero-sum game, nor are they contradictory goals. In fact, these are additive. You can take care of the self and the team.

In her book *Wolfpack*, soccer champion and *New York Times* bestseller Abby Wambach stresses the importance of thanking people for their assistance. "I've never scored a goal in my life without getting a pass from someone else. Every goal I've ever scored belonged to my entire team. When you score, you better start pointing."[119] The pointing she refers to is such a small move with such tremendous impact. We always want to be aware of who is in the spotlight and who is not. It is important to acknowledge, thank, and then move the spotlight to others on the team.

Who is the team? It isn't just the people with whom you directly work. It's also the supervisors, colleagues, and those you may oversee. It also means administrative and ancillary coworkers. While we stick to our message, your industry will never love you back.[120] Authentic connections with people lead to happier, healthier, and longer lives.[121]

In this chapter, we provide nine MicroSkills on how to be a team player.

MICROSKILLS TO BE A TEAM PLAYER:

1. Check in with the team.
2. Acknowledge the work and impact of your team.
3. Build and reinforce psychological safety.
4. Explore with people if they need an out.
5. Avoid scheduling meetings when people should be off.
6. Call in sick when you are not healthy enough to work.
7. Deliver kind, actionable feedback.
8. Ask for focused feedback.
9. Bring positivity to the workplace.

THE MICROSKILL:

1. CHECK IN WITH THE TEAM

WHAT IS THE ACTUAL SKILL?

Resist the temptation to consistently jump into the work when meeting with the team.

> **RESA**
>
> I belonged to a team where we started Monday weekly meetings with a ritual we called "Check-in." I learned the impact and effectiveness of this exercise thanks to a gifted emergency medicine leader and dear friend. One at a time, each person updated the group on what had happened over the last week. It could be something personal, professional, both, or neither. Some took a pass on their turns. At first, I myself kept it to work-related updates. Over time, I started sharing more personal things. "I am working on my roasting vegetable skills: currently brussels and cauliflower" or "I loved my recent podcast conversation with such and such a person." Through check-ins, I got to know the team and vice versa. I became convinced of the power and importance of this practice based on the people who arrived late and urgently asked, "Wait! Did I miss Check-in?" This really spoke to how people like to connect and share with the team.

WHY DO WE NEED THIS SKILL?

We want to feel welcome to share our authentic and well-rounded self at work. Amy Edmondson, Professor of Harvard Business School, coined the term *psychological safety* to describe a person's feeling about the negative consequences of taking a risk or making a mistake.[122] Google researchers collected data over a few years on team effectiveness. They reported that one team started a practice of beginning each meeting by sharing a risk taken in the previous week. This increased reported psychological safety ratings by 6%.[123] Check-ins and sharing a risk may have a similar effect on exposing the well-being of the group and may identify individuals in need of support. People want to feel valued. And a check-in, where everyone pays attention, allows time, space and attention for each person.

WHY IS THIS SKILL HARD TO ACHIEVE?

- You or someone you know does not want to participate.
- Psychological safety is not easy to create. Especially if trust has been previously broken.
- Check-ins affect staying on schedule when time is limited.
- Check-ins feel performative in a toxic workplace.

WHAT ARE THE CRITICAL ACTIONS FOR THIS MICROSKILL?

MAKE THE ANNOUNCEMENT: At the start of the meeting, frame the activity. "Hey, everyone. Can we go around and do a quick check-in?" If you are not the meeting leader but would like to initiate this practice, touch base with the team leader first. Simply suggest, "Do you mind if we do a quick check-in with the team before we get started?"

DESCRIBE A CHECK-IN: Not everyone may be familiar with this practice, and it may be a surprise for people to engage in this at work. Consider adding: "You can share something personal or professional, both, or nothing. It's no problem to pass." It might feel safer to talk about work. So start there. If you want to go more personal share your favorite book, a restaurant you tried, or what you did over the weekend. There can be a prompt for everyone: "What is the last good film you watched?" to help those who might be uncomfortable sharing personal content.

TIMING THE CHECK-IN: Check-ins are great at the top of the meeting but also could be done during a break or at the end. The most important part is that it happens: people come to rely on it as a grounding. Be sure to circle back if someone is late and missed out. Of note, these need not happen every single meeting, especially around tight deadlines or agenda full meetings. But when there is time and pressure for other work is light, thread them into your standing and ad-hoc meetings.

FOLLOW UP ON CONCERNS: A check-in helps create closeness and sometimes raises alarms. Trust your instinct and follow up privately with someone. If a person repeatedly passes on sharing anything, this could signal that you should check in with them after the meeting. "How do you feel about check-ins? How are you doing?" If you prefer not to address this alone, speak to the person's supervisor or their trusted peer about your concern. In these cases, keep as few people involved as possible, and maintain confidentiality.

SCHEDULE INDIVIDUAL CHECK-INS: In the world of remote work it is easy to never directly connect with peers. Having quick, one-on-one virtual meetings or direct messages just to say hello and check in should feel similar to going to someone's cubicle (if in person) to say hello. Keep the barrier of entry low: if you see them active, relaxed, and free, pop over to say hi. In the virtual world, ask "Would you mind if we catch up fifteen minutes before or after our next meeting?"

NOTICE CHANGES IN APPEARANCE: Unkempt personal appearance and hygiene can be a sensitive topic. It can be a reflection of lack of access to housing stability or laundering supplies, for instance. Personal hygiene or a change in attention to grooming and appearance can be a sign of depression or other struggles.[124] Compassionate conversation can be as simple as "Hey, I wanted to check in. I may be misreading you, but I've noticed a change in your appearance. Is everything okay?" Take caution here with intervening. We are speaking about a noticeable decline in how people intentionally care for themselves.

THE MICROSKILL:

2. ACKNOWLEDGE THE WORK AND IMPACT OF YOUR TEAM

WHAT IS THE ACTUAL SKILL?

Name people and generously give credit and attribution.

ADAIRA

For me, one of the hardest parts of working in the emergency department is taking care of pediatric patients who die. Each death—especially of a child—is memorable and impacts me deeply. I remember a traumatic case where a young child was fatally shot. It was in New York City right outside of a convenience store. His down jacket exploded from the gunfire and the feather material was all over his body. As the nurses and doctors were giving medications and doing CPR, a young technician picked all the coat material stuck to his exposed skin. I watched her and knew that she realized his parents would be viewing the body of their son shortly. I remember the scene vividly: she stood there and literally picked each feather off and cleaned his bloodied skin. And at the team debriefing of the code and death of this patient, the senior physician focused the light on the technician: her work, the love and humanity she brought to the patient, and the respect she brought to the family. I had seen many team debriefings at that point but never had I seen her position recognized so publicly.

WHY DO WE NEED THIS SKILL?

Acknowledging team members models a sense of gratitude and humility. This isn't just style, it's science: a gratitude practice is linked to better health, happiness, and sleep.[125] Making others feel good can help build a sense of positivity for the self. It also boosts what people think and say about you. We want you to be known as dependable, ambitious, and hardworking. But we also want you to be known as someone who generously shares credit.

WHY IS THIS SKILL HARD TO ACHIEVE?

- You may prefer to look out for the self first, foremost, and exclusively.
- Not everyone learns how to support the team.

- Toxic or competitive work environments can foster competition and minimize generosity.

WHAT ARE THE CRITICAL ACTIONS FOR THIS MICROSKILL?

THINK *WE* AND NOT *I*: Words are important. In most circumstances you can use *we*, as few tasks in the workplace are done completely alone. We understand in some cases you do the bulk of the work alone, and we don't want to undermine your hard work. However, in general there is someone to thank.

SELF-CENTERED	OTHER-CENTERED
"When I started this project, I spent so many hours working on it. I'm so glad I finished it."	"Though I managed this project, we brainstormed as a team, iterated over multiple meetings, and completed it together."

GATHER A LIST: Before addressing credit, stop, pause, and think about all of the people and systems in place which allowed you to get where you are and be successful. Check out the Acknowledgments section at the end of our book! Be mindful of erasing the work of women and racially and otherwise marginalized groups—as their service is more likely to be overlooked.[126]

OFFER THANKS: Thank people or groups by name no matter the medium. Say it aloud. Write an email. Send a letter. Let their supervisors know.

ACCEPT COMPLIMENTS: Related to the topic of praising others, get comfortable accepting a compliment. A simple *Thank you* is enough, or you can add the specific item for which you are thankful, e.g. *Thank you for the kind feedback on my slide design.* Sharing credit with others isn't a matter of dismissing the credit you deserve.

KEEP THE TEAM UPDATED: Part of acknowledging the work of the team is keeping them updated. Be thoughtful with sharing information with the team. Include them. Don't overlook them. When needed, share what is happening and offer a why. This keeps the team feeling connected and on the same page.

THE MICROSKILL:

3. BUILD AND REINFORCE PSYCHOLOGICAL SAFETY

WHAT IS THE ACTUAL SKILL?

Commit yourself to building and reinforcing a feeling of belonging for your teammates.

RESA

I was working in the emergency department, typing a patient chart, when the ECG technologist came over to the desk. "Dr Lewiss. The patient in room ten is here with chest pain every day. I went to do his ECG and he called me the 'N' word. I won't do his ECG if he talks to me like that." Born in Trinidad and living in the USA for decades, she and I had worked in the ED on a team together for years. I thanked her for letting me know, stood up, and walked over to the patient. He was stable, with no chest pain nor discomfort, and was smiling. "Hi Doc!" We shared racial concordance. "Mr. X, I am Dr. Lewiss. The ECG technologist told me you called her the 'N' word. Did you call her the 'N' word?" He seemed taken aback and slowly nodded yes. "Mr. X, we do not do that here. If you feel that you cannot act respectfully, if you feel you cannot refrain from using inappropriate, unacceptable, and disrespectful words, then you can go to another emergency department. Do you understand?" Slowly, he shook his head yes. I asked another tech to please do the patient's ECG and the patient was discharged after an evaluation that came back normal. Every time patients are verbally or behaviorally inappropriate—when they violate minimum standards and the ability for people to do their jobs—it creates psychologically unsafe situations. I have not always been good at upstanding in the moment. I definitely get caught off guard. Yet I tell myself I shouldn't, as these types of behaviors happen all the time. So I keep my guard up, awareness high, and ready to act when situations arise. I feel that responsibility to create psychological safety very strongly.

WHY DO WE NEED THIS SKILL?

Our best work is done when we feel safe and can focus our time and energy. What may interrupt and disrupt this focus? Bias, discrimination, microaggressions, slights, harassment, assault, unprofessional jokes, and more. When we feel unsafe, we are on alert and distracted, and energy is diverted to navigating a work environment that may be unfriendly. In other words, it's difficult to focus on the tasks at hand, and we cannot perform at our best.

WHY IS THIS SKILL HARD TO ACHIEVE?

- You are unaware of your own privilege. You may feel perfectly comfortable and not threatened at work. You may not realize others have a different experience.
- You are aware but are caught off guard and unsure how to upstand in the moment.
- You feel it's not your job to police or monitor other people.
- Directly or indirectly you have faced retribution for being an upstander.

WHAT ARE THE CRITICAL ACTIONS FOR THIS MICROSKILL?

IDENTIFY ALLIES: As always, it's important to know who you can trust. This might be a member on your team or your personal board of directors. It might be someone in a different department within the same company. If you feel you have no one internally, then check your external resources for support. When it comes to standing up for others, you should also recognize who is there to stand up for you.

START WITH CURIOSITY: If you want to address a moment that harms anyone's sense of safety, start with curiosity. "I'm wondering what made you say that comment about our peer?" or "I'm curious if you could explain that joke?" This opens the door for discussion. After their explanation you can then explain how the comment makes people feel unsafe or uncomfortable.

DOUBLE CHECK IDIOMS AND PHRASES: The world is evolving and creating space to be inclusive to people with different indentities and perspectives. One way this can be undermined is by the use of idioms or catch phrases—many of these have harmful origins. We want to emphasize compassion here—there might be a phrase you say often and you have no clue that it is offensive. For example, "peanut gallery," "blind spots" or "low on the totem pole." When educated on why a phrase is harmful, simply say, "I am sorry I was not aware. Thank you for sharing. I will try to avoid saying it going forward."

MIND THE TONE OF DIFFICULT CONVERSATION: Personal topics can get sensitive quickly, so it is really important to mind the tone and content of the conversation. Are voices being raised, unfriendly words used? Assess body language. Are arms now folded, eyes rolling? Is the person pale, flushed, or sweating? If any of these cause concern, then take a pause, deep breath, and determine the best timing to hold the conversation.

CHECK IN: After a comment affects a teammate, it's good to circle back. See how they are doing. Ask, "Are you doing ok?" or "Is there anything we can do to make you feel more supported?" And later, "How have you been since we last spoke?"

WEIGH THE OPTIONS: Reporting lapses of safety at work can be met with negative consequences, such as retaliation, being pushed out, and social isolation. Renowned researcher Jennifer Freyd describes *institutional betrayal,* which occurs when the workplace fails to protect individuals who report or to respond in a supportive or protective manner.[127] Given the risk, trust your instincts, and if needed, consult a friend or colleague who is external to the company.

LEARN HOW TO REPORT: Ask trusted colleagues. Learn the reporting process before you make calls or put things into writing so that you know you are involving the right key people. This could be addressed to your supervisor, an anonymous reporting line, the Title IX office, the office of professionalism, an ombudsman, or Human Resources. Trust us: before you report something take a pause and seek trusted guidance on wording, medium, and timing. You also want to confirm to whom to send the message. This sounds paranoid but once you declare an accusation or complaint it cannot be easily recalled.

THE MICROSKILL:

4. EXPLORE WITH PEOPLE IF THEY NEED AN OUT

WHAT IS THE ACTUAL SKILL?

Recognize when and how to offer an out when a person is not doing their part.

RESA

Offering people an out is a very powerful and generous tool. I will never forget the first time I was offered an out. A colleague called me to ask if I would organize a medical education workshop. The date was set six months from our first conversation. I said yes and quickly realized there was a misunderstanding on the timeline and deliverables. After I agreed to do the work, they started sending very frequent emails, reminders, and requests for updates. I was confused and felt certain there was a miscommunication. Nonetheless, I was not delivering as they expected so they asked me if I wanted an out. After thinking about it, I said yes I did. Things had not started off well and I knew I would not meet their expectations. I had never been offered this and generally, I would say I don't see this tactic taken. Even rarer do people take the offer. So, needless to say, the colleague was surprised. I thought it incredibly kind for them to offer and wise of me to accept. It gave me an out yet allowed them an opportunity to find someone else to complete the task and to meet their expectations. Since that experience, I try to generously offer people an out as an option when I sense something is awry.

WHY DO WE NEED THIS SKILL?

By giving someone an out, we mean providing a way for a person to step away, escape, or remove themselves from the project—without negative consequences. And we allow them to do it with grace. It seems obvious that if work is continuously stalled, you need to check in and intervene. But remember, there may be a reason a team member is uncharacteristically falling behind,[128] so it requires sensitivity and curiosity rather than judgment. Intervening may not be your responsibility but rather that of the team leader.[129] If someone is not putting in the correct effort, it can be unfair to the team and cause resentment or low morale. Especially if behavior is persistent and not addressed.

WHY IS THIS SKILL HARD TO ACHIEVE?

- You get distracted and neglect checking with people who are not keeping up.

- You are not in charge and do not feel comfortable holding a difficult conversation with the person.
- You prefer to avoid conflict and just do the work yourself.

WHAT ARE THE CRITICAL ACTIONS FOR THIS MICROSKILL?

GATHER CONCRETE EXAMPLES AND DATA: Hold on to your assumptions about why someone might need an out. The objective data is gathered not to belabor any point or to embarrass anyone. It is to make sure you have concrete facts: missed deadlines, unanswered emails, dropped projects. The conversation goes better with specifics rather than generalities.

SUBJECTIVE AND LESS EFFECTIVE	OBJECTIVE AND MORE EFFECTIVE
"I wanted to check in. How are you feeling about the project?"	"I wanted to check in. We missed you at the last three meetings and I noticed you stopped contributing to our virtual discussions."

PLAN THE CONVERSATION: Ask to speak privately with the person and decide upon the best medium, e.g. in person, by phone, or virtually. Text and email are risky because tone and emotion could be lost. Do not have the conversation when you are feeling frustrated or resentful. Give yourself time to process your emotions. Start from a place of curiosity, kindness, and genuinely exploring why someone might be behind. Since this can be delicate and make the person defensive, practice the conversation alone, aloud, or with someone you trust.

PROBE GENTLY AND OFFER THE OUT SINCERELY: Without confrontation, ask, "How are you doing?" Assess if there is anything holding up their ability to do their part. Try to discern if they recognize that they are holding things up—they might not be aware. "I was wondering if you noticed that some of the timelines have passed. I wanted to make sure everything is okay." Most people feel bad when they are not pulling their weight. Have some phrases that feel authentic to you and are not punitive, judgmental, or unkind. Try, "I just want to normalize that its easy for anyone to fall behind. I'm here to check in on how I can help you best."

OFFER THE OUT: Offer it sincerely and non-judgmentally. Talk about how it will be handled to ensure they would not be publicly embarrassed. Don't put the onus on them to fill in the gap or find a replacement. "I wanted to give you an out. An opportunity to step out of this project and focus on other areas where you are needed."

FOLLOW UP: Check in, either way. If the person takes the out, don't make a big deal when you circle back to them. If they choose to continue the project, plan for a check-in, and ask how they wish to hold themselves accountable for follow-up. E.g., "Do you mind if we set some milestones and touch base in two weeks on progress?"

THE MICROSKILL:

5. AVOID SCHEDULING MEETINGS WHEN PEOPLE SHOULD BE OFF

WHAT IS THE ACTUAL SKILL?

Be mindful of people's personal time.

> **ADAIRA**
> I was invited to participate on a weeknight panel. Ironically, the discussion topic was Wellness and Work-Life Balance. I felt conflicted about joining as a panelist: I wanted to help others, but I resented the time of the day. When I started the set up I heard my children crying behind the closed bedroom door as I logged in for the panel. They kept trying to open the door so I literally slid a dresser to keep them from entering. It was close to bedtime, and they needed me. I heard them banging on the door and saying, "Mommy, let us in." I found myself saying to the audience, "I'm sorry, my kids are crying in the background." Seconds later the moderator asked me, "Dr. Landry, can you share your approach to balancing family and work?" Not hilarious timing. I was not present for anyone—myself, the kids, and the panel. It was at that moment I realized it was a disastrous choice to sign up. Now I rarely commit to evening meetings.

WHY DO WE NEED THIS SKILL?

It is hard to change long-standing work-culture. Medicine holds early-morning meetings and late evenings all the time. We get that sometimes the team has to meet outside of business hours—people working across time zones, emergencies, etc. However, meetings outside of business hours should not be the standard. The Athena Swan Charter, which is a framework to shape and encourage workplaces to be more equitable, suggests that meetings be scheduled during the week and only between the hours of 10:00 a.m. and 4:00 p.m.[130] Early-morning meetings are not good for our physical health, home responsibilities, mental focus, or work engagement.[131] Late-day and weekend meetings also disrupt our ability to eat dinner and rest, either alone or with family. The argument for no early-morning meetings can be extrapolated to none at end of day or on weekends and holidays.

WHY IS THIS SKILL HARD TO ACHIEVE?

- You are told "Well, we've always done it this way."
- Leaders may not realize the practice is unhealthy and often places a greater burden on those with more household responsibilities.
- Calling out unreasonable hours is hard and may be met with retaliation.

WHAT ARE THE CRITICAL ACTIONS FOR THIS MICROSKILL?

SHIFT THE MEETING BY ONE HOUR: One additional hour makes a difference for people. This time is precious and personal for e.g. exercise, morning or evening rituals such as eating breakfast, drinking coffee, walking the dog, childcare, eldercare.

TRIM THE MEETING ATTENDANCE LIST: Are all of those people really necessary? Probably not. Save people's calendars by inviting people who truly must attend. This will open peoples' schedules.

ROTATE TIMES: If your team spans multiple time zones, especially if it's international, rotate the time so that the burden of early-morning or late meetings is shared. If some people have commitments in the early morning or the evening that can't be moved, consider rotating into midday to level the field.

RECORD THE MEETING: Share the recording for the team to listen to later.

THE MICROSKILL:

6. CALL IN SICK WHEN YOU ARE NOT HEALTHY ENOUGH TO WORK

WHAT IS THE ACTUAL SKILL?

Prioritization of your own health.

RESA

Calling out sick when sick is a foreign concept for many doctors. We generally do not do it. Culturally, it's considered "weak." In 2020, before vaccines were available, I got infected with COVID. I felt like I had the flu: tired, fever, body aches, plus a complete loss of smell and taste. Going to work was not an option: I had to stay home according to hospital policy. For sure, I felt shame—as if I had somehow failed myself, my team, and all of the profession of medicine. I consequently had to activate sick call for a few shifts. This means the on-call doctor had to work my shifts. Sure, they got paid and they knew getting called in is a part of the job. But before COVID, it was rare to do this. It's a silly masochistic badge of pride that doctors never call out. Since the pandemic, however, doctors are pushing back on this aspect of workplace culture. I see this as a healthy movement towards self-care and better patient centered care.

WHY DO WE NEED THIS SKILL?

Everyone has moments where they feel unwell—from the flu, a sports injury, nausea from pregnancy, to a chronic illness. We need to rest when our body limits our ability to work. The more we focus on self-care, the more future generations will see it normalized in the workplace. They won't feel intimidated speaking up for themselves because it will be standard practice to not work while sick. The COVID pandemic dramatically shifted our view of being sick at work. National organizations and experts such as the CDC instructed employees to stay home if they felt ill. That support shifted our practice of self-care.[132] And long COVID has shifted our ability to see that the human body doesn't always fully recover from illness. Between 2020 and 2022, 18% of patients with long COVID could not return to work for a year or longer after initially getting sick.[133]

WHY IS THIS SKILL HARD TO ACHIEVE?

- Culture change is hard: Your industry teaches it's "strong" to work while sick and "weak" to call in sick.
- You dislike the idea of adding work to your coworkers.
- You are afraid people will talk about you for calling in sick.

WHAT ARE THE CRITICAL ACTIONS FOR THIS MICROSKILL?

LEARN THE SICK-CALL POLICY: Check your benefits: understand the number of sick days provided by your employer. Learn the acceptable uses: likely you are able to call in sick for care of children or parents, but it's worth checking the specifics of your policy. Ask your trusted colleagues, "What happens if a person goes over the permitted number of sick days?"

SUPPORT OTHERS WHO CALL IN SICK: Whether you are the team leader or a team member, you should verbalize at meetings that if someone is unable to work due to illness, they should call in sick. "We can cover you while you rest and heal" goes very far in terms of support and compassion. If you get reprimanded for helping a team member, that could be considered a red flag for your company's work culture.

MODEL WHAT TO DO WHEN SICK: We know a lot of people who have worked an ED shift walking around with an IV in their arm, fluid running and medicines added. Migraine headache. Morning sickness. Food poisoning. We are not fans of this behavior. If you are sick and unable to work, stay home. Speak with your supervisor, and use your sick days. This is why they exist.

THE MICROSKILL:

7. DELIVER KIND, ACTIONABLE FEEDBACK

WHAT IS THE ACTUAL SKILL?

Deliver feedback that can be put to use.

RESA

Giving feedback takes practice, and I have definitely messed this up. One time, the faculty were talking about a resident and saying that their patient care was scattered and disorganized. Faculty could not rely on them to follow through on tasks. On my next shift working with them, I was at the doctor's desk and began a conversation without context. I said, "The word for you today is *focus*." They looked at me blankly and said, "What do you mean?" I offered, "Try not to do too many tasks at once. Don't pick up a new patient if you don't first complete care for the others." They continued to stare at me, confused. Clearly nobody had given her any feedback up to that point, and my suggestions had come out of nowhere. On my part, I considered it an epic fail because as I gave no background, no preparation, no frame of reference for the conversation. In retrospect, I should have prepared them and selected a better time and place. Prepare the person, give a heads up and be sure both of you are in a good headspace.

WHY DO WE NEED THIS SKILL?

It's going to happen: someone will ask you to provide feedback. Or, because of your position or perhaps something that occurred at work, you will need to give feedback without a request. You don't need to be a team leader to give feedback; it can be provided by anyone to anyone at any time. And sometimes it's indirect, via survey, rather than a one-on-one conversation. Delivering feedback is an essential way for the team to grow as you provide critical insight. It will also develop the self as we learn how to unpack our observations and then repackage for others to receive.

WHY IS THIS SKILL HARD TO ACHIEVE?

- You are unsure how to start, how to be effective, how to hold what could become a difficult conversation.
- There is comfort in generalities, while being specific with your feedback can be hard.
- You don't consider it your job or responsibility to provide feedback.

WHAT ARE THE CRITICAL ACTIONS FOR THIS MICROSKILL?

SEND EARLY NOTICE: Not all feedback is positive. If you need to have a difficult conversation, make sure the person is literally and figuratively in a position to hear feedback. Do not surprise them. Prepare them with a heads-up about the purpose of the conversation to avoid surprising them. This is ideally done in person or virtually with camera on so you can see and hear each other.

PRACTICE AHEAD OF TIME: These can be difficult conversations. Practice with a friend, a coach, a trusted colleague, a mentor, or perhaps someone whom you have seen do it well. Role-playing and working on your words can help you clarify what you want to get across.

START WITH A QUESTION: This allows the person to open up and grow comfortable with you and the topic. "How do you think you're doing? What are you curious about?" or "What are you hoping to work on?"

START SMALL: Pick one area that is concrete and give actionable feedback. Be specific and have a clear example. Actionable means that the issue is something that can be improved. People can improve the time it takes to get through a meeting or their ability to communicate about timelines. People cannot change their skin color or age, for example.

AVOID BIASED FEEDBACK: As the workplace diversifies, new behaviors, standards, and expectations arrive as well. These differences open the door for feedback based solely on the fact that we are all unique. Before you give feedback, ask yourself, *Is the message I am about to deliver rooted in bias and my preference for traditional norms?* If you don't know the answer, stop, put a pause on the process, and discuss best practices with trusted colleagues.

INCLUDE SOME POSITIVITY: Not everyone needs a thick layer of positive feedback before diving into the details; however, based on your exploration of how someone is doing, some authentic and intentional positivity might help. Avoid sandwiching negative feedback. "I'm going to give you some specific feedback on your communication, and I also want you to know that, overall, I think you are doing very well. Here is a specific example which shows an area that can be improved."

MIND SURVEYS: Remember that surveys are a great option to give asynchronous feedback to your team, supervisor, or executive company leadership. However it is important for you to remain respectful during this process. It is also critical that you recognize when feedback is confidential. Confidential feedback can in many ways be traced back to you. Anonymous feedback is more protected—meaning there is no way for the survey responses to be traced back to you. It is okay to ask, prior to answering questions, "Is this survey confidential or anonymous?"

DELAY MEETINGS, AS NEEDED: If you are not ready or if they are not ready, then meet at a later date. And be sure to get back to them and do not allow too long a period to elapse. Feedback is generally time-sensitive as recall can wane. If you must wait for an extended period of time, write down the details early on.

THE MICROSKILL:

8. ASK FOR FOCUSED FEEDBACK

WHAT IS THE ACTUAL SKILL?

Request focused feedback when you want to work on specific skills.

ADAIRA

I was working with a motivated emergency-medicine resident, Dr. Alister Martin. When we started the shift, he said, "Dr. Landry, today I want to work on my documentation. Do you mind reading my notes in real time and giving feedback?" On our next shift together, he said, "Can you observe the way I speak with patients?" And on a third shift, he said, "Today I want to work on my teaching skills when I work with the medical student." His clear, focused feedback request made my role easier. I knew the task up front, versus if he waited until the end of the shift and asked. This helped me direct my observations and focus my attention.

WHY DO WE NEED THIS SKILL?

Remember you determine your own degree of engagement with work. It is reported that 43% of highly engaged employees receive feedback at least once a week, compared to only 18% of employees with low engagement.[134] Stay curious and invest in your own growth and learning at work. The premise of Doug Stone and Sheila Heen's book, *Thanks for the Feedback: The Science and Art of Receiving Feedback Well*, is rather than working on giving feedback, we should work on requesting, being open to, and receiving feedback.[135] Request specific feedback: "What's one way I can improve how I deliver project updates?" This is easier for your team to give feedback on than a general question such as "Do you have feedback for me?" In our world, a medical student may ask at the end of shift, "How did I do?" We can answer; however, it's more difficult without specificity.

WHY IS THIS SKILL HARD TO ACHIEVE?

- You dislike asking for feedback because you view it as adding work to someone's plate.
- It's hard to ask for feedback if you are afraid of what you may hear and are not emotionally ready.
- It's hard to remember to ask for feedback, and you may not time the request well.

WHAT ARE THE CRITICAL ACTIONS FOR THIS MICROSKILL?

PICK ONE THING AND BE SPECIFIC: Identify a nuanced skill or task on which to focus. No matter the topic, be specific about what you want to improve.

LESS CLEAR	MORE CLEAR
"Can you let me know how I did running that code of the patient in cardiac arrest?"	"When I ran that code, could you hear my voice above the noise? Was it clear I was leading the resuscitation? Did I keep the team organized?

ASK EARLY: Instead of asking at the end of a meeting, presentation, or workday and make the request early. "I'd love to get feedback on how I run a meeting. Would you be able to join and observe me?" We understand how observation works. One phenomenon is called the Hawthorne effect, and we respect its findings: if you know you are being observed, you will change your behavior. But in this case, the specificity will give the observer something to focus on. And we hope you will bring your best self for them to evaluate.

PROBE VAGUE FEEDBACK: Remember that not everyone is comfortable or facile with communicating feedback, and this may only become obvious after the fact. It may be vague or may not contain specifics or actionable items. You could gently probe for further details. Ask, "Would you be able to elaborate on why you said my report was great? Is there one thing you can identify that was great?"

RECONSIDER UNHELPFUL FEEDBACK: You may not agree with what you hear. You may not trust the source. Remember that you don't have to act upon everyone's feedback. Perhaps it's too vague or not grounded in specific examples. Maybe it's subjective or inconsistent with others. Feel free to hear the person, thank them for the feedback, and later reconsider if there was anything valuable that you can incorporate going forward. Remember, though: if you hear a theme, check in with yourself and examine if you are being defensive and closed to something helpful.

THE MICROSKILL:

9. BRING POSITIVITY INTO THE WORKPLACE

WHAT IS THE ACTUAL SKILL?

Recognize the impact of perpetual indifference or negativity.

ADAIRA

Every year I have an annual review with two of my very supportive supervisors. They review my performance metrics such as how many patients I have seen per hour and how long patients are in the ED under my care. All this data goes into a bell curve alongside my colleagues. I fall exactly in the middle every year. During the annual review meeting I disclose that I have little interest in moving faster unless they are concerned about my performance. The reason why I don't want to move faster is that during slow parts of the ED, I enjoy socializing and checking in with the team. I check in with the techs, nurses, residents. I also enjoy getting to know my patients and taking longer histories. We laugh, we share photos of kids, we talk about restaurants and gardening. All of this allows us to feel comfortable with each other andcommunicate smoothly. This morale boost also helps us care for patients better as we energized and enjoying the shift. My written feedback always shows comments about how I lighten the spirit on days I work, and that people look forward to working with me. I think a large component of this stems from being positive at work.

WHY DO WE NEED THIS SKILL?

Positivity at work can occur even on the worst of days. There is usually at least one positive thing you can say about any scenario. Even adding, "Well, at least the coffee machine is working" can lighten a dark mood. The point is that we aren't asking you to be fake. We are asking you to take inventory of the moods and morale around you. Both of these affect the self, the team, and the work. While it might not be your responsibility to make everyone laugh, positivity is a gift that we can offer others.

WHY IS THIS SKILL HARD TO ACHIEVE?

- This is not your nature.
- You equate positivity with a humorous, gregarious nature.
- You find it taxing and time consuming.
- You think adding joy and positivity seems disingenuous.

WHAT ARE THE CRITICAL ACTIONS FOR THIS MICROSKILL?

SHIFT THE FOCUS: When we say bring positivity, we mean tell people "good job" or "congrats." It's a matter of keeping the morale high so that people still have hope. It's also a matter of holding on to your negativity instead of processing it. It's very easy to get stuck in the world of negativity, discouragement, cynicism. When you notice yourself doing that, break the cycle.

LOWER THE BAR: Being positive at work doesn't mean making people laugh or blowing up animal balloons. We just want you to recognize that saying small phrases, such as "we did it!" causes the team to recognize that their work and effort was recognized. We know this can be tiring and draining for some, so considering doing this only when you have the emotional bandwidth and time.

BE AUTHENTIC: Some days you will not feel positive. And no matter how much you try to muster up good words of encouragement or excitement, you cannot. We aren't asking you to further your personal or interpersonal struggles for us. This isn't about putting on a fake face.

CONCLUSION:

Upstand and create psychological safety for yourself and for your team	Check in and get to know your colleagues one-on-one.	Model support and compassion for each other: call in when sick, and be someone who takes a stand.

SUPPLEMENTAL RESOURCES:

TED Talk
Patrick Lencioni

The Visible
Voices

Forbes

8

MICROSKILLS TO GROW YOUR NETWORK

RESA

I was too early in my career to understand the importance of professional networks or that I even had one. I was a medical student. It was the month I decided emergency medicine was the specialty for me. The doctors embodied the intelligent, compassionate, hardworking, down to earth, and able to handle anyone who came through the door persona I sought. The chief resident really impressed me. He was super effecient, kept his emergency department tasks organized, and took excellent care of patients. I never saw him abandon his kindness, sense of humor, or focus. Years later, I ran into him, reintroduced myself and shared the impact he made on me. In that moment, I realized that four weeks of working beside him in Philadelphia, trying in my medical student way to help care for the patients injured by knife or gunshot wounds, the pregnant patients with vaginal bleeding, the intoxicated patients who fell with head injuries created a bond of connection. We were a part of each others network. He calls for advice about ultrasound. I have called him to talk about leadership and managing a team. We called each other during COVID just to connect, check on each other, and share how we fared and what we did to keep healthy.

Your network consists of the people you are meaningfully connected with. And, trust us, you are connected. Your connections started before grade school and have continued to grow since. Perhaps you haven't kept in touch with everyone. Or maybe they didn't follow the same career path as you. But the point remains: your connections are not starting from zero. You have a base. And your base stems from family and friends.

Early in our careers we went to panels and lectures to hear about the benefit of connecting. Speakers would say that having this or that connection changed their lives. And at the end of the session, there was a call to action: *Go out and network!* But nobody discussed the how-to of it. What we needed was a concrete step-by-step guide on how to establish, nurture, and grow a network.

Growing your connections does not follow a linear pattern over time. Some relationships happen organically; some take active effort and intention. It's not about superficially collecting names and contact information. We want you to truly link up with people you can call for questions, advice, or even just to chat and speak at a human level. Your network is there to help you grow, learn and fill in your gaps. And remember that you have lots to offer in return.

Many people hesitate to network. They wonder, *I don't know what I want to do with my life, so what do I even need from others?* This question stalls early-career professionals from moving forward. We want to push back on that mindset. You don't need to know exactly what you want with your career to start networking. In fact when our mentees often ask, "How did you decide what to focus on?" we share how much networking helped us chisel our career to be what it is.

In this chapter we discuss the eight MicroSkills needed to realize and grow your connections.

MICROSKILLS TO GROW YOUR NETWORK:

1. Discover your networking needs.
2. Understand the difference between a conversation and a commitment.
3. Overcome discomfort with networking (for introverts).
4. Create meaningful relationships that stick.
5. Leverage your existing network to build a bigger one.
6. Demonstrate your expertise to an audience.
7. Avoid networking faux pas.
8. Share your network to help others.

THE MICROSKILL:

1. DECIDE YOUR NETWORKING NEEDS

WHAT IS THE ACTUAL SKILL?

Understand how networking will help your professional success.

ADAIRA

A few years ago I approached the chair of my department, Dr. Mike VanRooyen. At that point I had a small network. I told him I wanted to meet senior-level Black women who were great leaders. It did not matter what field they were in. My goal was to find someone who looked like me and understood how to become a leader. I didn't need to collaborate with the person. I didn't need them to hire me. I wasn't looking for potential customers. I just wanted to learn about leadership from the person he recommended. He suggested that I meet with Dr. Paula Johnson, an amazing woman who has accomplished extraordinary growth as a leader: she'd been a professor of medicine at Harvard Medical School, professor of epidemiology at the Harvard TH Chan School of Public Health, and when we were first introduced, she was at the time the president of Wellesley College. She provides an immense amount of insight and clarity. She also normalizes for me that Black women can be incredibly successful in the workplace.

WHY DO WE NEED THIS SKILL?

Humans are social creatures. The work environment requires social interactions and engagement. Though possible, it's challenging to achieve success without the help of other people. And it really pays dividends when you have people to whom you can ask questions. Why is that? They steer you in a direction. They hold you accountable. They teach you humility. And perhaps most importantly—you help them in return.

WHY IS THIS SKILL HARD TO ACHIEVE?

- You think its time consuming and low yield.
- Networking feels uncomfortable and/or contrived.
- You think your current network is enough.
- You don't realize the benefit of helping other people through networking.

WHAT ARE THE CRITICAL ACTIONS FOR THIS MICROSKILL?

LEARN WHAT OTHERS GAIN FROM NETWORKING: Get inspiration from your closest friends, family, and colleagues. Literally even a text could be the start of this conversation. "I'm trying to understand the perks of networking. Can you share your experience?" To get you started, we asked some of our people how networking helped their career. Here's what they said:

NAME	ROLE	BENEFIT OF NETWORKING
Amorina Lopez, JD	Medical Malpractice Lawyer	I think the most recent and biggest example is how easily I was able to find a new job and seamlessly transition from one firm to the next because of the relationships I have built and cultivated over the years. The partners that hired me are friends since I've been socializing with them for years at different conferences and events.

Peilin Chou	Academy Award–Nominated Film Producer	I have to admit the notion of "networking" has never been really appealing to me. Especially in the early days of my career in Hollywood, I always marveled at those that were scheduling breakfast, lunches, drinks and dinners every day, trying to connect and meet with as many people as possible. I could tell it energized them, but to me it just felt exhausting. So much so it actually made me wonder if I could be successful in an industry where so much was built on relationships and who you knew. I came into this industry literally knowing nobody. Over the course of my career, I've found that I made my strongest connections in a slower and more organic way. It's been a lot through people I've worked with who share common passions, values or beliefs. Whether it's love for a story that we all feel must be told, or a shared fervent belief in the importance of representation in storytelling, that's where the long lasting and meaningful connections have come from.
Heidi Messer, JD	Chairperson, Cofounder, Collective[i]	It takes time and effort to build a network but that investment will give you exponential advantages. To start, you have to be willing to be a connector. Connectors are people who thrive sharing what and who they know to help others succeed. They are givers and ready to offer their network advice, referrals, knowledge, and introductions that create tremendous opportunity. In my experience, helping others in business in this way pays tremendous dividends. People remember and want to reciprocate. It becomes a virtuous cycle. The most successful people I know got there because of the help they provided others along the way.

Serena Murillo, JD	Judge of the Los Angeles Superior Court	Graduate programs train you on how to do a job, but they don't necessarily equip you with the tools you need to navigate the workplace or advance your career. When I speak to new lawyers, I advise them to join three attorney bar associations: one for their region, one for their practice area, and one that supports them as a person. I didn't do that until much later in my career, but in short order, the people I met in those groups helped me develop as a professional, provided me with leadership opportunities, and encouraged and supported me on my path toward becoming a judge. I couldn't have done it without them and I wish I had known the value of networking earlier in my career.

Learn what others have gained from networking by asking your closest friends, family, and colleagues.

ASSESS YOUR NETWORKING NEEDS: Think of where you are currently. Measure the distance from where you are and where you would like to be e.g. you are hoping to be a CEO but you are currently an entry level employee. You want to be an award-winning author, but you haven't written a sentence in years. Be honest and ambitious. And let yourself realize that it will greatly help to have people guide you. And it's very strategic to network and meet people on the same path (farther along, peer level, more junior, and at all levels). It's also okay if you feel unsure or lost when it comes to career mapping. If that is the case it will be even more helpful to connect with people who may guide you. Finally, know that you are not obligated to stick to any path. So even if you pick a path as a placeholder, know that it can be changed over time.

BRAINSTORM TOPICS: Now that you have considered where you want to be, you need to brainstorm the topics you need to learn to get there. Make a list of areas on which you seek input and advice. Think about areas you wish to work on. Select something that you want to take to the next level.

EXAMPLES OF DISCUSSION TOPICS
☐ Speaking and Designing Slides
☐ Time Management
☐ People Management and Conflict Resolution
☐ Leading Meetings
☐ Budget and Finances
☐ Politics and Advocacy
☐ Workplace Wellness and Burnout Prevention
☐ Sponsoring and Mentoring
☐ Teaching, Evaluating, and Competency Assessment
☐ Writing Proposals
☐ Product Design
☐ Web Development and Design
☐ Leveraging Artificial Intelligence
☐ Founding A Start-Up

Making a list of areas on which you seek input and advice can help you decipher your networking needs and grow your circle.

ASK FOR A MEETING: Email people. Yes, we know this can be uncomfortable. Do not fret if you get no response or a "no"—it happens. Assuming you were polite and professional, they aren't mad at you for asking; they are just busy. Move on and ask someone else. Example of an email request to meet:

FROM:

TO:

CC:

BCC:

SUBJECT: Meeting Request to Discuss Next Professional Steps

MESSAGE:

Hello Resa,

I hope you are well.

I have been a physician here for seven years. I am at a crossroads and am looking at my next professional steps. I value your expertise as an educator and mentor. How is your calendar in the next one to two weeks to chat for twenty minutes? Here are some options and I am glad to look further out if none work:

Mon 21st, 2–4 p.m. EST
Fri 25th, 10–11 a.m. EST
Mon 28th, 2–5 p.m. EST

Let me know what works, and I can send a calendar invite with video conferencing link.

Best,
Adaira

Ask for a meeting with people to grow your network.

BE PROACTIVE: When scheduling a meeting be accommodating of their calendar and time. After a meeting is confirmed, send a calendar invitation. Just prior to a meeting, send a meeting reminder. After the meeting, send a thank you note.

TAKE YOUR TIME: Relationships take time to build. Enjoy getting to know people and expanding people in your network. The process should not feel like a burden. You may only reach out to meet someone a few times a year. Or perhaps you only meet with these individuals annually. There is no need to rush and pack your calendar. Get to know one person, learn the cadence and the how to of connecting. Let your network slowly grow.

THE MICROSKILL:

2. UNDERSTAND THE DIFFERENCE BETWEEN A CONVERSATION AND A COMMITMENT

WHAT IS THE ACTUAL SKILL?

Accept that a networking conversation need not translate to more work.

ADAIRA

It took a few times for me to realize I did not have to collaborate with every new person in my network. When I first intentionally started growing my professional connections, I'd somehow leave every meeting with more projects on my plate. I'd set up a meeting based on a cold email or a warm introduction. Then, in the meeting with that person, many amazing offers started coming my way: "Well, why don't you join me in this project?" or "You know, I was thinking about working on this idea, Adaira. Would you like to join me?" I felt obligated, even pressured, to say yes. So simple conversations turned into hefty commitments. I'd accept the invitation on the spot. No thought, no reconnaissance. I wouldn't even check my calendar. I'd just say, "Yes, I'm interested. Let's do it!" I soon realized that while many of the ideas were great, they were often not great for me. So, I'd end up with more on my task list and perhaps less clarity on who I was and what I wanted for myself professionally.

WHY DO WE NEED THIS SKILL?

Growing your network starts with communication, a conversation. Doesn't matter the vehicle: phone, direct message, video call, email, or in person. However, we need to understand the boundaries of a professional conversation and normalize that it is fine to just chat; there is no obligation to commit to more work, if offered. The pressure to please others is real. And the pressure to accept an opportunity from someone you respect is real. But knowing your boundaries will help you explore the professional relationship without obligation.

WHY IS THIS SKILL HARD TO ACHIEVE?

- You have been told to say yes to everything.
- You worry you will be seen as lazy, unappreciative, or unfocused.
- You worry you won't get another opportunity.
- You feel obligated, so it's anxiety-provoking to decline.
- You don't know how to decline an offer.

WHAT ARE THE CRITICAL ACTIONS FOR THIS MICROSKILL?

CLARIFY WITH YOURSELF THE GOALS OF A MEETING: Before you meet with someone, clarify with yourself what you want. If it's to get to know someone, that's fine. If it's to share what you are doing and ask for advice, that's great. If you want them to help you fill a skill gap, perfect. And if you prefer to keep your plate clean, then remind yourself of that. No need to state that up front however practice your response if the conversation gets to that.

BE CURIOUS ABOUT THE PERSON: Focus on the other person. The person you meet with is a font of information. Ask about their current or future projects or goals. "Why did you choose that particular project?" or "How did you learn that skill?" Give them time to share about themselves. This allows them a chance to speak openly, you to learn, and bonds to be formed. Brainstorm how you can help them. Be curious about how they can help you and also, how you can return the favor.

LESS CLEAR	MORE CLEAR
How do I become a better leader?	What are three of the best lessons you learned about leadership? Where have you or someone you know failed as a leader? What is one thing you did to become a leader of this company?

UNDERSTAND THE ROLE OF THE PERSON IN YOUR NETWORK: Not everyone in your network serves the same role. Some people are mentors or coaches, some are sponsors and some collaborators—and the same person may change roles over time. Some become your friends.

MENTOR	They offer knowledge, development, guidance, advice or expertise to you for your professional development.	"I'd like to be sure our meetings are mutually beneficial. Please let me know your pain points and where you find yourself stuck."
ADVISOR	They give specific advice and guidance and the relationship is less of a two-way.	"I'm here to give you specific, concrete advice on decisions you need to make."
SPONSOR	They help you get to your goals by nominating and advocating for you. The relationship is less personal and this is not someone with whom you meet regularly.	"I will say your name and suggest you when openings or opportunities come up."
COACH	They can teach you a focused skill.	"I will work with you on giving oral presentations."
COLLABORATOR	They work with you on projects together and partner.	"We are equal partners on this project and are committed to the same goal."

Understand the roles of different people in your network.

EVALUATE OPPORTUNITIES OFFERED TO YOU: Be ready for an offer. If you get along with this person, you may be offered a project to join, a paper to write, etc. Remember and stick to your meeting goals. And respond warmly, authentically and in a way to keep the dialogue open for future collaboration. Always close the communication loop in real time. Adaira always advises her mentees, "Don't say yes. Say, tell me more." This approach allows you to explore further without immediately declining. You'd be surprised the type of potential red flags you will uncover if you probe deeply enough.

EXAMPLES OF HOW TO DECLINE AN OFFER
"Thank you for thinking of me. Unfortunately I think this opportunity does not align with my goals right now." "Thank you for the offer. Let me look at my schedule to check on my bandwidth for more work right now. I will circle back in the next 1-2 days." "Thank you. I would welcome the opportunity to work together in the future. Right now, I have a lot to clear off my plate." "Can you tell me more? What is the timeline? Who is on the project? Is there a draft available? I'm interested in timelines."

THE MICROSKILL:

3. OVERCOME DISCOMFORT WITH NETWORKING (FOR INTROVERTS)

WHAT IS THE ACTUAL SKILL?

Learn adaptive techniques for networking if you are an introvert.

RESA

It took me years and many emergency medicine conferences to learn habits that help me navigate these professional events. I tell people I am socially adept and not shy; yet, I am deeply introverted. And these attributes are not in conflict. I can lead a meeting, speak before hundreds or thousands of people, and be comfortable at social events with strangers. And also, I recharge, regroup, and get restored in quiet and solo environments. Reading books, walking in nature, and connecting one-on-one are my go-to's. Consequently, professional conferences and socializing in large crowds are not my preferred way to connect. For conferences, I stay in accommodations close to the venue but usually not at the venue. This allows me to escape for quiet breaks when needed. I eat meals or drink coffee solo or organize small groups in lieu of large dinner events. This has really worked well as a comfortable way to grow my connections.

WHY DO WE NEED THIS SKILL?

For the longest time and for many industries, the culture around networking has been defined by large events with many people and a lot of social stimulation. This works if you are an extrovert. According to Myers-Briggs Company, 56.8% of the world is introverted.[136] Thank goodness there is more awareness around managing both extroverts and introverts in the workplace.[137] To be clear, being shy and introverted are not the same thing. *A shy person* is someone who is anxious about social interactions. An *introvert* is someone who is not shy but is drained by large-group interactions and recharges with alone time and prefers small-group or one-on-one socializing.[138]

WHY IS THIS SKILL HARD TO ACHIEVE?

- Many industries and work environments have social and networking events built for extroverts.
- People interpret your introversion as being rude, standoffish, or antisocial.
- Unless you learn adaptive socializing skills, you may skip out on all networking opportunities.
- It's hard to advocate and request that the team host networking events that feel comfortable for introverts.

WHAT ARE THE CRITICAL ACTIONS FOR THIS MICROSKILL?

TAKE TIME TO REFLECT: Consider the social spaces and conversations and situations which are most comfortable and joyful. Take time to consider when you are with others and at ease. Remember the prior instances where you felt unfulfilled and lacked meaningful connection to others. There is a spectrum of preferences so it is helpful for you to think of the nuances. Perhaps you enjoy dinners but with small groups, less than four. Perhaps you like conferences, but you stay at a smaller off-site hotel.

PROTECT YOUR ENERGY: Plan ways to protect and recharge your energy. Decline the offers that make you uncomfortable. Reply with, "Thank you so much for the invitation to the party. I'm unable to attend but might you be willing to meet separately at a different time?" A one-on-one walking meeting can yield a meaningful connection and professional relationship, sometimes more than a cocktail party with numerous light conversations.

COMMUNICATE YOUR NEEDS: If you feel your hesitancy with socializing is taking a toll on your reputation and ability to network, speak with the team. Explain how being an introvert translates. Tell them you are not rude or aloof or even shy. Many may express relief because they feel the same way.

THE MICROSKILL:

4. CREATE MEANINGFUL RELATIONSHIPS THAT STICK

WHAT IS THE ACTUAL SKILL?

Nurture your connections through kind, professional, polite, and authentic follow-up.

RESA

At a professional conference, I met a physician and dean of a medical school who was accomplished and an inspiring medical educator. I was sure he would be an excellent mentor. I asked if I could follow up with him to meet back in our home city. After six months of outreach, we finally met. At that meeting, I felt even more enthusiastic about forging an ongoing mentor-mentee relationship. I saw myself professionally following a path he had walked. I prepared questions. I sought his insights. Yet, after the meeting and in follow-up, he was not email-responsive. His availability was limited, and after he rescheduled our meeting twice, I realized that the relationship was not sticking. I took a step back and was able to point to the professional relationships I had where meeting, communicating, and the mutual interest in the relationship took little effort. This really drove home the point that connecting and developing meaningful connections at work required that both parties be invested and prioritize the relationship. The next time this happened, I was quicker to move on.

WHY DO WE NEED THIS SKILL?

We readily discover the value of our relationship when there is an urgent need to fix or resolve an issue. During moments of stress is where we may tap our network for support. We want those relationships to feel strong and stable. We could always cold-call someone—but that might feel uncomfortable, especially if there is no established history or no recent contact. Maintaining ongoing communication with a network builds a strong foundation and fosters organic growth of the relationship—it also creates a symbiotic relationship where both parties benefit.[139]

WHY IS THIS SKILL HARD TO ACHIEVE?

- Consistent communication is an investment of time and energy.
- It can be challenging forging a path to naturally stay connected. You do not know when or how to reach out to someone.
- Asking how others want to communicate and create a sustainable relationship can feel intimidating.
- It may be hard to recognize or let go when a relationship is not working.

WHAT ARE THE CRITICAL ACTIONS FOR THIS MICROSKILL?

DEVELOP THE RELATIONSHIP OVER TIME: Not all relationships require a daily conversation. Some people you might not need to connect with regularly, while others you might. We all have a zone of connectedness that, in the background, places our network in different locations. Core contacts are part of your inner networking: you might connect daily or multiple times a week. Farther out you have a more peripheral group: you are aware of each other's lives but not in regular contact. Finally, you have distant contacts with whom you meet irregularly and often only when there is a specific purpose, goal, or need.

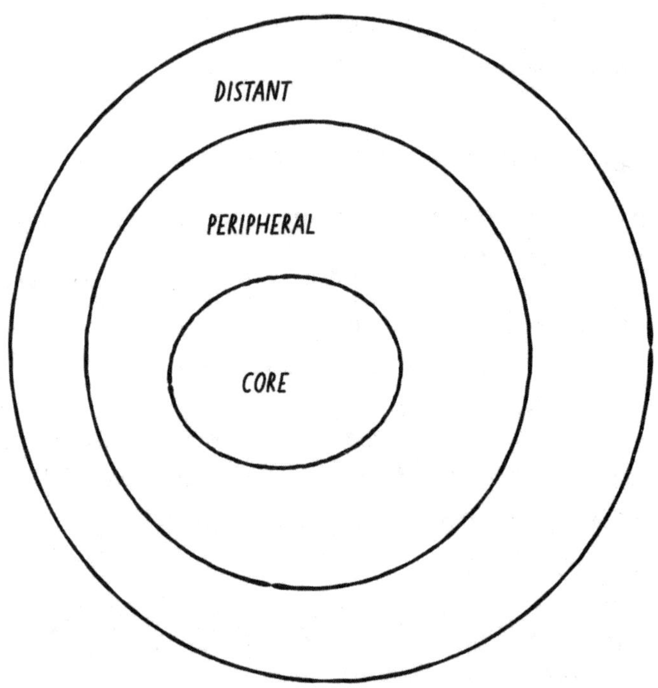

ZONE OF CONNECTEDNESS: Core contacts are part of your inner network. Farther out you have a more peripheral group, aware of each other's lives but not in regular contact. Finally, you have distant contacts with whom you meet very irregularly and often only when there is a specific purpose, goal, or need.

TIME THE COMMUNICATION: Determining how often to reach out to someone can be a challenge. We are certain there are people you'd love to meet regularly, but that may just not be feasible or necessary. When determining the frequency of communication, consider three principles:

1. **NEED:** Is there an immediate need? If you don't have to meet with them over the next few days, weeks, or

months, consider aiming for a quarterly, semiannual, or annual cadence.

2. **AVAILABILITY:** Consider how available you and the person are to meet. At the bare minimum, an annual meeting or email is reasonable. For some forms of networking you might need to meet daily or weekly e.g. for an active project.

3. **IMPACT:** Is this a contact who inspires, motivates, or revolutionizes your life every time you meet? Nurture that relationship and keep those people on your radar. You might want to meet at the peaks and valleys of your professional journey to feel inspired.

GIVE AN UPDATE, ASK A QUESTION: Updates on your life and career are wonderful gifts for people with whom you are connected. Be specific and intentional, e.g. tell them if you got published and attach a copy if it's an article, had another child, enrolled in an advanced-degree program, or joined a new company. Use that as an opportunity to get their opinions.

OFFER VALUE IN RETURN: Be sensitive to one-sided asks and relationships. Try to show you have something to offer. Share a webinar, article, or social-media post you think would interest them. You can also send them a thank-you note that says *I just wanted to say that I appreciate you and the time you have given me*. Schedule calendar reminders for yourself about people's birthdays. Do not feel pressured to spend money. You can send an appreciation letter to their supervisor.

LET YOUR CALENDAR HELP: When you finish a meeting discuss and calendar the next one. This is not required and yet completely helpful. At the very least, put a calendar reminder for yourself to reach out within a certain amount of time. We want to emphasize one tip—stop relying on your brain to remember extraneous details.

THE MICROSKILL:

5. LEVERAGE YOUR EXISTING NETWORK TO BUILD A BIGGER ONE

WHAT IS THE ACTUAL SKILL?

Ask your current network if they have anyone else they recommend you meet.

ADAIRA

I meet with about three to five students a week. Some are in college, others in medical school. Occasionally, I realize some of their needs are out of my skill set and expertise. So at the end of the meeting we use the *snowball effect*. I give them a name of someone else I think they should meet with and we discuss how they can create that connection. This way they use my existing network to build their own. I like this strategy because it takes advantage of my already curated list of contacts—which is less risky for the student compared to them sending a cold email to a stranger. I remind them that I am happy to push them toward finding their core network, and I can remain in their peripheral network.

WHY DO WE NEED THIS SKILL?

You want more than one person in your network. But you don't want to pack your contacts list with names just for fun. The goal is meaningful professional relationships. Some say you should have no more than six.[140] There's some validity to having a smaller, contained group, especially in your core network. Leveraging the network of people you trust to expand your own network can help you meet others strategically and at a do-able pace.

WHY IS THIS SKILL HARD TO ACHIEVE?

- You worry asking for an introduction might be perceived as abusing or exploiting the current relationship.
- You don't know who your current network is associated with.
- You believe you have no connections to offer in return to other people.

WHAT ARE THE CRITICAL ACTIONS FOR THIS MICROSKILL?

CONSIDER YOUR SCHEDULE: If you are already struggling to make meetings, asking for more is not the right move. Wait until you have more bandwidth. We don't want you setting up meetings and cancelling. While a cancellation is understandable here and there, too often is not optimal for your professional reputation.

TAKE INVENTORY: Think about your connections. Look at your phone and email contacts. These may be family and friends from childhood, all your education stages, hobbies, part-time jobs. Everyone counts. Consider *What is this person really good at doing?* If you feel comfortable, kindly request a 15–20 minute conversation with a focused ask.

ASK CAREFULLY FOR A NEW CONTACT: Ask a contact to introduce you to their contact. One way to phrase the request: "Thank you for our meeting. I'd love to stay in contact. And I'm also curious if there is anyone with whom you think I should connect."

FOLLOW UP: Allow time for your established connection to make their outreach. If they offer to introduce you to someone, give them 1–2 weeks for that to occur. When they do set up an introduction, be sure to be professional, polite, and follow through with your promises. If there's been radio silence, you can circle back with your point person. Ask, "Hello, I'm really glad we were able to speak last week. Might you have any updates re: the introduction we discussed? If it is easier, I am glad to reach out directly and CC you?" Here's some behind the scenes insight: when we want to introduce one person to a second person, we almost always check with the second person out of respect and get an "ok". We want to make sure they have the space and time for the new contact.

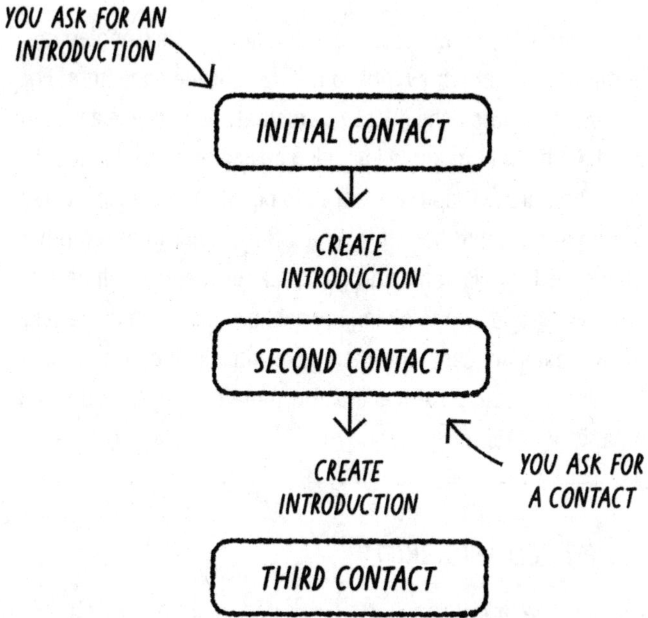

Once your established connection has made their outreach, be professional, polite, and follow through.

THE MICROSKILL:

6. DEMONSTRATE YOUR EXPERTISE TO AN AUDIENCE

WHAT IS THE ACTUAL SKILL?

Make it known why people should connect with you.

RESA

I remember the conversation in a podcast episode when I realized that I needed to more intentionally let people know my expertise. Two guests joined me. We were all physicians with leadership experience. One guest knew me. The other guest was meeting me for the first time. Up to this episode, I thought guests Googled me, read about me, or somehow looked me up. Not the case here. For the first twenty minutes, the guest was distant and spoke in a way to suggest that she did not know I am also an academic and a doctor. In the conversation, I made references to people and places we had in common and I noted her shift. She let down her guard and her tone changed. This was amazing feedback for me. Ever since that conversation, in addition to giving my background by email, I make sure to start each podcast recording by re-introducing myself more intentionally. The conversations are now more friendly, smooth and psychologically safe for everybody.

WHY DO WE NEED THIS SKILL?

We know the workplace is full of bias and the world is not equal. We do not begin at the same starting line, so asserting your skills and qualities will catch others up to speed. Nobody really knows you until you share some information about your background, interests, values, expertise. We want to normalize that it is okay to share your interests and accomplishments. In fact, it helps other people share theirs. In our article, "7 Ways to Promote Yourself on Social Media without Bragging," we write "Recognize that what one might see as boasting, another person, perhaps historically excluded from opportunities, may appreciate as intel and guidance. Informing and supporting others makes the world a better place."[141]

WHY IS THIS SKILL HARD TO ACHIEVE?

- You don't know how to demonstrate expertise while remaining humble.

- You do not know what to highlight from your bio when you meet other people.
- You assume people know your accomplishments.

WHAT ARE THE CRITICAL ACTIONS FOR THIS MICROSKILL?

PRACTICE INTRODUCING YOURSELF: Practice introducing yourself in one minute. Or two minutes. Role-play this with a member of your personal board; pick someone who is good at giving feedback. You can even start with, "Is it okay if I tell you a little bit about myself?" or "I would love to tell you more about my professional path; is that okay?"

BE VISIBLE: An opinion does not mean much unless you share it. Speaking, writing, and holding leadership roles related to a topic, do establish expertise. You do not need to be an award-winning writer to publish. You do not need to give a TED Talk to be a speaker. You just need an idea, the ability to tell it clearly. Find the opportunity or make the opportunity.

AMPLIFY YOURSELF THROUGH SOCIAL MEDIA: Social media is not going away. Watch how other people self-promote and share their voice—and therefore see how you can comfortably assert your expertise. If you don't participate in social media, then it will be harder—though not impossible—to grow your network.[142] Share an award, lecture opportunity, or anything else. Share what you are working on, e.g. "Excited to share that I [insert opportunity]. I want to thank [insert names or handles]." What we saw when we started promoting, voicing opinions, and commenting is that more people joined our networks. They reached out, friended us, invited us to speak and to collaborate on projects.

WRITE BIOS OF DIFFERENT LENGTHS: Have a brief bio and a longer one written and ready to share. The shorter one highlights concrete specifics of who you are and why someone should want to connect with you. As you are early in the career—a brief bio might feel sufficient. As you gain more experiences and opportunities, consider three-to-six sentences for that version and two-to-four paragraphs for the extended one. Ask friends for their examples on which you can model yours. Be proactive and send this to people so they can get to know you before meeting.

SAMPLE BRIEF BIO SKELETON	SAMPLE EXTENDED BIO SKELETON
Sentence 1: Name **Sentence 2:** Current title **Sentence 3:** Relevant training and key prior jobs/roles **Sentence 4:** Current responsibilities **Sentence 5:** Future aspirations	**Paragraph 1:** Current Name, Title, Schooling, and Responsibilities **Paragraph 2-4:** Past experiences, current experiences, prominent awards, publications, speaking gigs, future goals

Have ready to share a three-to-six sentence bio highlighting concrete specifics of who you are and why someone should want to connect with you. Write a longer two-to-four-paragraph bio to share more in-depth your experiences and opportunities.

CREATE A WEBSITE: A simple website that has your name, photo, and biography, your abridged résumé, a few examples of your work, and a way to be contacted is enough. Be consistent and clear about your expertise. Link your website to social media.

ATTEND CONFERENCES: Conferences are a centralized way to meet people with similar interests and expertise. Connect with people before the conference begins—even virtually—by sending an introduction. For example, "I saw you are speaking at [name of conference]. I know you will be busy and I'd love to try to connect there. What may be some windows to connect?" If they say it's not possible, then offer that you will introduce yourself after the lecture and hope for a later date.

THE MICROSKILL:

7. AVOID NETWORKING FAUX PAS

WHAT IS THE ACTUAL SKILL?

Knowing what not do when networking is more important than knowing what to do.

RESA

I had just finished a visiting faculty lecture. In particular I told a story on how I learned to develop the courage to stop waiting for things to happen for me and how to start asking for what I needed at work. In doing so, I was encouraging the audience members to speak up and to just ask for what they needed or wanted for their professional development. The talk ended. I was standing on stage by the podium and a few people came up to ask questions one on one. A shy appearing man began:

HIM: "Hi. Will you write a letter of recommendation for me?"

ME: Smile. Pause. Not sure what to say.

HIM: "You just talked about asking. So I decided to start now. And ask you if you would write a letter of recommendation for me."

ME: I decided to diffuse kindly and professionally. We had never met. "Let me give you my email and please reach out. Let's continue the conversation there. Also, I want to be sure you are connected with your mentors on this."

To be clear, there was nothing devastatingly wrong with what he did. The situation was awkward because he interpreted the advice very literally. Asking for something still requires careful timing and some reflection: who to ask and how to ask. In this case, there was no established connection. My gut reaction told me that I was not the right person to write the letter. And I could help him navigate to the right person.

WHY DO WE NEED THIS SKILL?

Rest assured, you will make networking faux pas. To a certain extent, we all do. We may forget to call someone back, or send an email, or accidentally call someone the wrong name. In isolation, these are all forgivable. And we love self-compassion, so we don't expect you to be perfect. However, small mishaps are different than repetitive faux pas: coming across as rude or selfish, thinking only about the self, or speaking and interacting in a way that is contrived, disingenuous, or salesperson like. Believe us, people recognize all of that.

WHY IS THIS SKILL HARD TO ACHIEVE?

- You miss social cues or lack situational awareness.
- Networking makes you nervous or prone to social errors.
- You have difficulty knowing and keeping boundaries.
- You fear that people will not forgive you if you misstep.

WHAT ARE THE CRITICAL ACTIONS FOR THIS MICROSKILL?

RESPECT BOUNDARIES: Take your time when it comes to meeting people. There is no rush or expectation to become best friends overnight. Networking is a process where you meet someone who can help you develop your career. Just start by having conversations, and let the connection gradually build.

BOUNDARY FAUX-PAS	EXAMPLE
Communicating in off-hours	Phoning your supervisor or coworker for something nonurgent at ten o'clock at night
Communicating using a method that is too intimate	Regularly text messaging someone who does not have you in their contacts list and who did not give permission

Communicating with someone too informally	Calling someone by their first name or nickname without them offering you to do so or you first asking "What would you like me to call you?"
Communicating too frequently	Emailing multiple times for nonurgent issues within a short time period
Communicating high demands	Asking to be introduced to others (especially executives or senior level individuals) every week or month

Respect boundaries and take your time meeting people. Networking is a process.

BE HUMBLE AND GROUNDED: When mingling, don't overshare or boast. We understand being nervous and being focused on making sure you share your accomplishments. However, take two slow, deep, cleansing breaths. Be an active listener and observer. Avoid a tone of entitlement, name-dropping, or one-upping other members of the group.

BE POLITE: This may sound obvious, and we are not social etiquette experts: simply remember to say *Please* and *Thank you.* Be patient when asking questions. Do not overstay if there is a natural ending to a conversation. Avoid hurtful language.

HAVE PERSON SPECIFIC QUESTIONS: Invest in getting to know the person. If you are meeting with someone, especially someone more senior to you—Google them, read about them, listen to podcast episodes with them and their work ahead of time. Integrate that into your conversation, e.g. "I read your latest blog post on climate change. How do you think we course correct in the face of a growing population?"

FOLLOW UP WITH CONTACTS: Be sure you have a way to follow up. You miss an opportunity if you leave a conversation or a conference or a meeting without an email address, phone number, or other way to keep in touch. Just ask and be sure to say, email, or handwrite a thank-you.

DIVERSIFY CONNECTIONS: Be open and social and ready to speak with anyone. Don't be the person who only focuses on connecting with people who look like them or who are more senior for that sake. Consider peer networking and connect with people outside of your company and field. Diverse and inclusive connections are super rewarding.

THE MICROSKILL:

8. SHARE YOUR NETWORK TO HELP OTHERS

WHAT IS THE ACTUAL SKILL?

Introduce people in your network to each other.

ADAIRA

A few years ago, I mentored a woman who wanted to train at a particular residency program on the east coast. I happened to be slightly familiar with that program's leadership team. She applied and had not received an interview. She came to me for advice. I offered to leverage my connections. I knew this student well and could vouch for her academic record—she compared similarly to amazing medical students I had worked with. I had no doubt that her qualifications were stellar so I emailed one of my contacts a simple message, "Just wanted to see if you could take a second look at an applicant applying who hasn't received an interview yet." They took a second look at her application and saw her potential. And years later, I hear she is thriving in the program. Her success fuels me, brings happiness into the world, and my advocacy for her caused me literally no harm. There is hardly ever a reason to keep your network locked away.

WHY DO WE NEED THIS SKILL?

There's very little to gain from keeping resources to yourself. And you want to try to help contribute to the professional growth of other people. Think of your network as an asset. And this is an asset to share. Second-degree connections are the people connected to your first-degree connections.[143] More than half of the connections you make will be friends of friends or second-degree connections.[144] By introducing your people to others, you help them meet collaborators, peers, and even experts. This positions you to go further when your interest in helping other people is genuine. They will remember you helping with accessing a job interview or a meeting with someone, they otherwise could not access. They in turn are more likely to help you when the situation is flipped.

WHY IS THIS SKILL HARD TO ACHIEVE?

- It takes time and energy to make a connection.
- It's hard to know if a connection will prove helpful to you or others.

- Sharing your network may feel like an invasion of privacy or giving away your hard work.

WHAT ARE THE CRITICAL ACTIONS OF THIS SKILL?

ASK PEOPLE TO BE SPECIFIC ABOUT WHAT THEY NEED: When you're speaking with someone, ask them what type of connection they need. If you plan to connect a person to another person think about the connection's bandwidth and their history with mentorship and collaboration. Be mindful of referring to the same person repeatedly.

BUILD VARIETY: Create an intentionally diverse network. This means having people from all different backgrounds and industries. This makes you more helpful to contacts with various needs. Variety can be with personal identifiers, geography, fields of interest, levels of expertise.

ASK YOUR NETWORK IF THEY WISH TO BE CONNECTED: Avoid giving out emails and phone numbers without asking first. Always ask a person before making the introduction. For example, "Hello, I have someone who might benefit from meeting you. Can I connect you? It is okay to decline." Check if they prefer to be connected by email, text, phone, etc.

MAKE THE CONNECTION FOCUSED: If you are doing an introduction for two or more people keep introductions brief—a high-level introduction of each of them can be done in one to two sentences. Allow them to do deeper introductions of their own. Then inform the parties that they can start their own thread. It also makes the practice less of a burden for you—and that is important for self-care and sustainable behavior. E.g., "Please connect directly. No need to include me in further emails." This frees up your inbox.

RECOGNIZE THE BENEFIT OF HELPING OTHERS: Maybe your network feels like it belongs to you. You may want to safeguard those contacts and share sparingly. Your people deserve privacy and respected boundaries. Plus every time you make a connection that judgement call is a reflection of you. However, if someone comes to you for help, and you know a person who can assist, kindness and generosity win. Giving to others keeps us connected, feeling good, and is a positive reflection on you.

CONCLUSION:

You may not realize you already have a network.	Grow your network beyond the workplace intentionally and organically.	Share your network kindly and generously.

SUPPLEMENTAL RESOURCES:

TEDxPortland

Networking School

LinkedIn

9

MICROSKILLS FOR NAVIGATING CONFLICT

RESA

In the emergency department, we navigate conflict a lot. Patients are definitely a piece of this; however, much of this tension is actually between colleagues. My mentee told me about a situation at work. When she first onboarded, people told her about a colleague, who was known for inciting conflict. They were the first person everyone brought up to her: "Let me tell you about my experience with them," and "How's it going with them?" They were known to lose their temper and kick residents out of the emergency department. They lost their temper at her, at other teammates, and even at their supervisor. From what she could tell, nobody wanted to address the conflict and it had persisted for many years. People avoided them, and instead whispered about them behind their back. People shared that they felt bullied, demoralized, and distrustful of the department leadership because nobody handled them. Meanwhile the colleague kept getting promoted. When my mentee and I talked about it, we understood how tempting it was to avoid difficult conversations and to live in hopes that the conflict would go away. It never did of course. Mostly, we talked about how leaders should frame this as an opportunity when they have an employee causing conflict: to hold difficult conversations, to address bad behavior, and to create psychologically safe working conditions so people can really focus on their patient care.

Here's an unavoidable reality: Conflict is almost inevitable. It is reported that 85% of employees face it, and in the USA almost three hours per week are spent on conflict at an annual cost of 3.5 billion dollars.[145] Given its frequency and its impact on a company, it's in your best interest to learn about conflict. And here's where we drop the mic: How you handle conflict is just as important as the core issue itself.

Think of conflict as an opportunity—to clear up a misunderstanding, to get emotions off your chest, to develop communication skills. No matter the cause, conflict provides a chance to grow. But actually turning it into a net positive is not simple, as it often reveals a side of someone that was previously unappreciated or unnoticed.

As children, we are taught to share and play nice in the sandbox. But in the workplace you cannot just walk up to someone and grab your toy back and walk away. Just as you notice the behavior of others around you, people take note of your approach to conflict resolution. In the workplace you often need to find a way to work together even after the conflict is theoretically resolved.

Barriers to conflict resolution run the gambit: identifying the cause of conflict, holding a difficult conversation, addressing the miscommunication, sharing perspectives, contesting a hierarchy, reporting harassment, hiring legal representation, and reconciling a fear of retaliation. Sometimes it requires involvement of disciplinary bodies, lawyers, advocates. These barriers can foster fear and demotivate us from ever moving forward.

Additionally, these factors can be harder for marginalized groups to navigate, such as women, people of color, people with disabilities, members of the LGBTQ+ community.[146] In 2022, gaslighting was Merriam-Webster's word of the year.[147] Gaslighting is the psychological manipulation of a person or persons usually over a period of time, thus causing them to call into question their experience. Gaslighting occurs when someone has a complaint and then that complaint gets minimized, ignored, invalidated without contemplation. Imagine being offended by a comment and then hearing the phrase, "I think you are just blowing things out of proportion. That's not at all what I said to you."

One specific manifestation of gaslighting is a phenomenon called DARVO (Deny, Attack, and Reverse Victim and Offender).[148] DARVO is used by a perpetrator to control a narrative and to maintain power and control over a victim.[149] A person who employs DARVO is defensive, avoidant, and plays the victim when in fact, they are the root of the problem.

We do not want you to ignore your feelings or the words and behaviors directed at you. Too often we see our colleagues reporting, "they were screaming and yelling at me" and then tie the complaint up in a nice bow, such as "but, you know, they are a good person and they didn't mean it." Addressing and naming your feelings is healthy. Tell yourself, "This happened. I am not making it up." Minimizing our responses is how bad behavior is allowed to pass.

There is a name for the person whose behavior is at once egregious and unprofessional and is subsequently excused: this is the perpetual "good guy."[150] And to be clear this person is not a good guy. And they are truly not just men. Women exhibit bad behavior too. We don't want you to talk yourself out of what happened. Call it out, even if it is to yourself alone: "I don't like that person. They are verbally abusive. And I am not obligated to protect someone who has caused me harm."

This is our part of the book where we tackle some of the more challenging aspects of the workplace. We do not claim to know all of the answers. Yet, we have experiences that inform our commitment to radical honesty. We hope that this chapter with ten MicroSkills supports you to better manage conflict at work.

MICROSKILLS FOR NAVIGATING CONFLICT:

1. Learn to recognize conflict.
2. Acknowledge your role in conflict.
3. Create psychological safety for your coworkers.
4. Receive and reflect on feedback, and then move on.
5. Learn to interact with difficult personalities.
6. Intentionally practice and hold difficult conversations.
7. Balance competence and confidence.
8. Keep a paper trail.
9. Learn who Human Resources serves.
10. Reporting and ignoring bad behavior.

THE MICROSKILL:

1. LEARN TO RECOGNIZE CONFLICT

WHAT IS THE ACTUAL SKILL?

Pay attention to the emotions and behaviors in workplace interactions.

ADAIRA

After college I worked for a test-preparation company teaching the SAT. Private sessions were one hour long and expensive. Because of the high cost and out of respect for the customer, I'd show up a few minutes before the hour started so that by the time we were situated the students would get their full hour of tutoring. One student always arrived late, and his mother sat in on the sessions. One time she asked me to stay an extra fifteen minutes over to compensate for their quarter-hour-late arrival. I told her I couldn't accommodate the request. That extra time would have eaten into another student's time. After that, she avoided me, never asked again, and instead sat in the car during the sessions. Recalling how drastic her involvement changed, from being engaged to removing herself, I suspect she was really upset with me and my decision to not stay late. If I could do it all over again, I would ask her meet and talk about it.

WHY DO WE NEED THIS SKILL?

Conflict can manifest as screaming and shouting or something more subtle and quiet such as ignoring or walking away. Recognizing and dealing with conflict decreases the chance of it festering, becoming disruptive, and eating away at people's morale and productivity—and mental health. Why resolve conflict? Well, unresolved conflict dissolves the sense of safety we all deserve. In one study, 25% of employees said that avoiding conflict led to sickness or missing work.[151]

WHY IS THIS SKILL HARD TO ACHIEVE?

- You explain the situation away assuming someone is stressed, or going through a personal issue.
- You are conflict avoidant and excuse the situation as someone just being stressed or going through a personal issue.
- Conflict may just be a part of the workplace culture.
- The conflict is subtle, so you begin to question your perception that it exists.
- You are caught off guard when conflict appears, you feel unsafe, and unsure how to proceed.

WHAT ARE THE CRITICAL ACTIONS FOR THIS MICROSKILL?

PAY ATTENTION TO TONES AND BEHAVIORS: Take note if the tone or the emotion between people grows tense, uncomfortable, bullying, angry, passive-aggressive, etc. Listen and watch people interact with each other and with you. Note the jokes and humor that are passed around the workplace. Do not ignore your discomfort or what you are feeling.

SPEAK WITH YOUR CONFIDANTS: Run an uncomfortable or heated situation past a trusted friend or colleague to get their impression and decide what to do. Maybe you are misreading the situation. Maybe you are responsible for the conflict. Maybe not.

NOTICE YOUR WORDS OR ACTIONS THAT TRIGGER OTHERS: We all have bad days and can accidentally say words in error or use too direct of a tone. Perhaps our facial expressions are too revealing of our disapproval. If you notice a pattern, everytime I do or say this someone gets upset, consider it a goal to create a change and remove that behavior.

NOTICE THE WAY THE TEAM TRIGGERS EACH OTHER: Look around. It's helpful to recognize conflict between others on the team. It might not be your responsibility to resolve, but you can at least notice how it is being identified, named, and resolved.

ANTICIPATE AND ACT IF CONFLICTS BECOMES PHYSICAL: Be aware of how close someone approaches you physically. As emergency doctors, we are vigilant re: never allowing an agitated or behaviorally distraught patient to get between us and the safe exit door.

DEVELOP A SAFETY PLAN: Make supervisors aware of conflicts on your team. Download, read and learn your company's safety and security policies. If you are in-office, ask where you can locate security call buttons and find out where security sits. If you are virtual, save texts and emails if you are being harassed, bullied, threatened. Keep documentation protected until you discuss next steps with your supervisor, trusted colleagues, or lawyer.

THE MICROSKILL:

2. ACKNOWLEDGE YOUR ROLE IN CONFLICT

WHAT IS THE ACTUAL SKILL?

Resist universally placing the blame on other people.

ADAIRA

When I was an emergency-medicine resident, a trauma-surgery resident would enter the trauma room and order everyone around. He was overconfident in his abilities. And, one time his confidence went too far. We had a very critical and unstable patient. He had fallen off of a scaffold while washing windows. The resident came in, interrupted me while I was delivering orders, and loudly talked over me. Each time I tried to speak, he put his hand up, palm toward my face. This felt aggressive, offensive and intrusive of my personal space. I looked him in the eye and spoke deliberately, loudly, and very directly to him: "Do you mind not speaking over me? And do you mind not putting your hand in front of my face?" Later when we debriefed the case. He apologized, and I acknowledged that I was sorry for escalating the situation with the volume of my voice. To be clear, I was still angry at how he had treated me (and other people on prior occasions), and I also felt that I personally could have behaved better.

WHY DO WE NEED THIS SKILL?

Success at work requires taking responsibility for ourselves—our words and actions. When we reflect on a conflict we should ask, *What happened? What was my role in this? What could I have done differently and better?* Self-reflection and taking responsibility are important. Looking inward can help you grow and realize the potential ways to act and speak differently. Realizing that you play a role in the conflict is an open and mature way to demonstrate your growth.

WHY IS THIS SKILL HARD TO ACHIEVE?

- You are tempted to point the finger at others and not own your part in the conflict.
- Apologizing can be difficult due to the feelings involved, such as embarrassment, pride, and shame.
- Acknowledging your part takes emotional maturity and self-reflection.
- Apologizing is not a part of your workplace culture.

WHAT ARE THE CRITICAL ACTIONS FOR THIS MICROSKILL?

STOP AND SELF-REFLECT: Put your ego into a time-out. Take time to think about the conversations and interactions, and discern your contribution. Reflect on your actions—the particular moments you control. When we reflect on a conflict, we should ask *What happened? What could I have done differently and better?* Perhaps you didn't cause the conflict, but there still may be skills to learn: how to de-escalate, how to listen, how to speak, how to monitor your body language.

ASK A TRUSTED PERSON FOR FEEDBACK: Ask your best friend, partner, coach, or therapist to give you feedback. Listen. Don't interrupt, and resist being defensive. "Am I hard to get along with, difficult, too particular, selfish, high maintenance?" or "Do you think I cause conflict?" If they know you over time then give them license to share. Brace yourself for impact. You could be the problem. If you shut down the conversation, then you close off your chance to learn.

SEEK ADVICE OR COACHING: If you feel like your involvement in conflict is an issue you can fix alone, great. Write down strategies to change. Take note of your thoughts and feelings. Read books. Meditate. Another option is a conflict resolution coach. Your company may be able to fund this training so speak with your supervisor.

WHEN INDICATED, APOLOGIZE: A sincere apology is the most effective predictor of being able to resolve conflict.[152] When ready, offer an authentic apology. It should not feel performative, offered just to avoid negative attention or discipline. It should also not focus on the ways you have been wronged. An insincere apology is worse than none at all. Good apologies come from places of regret, guilt, maturity, and responsibility.[153] Be mindful of your nonverbal communication too, as sincerity can be detected by facial expression, hand gestures, and posture.[154]

LESS IDEAL APOLOGY	MORE IDEAL APOLOGY
"I am sorry I am late, but I'm sure you understand. These things happen. I'll try to be earlier."	"I've been late to our meetings which is causing us to get behind on work. I am sorry. I will leave home twenty minutes earlier so it does not happen again."

— *With the less ideal apology there is no clear signs of reflection. No demonstration of growth.*

The more ideal apology shows the effect of their actions and their plans going forward to mitigate the same error.

COMMIT AND FOLLOW UP: Once you commit yourself to doing better and not repeating a behavior, check in with people. Ask if they observe a difference.

THE MICROSKILL:

3. CREATE PSYCHOLOGICAL SAFETY FOR YOUR COWORKERS

WHAT IS THE ACTUAL SKILL?

Create work environments and cultures where you feel safe and your teammates feel safe.

RESA

Emergency nurses are particularly vulnerable to violence in the department. Verbal and physical attacks by patients create an unsafe environment. Historically the "it's just a part of the job" mindset only made the situation more emotionally taxing.

Once, a patient very intoxicated from alcohol came in to the emergency department stumbling talking very loudly and stating that he had chest pain. He was immediately brought to a room for evaluation. The ECG tech and nurse went in and soon the nurse found me and asked that I come quickly as he was refusing care. I walked into the room as he was trying to stand up and get out of the bed.

ME: Sir, my name is Dr. Lewiss, I need you to please lie back in the bed. We need to do an ECG and place you on a monitor.

HIM: Doctor, I want to leave.

ME: Sir, are you having chest pain?

HIM: Yes.

ME: Sir, we cannot let you leave yet. You are intoxicated and we need to do an ECG and other tests for your chest pain.

Simultaneous to the conversation, the nurse put a blood pressure cuff on his arm and the pulse oximeter probe on his finger. The patient swung with his other hand and tried to grab the nurse and pull her towards him as if to hug her.

HIM (TO THE NURSE): Hon, what's your name?

ME: Sir. Please do not touch her. And do not call her hon. Her name is not hon. Please call her by the name she requested you call her.

The patient cooperated and we were able to continue his evaluation. Outside the room, the tech, the nurse and I debriefed the encounter. We checked in with each other—Are you ok? Yes, are you ok? Yes. I'm ok. Teams really need to look out for each other.

WHY DO WE NEED THIS SKILL?

Psychological safety is what makes individuals and teams successful. It has been defined as "a belief that one will not be punished or humiliated for speaking up with ideas, questions, concerns, or mistakes, and that the team is safe for interpersonal risk-taking."[155] People working in psychologically safe workplaces are five times more likely to be productive and innovative.[156] Toxic cultures are ten times better than compensation at predicting employee turnover.[157] A space with a lack of psychological safety feels tense. People withdraw. Communication falls apart. Morale drops. And work can come to a standstill.

WHY IS THIS SKILL HARD TO ACHIEVE?

- It is hard to identify concrete changes that could create psychological safety for you and your team.

- You feel it is the organization's duty to create a sense of safety and question your individual responsibility.
- You feel threatened and insecure making requests that would ensure psychological safety.

WHAT ARE THE CRITICAL ACTIONS FOR THIS MICROSKILL?

DESCRIBE PSYCHOLOGICAL SAFETY FOR YOURSELF: Think about the people who or places which create a sense of safety for you. Consider what they offer. Perhaps you feel welcomed to express concerns, pitch undeveloped ideas, and ask basic questions. Start by thinking of moments where you have really felt protected. Then compare that environment to prior or current unsafe environments. Reflect on the differences.

CREATE SAFETY FOR YOURSELF AND OTHERS: While you may not be in charge of a team, you can still nurture their sense of safety. In fact, give your teammates the safety you desire for yourself. Safety looks like people feeling comfortable being present and speaking with fluid communication in meetings. Safety looks like advocating for the teammate who looks uncomfortable, ignored, shamed, or threatened. Creating safety looks like, "I worry we just dismissed their suggestion—can we go back and hear more?" This shows others that you're there to respect everyone and participate in a positive workplace environment.

5 EASY WAYS TO CREATE SAFETY WITH OTHERS ON THE TEAM
a. Apologize for errors, when indicated. b. Support those who ask questions by saying "good question." c. Encourage creativity to exploring new ideas before they are dropped. d. Acknowledge if someone isn't being heard or included. e. Talk about your mistakes, failures, insecurities.

Create safety for yourself and others by adhering to this checklist of actions you can follow.

SPOTLIGHT OTHERS: Tell people what they do well. Tell them often and publicly. It doesn't cost anything but time and helps everyone feel recognized. Make sure you are spreading out the positive feedback, not focusing on the same person.

Send an email and CC a boss

Say something during a meeting

Nominate a colleague for an award

Put a shoutout on the company whiteboard or a digital community like Slack

THE MICROSKILL:

4. RECEIVE AND REFLECT ON FEEDBACK, AND THEN MOVE ON

WHAT IS THE ACTUAL SKILL?

Be receptive to solicited and unsolicited feedback, but don't let it stop your forward momentum.

ADAIRA

As residents, we had a yearly evaluation meeting with our program director and team. One of those meetings stuck with me for a long time. I needed to learn how to move on from constructive feedback. During that meeting, we reviewed the comments and feedback submitted by peers. For the most part, the comments were wonderful and supportive. Funny, though—I don't remember any of those in detail. What I do recall vividly is that one peer said that I should be nicer to the technicians in our department. (Technicians are the staff who help move stretchers, draw blood samples, and place stickers and wires on patients connecting them to the monitor.) I was surprised: I thought I was nice to all of them. It was hard for me to process it. The leadership team wanted to move past the single comment and finish the meeting; yet, I was so mentally distracted and discouraged and couldn't get past that constructive comment. Clearly years later I think about it and make sure to pay extra attention to how I treat our technicians.

WHY DO WE NEED THIS SKILL?

Feedback comes in all forms: direct and indirect, formal and informal, brief and comprehensive, positive and constructive. Most of us won't dwell on positive feedback. However, our response to constructive criticism is less predictable. Experts have long argued that constructive criticism can improve job performance and also lower turnover within a workplace.[158] And relatedly, some people want to hear this type of feedback.[159] But not all share this sentiment. One study showed that people with high levels of anxiety at baseline were more likely to see constructive criticism negatively and feel threatened.[160]

WHY IS THIS SKILL HARD TO ACHIEVE?

- Constructive criticism feels bad, even on days when you are not feeling fragile, defensive, or insecure.
- Building self-esteem, inner strength, and confidence takes work and can be easily backpedaled.
- If you do not trust the person giving you feedback, you doubt their intentions.
- Some feedback undermines or attacks your identity and can feel culturally insensitive.
- You resist admitting that you need help and have room to grow.

WHAT ARE THE CRITICAL ACTIONS FOR THIS MICROSKILL?

TAKE TIME TO DIGEST: When you hear feedback, resist the urge to be defensive. Your initial response may be to immediately respond "Well, what I was trying to…" or, "But, that only happened once." Hold those words. Resist being defeated. Your initial response may also be to respond with "I'm such a failure. I'll never be good at anything." Let the comments sit for a bit. Let the feedback-giver deliver the complete message. You have time from then to digest its meaning and significance.

ASSESS THE FEEDBACK: Realize that you have the ability to accept or table direct feedback given to you. Before you write off the feedback, share the comments with trusted others and if they agree, take it seriously. If you do not trust the person providing feedback and others agree with your interpretation, table the feedback and see if a pattern emerges from other sources.

RAISE CONCERNS OF BIAS: It is very possible that the feedback you are given is biased by or rooted in racism, ageism, sexism, transphobia, etc. You can raise this as a concern. When ready—and it might not be in the same meeting—you might say e.g. "This feedback I'm getting feels targeted or personal. I am the only woman of color in this department, and it seems like no matter how polite I am, I am seen as aggressive. Could this be an issue larger than me?"[161]

ASK FOR SPECIFICS: The more specific feedback you seek, the more you are able to find areas to improve. If you are told you're not a team player, follow up that comment with an inquiry, such as "Could you provide specific examples of when I did not seem like a team player?"

RESPECT THE PERSON'S INTENTION: Giving feedback to anyone is hard: it takes time, it can be uncomfortable, be poorly received, and make things worse. Typically, those truly invested in your success will take the time behind the scenes and put in effort to deliver what needs to be said.

WHAT YOU DON'T SEE:

"WE'VE ALL HEARD COMPLAINTS. I THINK IT'S TIME TO GIVE HIM FEEDBACK."

"I NEED TO MAKE SURE I GET THE LANGUAGE RIGHT WHEN I GET HIM THIS FEEDBACK."

"CAN I GET YOUR ADVICE ON GIVING SOMEONE CONSTRUCTIVE FEEDBACK?"

WHAT YOU SEE:

"I NEED TO TALK TO YOU ABOUT YOUR COMMUNICATION"

Giving feedback to anyone is hard. Those truly invested in our success will take the time behind the scenes and put in effort to deliver constructive feedback.

THE MICROSKILL:

5. LEARN TO INTERACT WITH DIFFICULT PERSONALITIES

WHAT IS THE ACTUAL SKILL?

Learn to manage yourself when working with people with difficult personalities.

RESA

Sometimes my "aha" moments come during a conversation recording with a Visible Voices guest. This completely happened when I spoke with Amy Gallo, author of *Getting Along: How to Work with Anyone (Even Difficult People)*. I shared that I had worked with a teammate—someone academically accomplished on paper and pleasant in person. I just could not figure this person out. They volunteered for tasks, agreed to the timelines the team set...and then... nothing. They rarely responded to emails and so the team had to resort to dividing up their work. I was so confused because face to face, they promised: "I will send updates on the project today." And then no email. I could not put my finger on what was happening. We had had a check in and there were no problems with their health or in their home. In our podcast conversation, Amy described the passive-aggressive coworker. "This is someone who doesn't feel comfortable or isn't able to, for whatever reason, express their ideas, thoughts, opinions, in a straightforward way."[162] Workplace mystery solved. This person wasn't comfortable telling the team they either didn't want to do the work or didn't have the time, or didn't know how to do the work. Although they never grew comfortable communicating honestly, I better understood them and could manage expectations for the team.

WHY DO WE NEED THIS SKILL?

Have you ever filled out the personality types or strengths-finder exercises, such as The Meyers-Brigg questionnaire?[163] These tools can be helpful in determining your personality type, but they cannot predict how to navigate conflict between individuals. Everyone around you is different. In fact, there are at least 16 different personality types.[164] And likely each of these personality types can present along their own gradient. Sometimes this degree of variety can lead to unpredictable and uncontrollable conflict. We often work around people with difficult personalities rather than dealing directly with the person. And yet, over time your personality and another person's may conflict, and you should be ready to learn to navigate around all kinds of people. We often check our intuition by asking trusted peers who know the colleague, "Do I have the right impression or am I misreading something?"

WHY IS THIS SKILL HARD TO ACHIEVE?

- It is hard to read personalities and moods—especially virtually.
- Difficult people have a long track record at work that can be tough to break.
- We work around people with difficult personalities rather than dealing directly with them.
- You find yourself arguing with the person instead of having productive conversations.

WHAT ARE THE CRITICAL ACTIONS FOR THIS MICROSKILL?

REFLECT TO FIND A LARGER ISSUE: While it's great to trust your gut and interpretation of who someone is, it's also wise to explore if you have the wrong or an unfair impression. What we may interpret as difficult or challenging behavior could just be representative of stress, lack of information, fatigue, or burnout. You may also have an incorrect assumption or expectation of how someone should behave that could lead you to address another as "difficult" or "hard to work with."

CONSIDER EASY SOLUTIONS: If the truth is that the person is universally difficult, the next question you should ask is, *Is there an easy solution to this problem?* Granted, it may not be your job to find the solution, but it is your job to get your work done—and sometimes that means dealing with a difficult personality. Consider offering solutions to help with your own productivity. Here's a small tip—before offering solutions, ask if they are interested in your help. If so, you can inquire about the issue: why they think it exists, what they have tried to resolve it, and then offer a possible solution if you have one in mind.

PROBLEM	FEEDBACK
The person always says negative things in meetings, and it affects team morale.	Check in with the person regarding their health and wellness. Brainstorm how to bring positivity and explore easy fixes.

The person never meets timelines despite agreeing to them.	Ask how they organize their time. Ask if increasing the frequency of check-ins would help. Explore how they wish to show up for the team.
The person feels targeted and bitter that they are left out of professional growth opportunities.	Share a calendar and list meetings and growth opportunities transparently.

SPEAK LESS, DOCUMENT MORE: Try to avoid back-and-forth arguments, which are emotionally draining. And can get you into trouble. If an exchange gets heated and threatening, pause the discussion. Document details with direct quotes and summaries of conversations. Save for later, if ever needed. Your ability to protect yourself—and your mental health—should never be sacrificed. Cool off. When calm, develop an action plan with a trusted contact or supervisor on how to deal with the person. Document details with direct quotes and summaries of conversations.

THE MICROSKILL:

6. INTENTIONALLY PRACTICE AND HOLD DIFFICULT CONVERSATIONS

WHAT IS THE ACTUAL SKILL?

When navigating workplace conflict, do not avoid necessary conversations that might be difficult.

RESA

I definitely have not solved the puzzle to mastering difficult conversations. However, I know they are important to hold and I know they get easier and everyone gets better with practice. I remember one of my colleagues asked our supervisor for a salary increase and a decrease in the number of shifts at their one-to-one annual review. Without question, my colleague was outperforming teammates at their level, and they were taking up the slack of an underperforming teammate. However, our supervisor did not want to grant the requests. Instead of telling them directly, the supervisor told me that I should tell them. I was not part of the evaluation process, and I had no control over salary and shift resources. Initially, I thought it would be good practice for me then quickly realized what the supervisor had done: handed the difficult conversation off to me. Ultimately, my colleague felt mistreated and disrespected when they realized what our supervisor did. Important feedback for me: I learned that handing off a difficult conversation is not the way to go.

WHY DO WE NEED THIS SKILL?

People speak approximately 16,000 words a day and spend a third of their day at work.[165] Given how many interactions occur, it is a worthy investment to learn how to navigate a difficult conversation. Since, if not done well, an initial difficult conversation gone awry can lead to amplified problems. Avoiding difficult conversations can allow bad behavior or personalities to go unchecked and then become someone else's problem. Also the avoidance can cause you to resent work and feel psychologically unsafe. We need to be forthcoming: this skill is a challenge and not fun. We too are tempted to avoid addressing conflict. However, we believe that calm engagement is sometimes the only way to resolve the tension.

WHY IS THIS SKILL HARD TO ACHIEVE?

- Difficult conversations are emotional.
- Power dynamics must be respected and approached with caution.
- You fear saying the wrong word or phrase and being misinterpreted.
- You want to avoid the situation and assume someone else will address the issue later.

WHAT ARE THE CRITICAL ACTIONS FOR THIS MICROSKILL?

PREPARE YOURSELF AND OTHERS: Write out what you would like to cover in the meeting. Don't expect the meeting to go according to your plan; but it is helpful to map points you'd like to address. Give a direct heads up to the person. Do not surprise them with the content of the conversation at the time of the meeting. And do not be vague when you reach out to schedule.

LESS CLEAR COMMUNICATION	MORE CLEAR COMMUNICATION
We don't seem to be on the same page. Can we speak at some point?	Can we check in? When is a good time to speak this week about the proposal? I want to brainstorm how to divide up tasks and set a timeline that works for us both.

PRACTICE THE DIFFICULT CONVERSATION: Practice the difficult conversation ahead of time, by yourself or with another trusted person.[166] The goal is to be calm and clear and illustrate with examples: "When I suggest a deadline, you shake your head and roll your eyes. It's happened three times now. It made me anxious about the collaboration. Am I misreading your response?"

CREATE PSYCHOLOGICAL SAFETY: You cannot predict precisely the other person's responses. Be prepared for strong emotional reactions. Align where there is agreement and point to positive aspects of the situation. "It seems we agree that our communication could be more frequent. How do you perceive our conversations? What could we do better?"

PRACTICE ACTIVE LISTENING: We know you have much to say. But remember to listen and avoid interrupting when another is speaking. Try to have the other person share equally in the conversation. Echo back what you heard, and ask if you have it right. Ask the other person to share what they have heard from you.

DON'T BLAME: Give concrete examples, and acknowledge there could be a misunderstanding. Respect that everyone has a perspective on a situation, and this is not about right or wrong, casting blame, or shaming. It's about respectfully finding the cause of conflict and finding solutions.

CREATE ALIGNMENT: Even if you disagree with someone it is great to identify and call out a source of alignment. "It seems we have different perspectives on who caused the error. It also appears that we can agree its important for this error to not happen again. Can we focus on ways to move forward?"

BUILD AN EXIT: Conversations can't go on forever. Especially if they are not productive and causing further harm. Build an exit strategy: set an alarm or timer on your phone as cue to wrap up the meeting. Tell the person, "I'm so sorry, is it okay if we wrap up here? I have to take care of another task." And perhaps that other task is just separating yourself from an ineffective meeting.[167]

FOLLOW UP WITH THE PERSON: At the end of the conversation, ask them if it's okay for you to follow up with them. See if there is anything further to discuss. Work together to move the relationship forward and positively to the best of your ability.

THE MICROSKILL:

7. BALANCE COMPETENCE AND CONFIDENCE

WHAT IS THE ACTUAL SKILL?

Be confident but do not overcompensate for any lack of competence with overconfidence.

ADAIRA

When I was a resident physician, I was working in the ICU for a month. A patient needed a procedure called a paracentesis. He had a very large amount of fluid in his abdomen that was floating around his organs. This fluid can be uncomfortable and even get infected.

So the paracentesis would remove the fluid from his abdomen using a needle and syringe. My senior resident and I were available to do the procedure. I saw my senior resident heavily reading articles and watching videos just before we were about to start. It was natural to review material prior to a procedure so I didn't question it. However, her nervousness appeared beyond typical. I asked if we should ask for support and she said, "Nope, I got it." When we set up the equipment she seemed a bit confused. But she figured it out over time. And finally we started to insert a needle through the patient's skin. However instead of fluid draining I saw brown liquid come into the syringe. She had accidentally punctured the bowel and stool was draining into our tubing. Thankfully, the patient was ultimately okay. This is a known risk of the procedure and admittedly, in medicine we all make mistakes. Myself included. Still, it was a great lesson for me to avoid confusing my confidence with competence. The culture of our field is to act confident when we are not and many workplace cultures reward that behavior. However, given her uncertainty, it would have been safter for her to call in a supervisor to assist her with the procedure.

WHY DO WE NEED THIS SKILL?

Confidence and competence. Accomplished leaders have a healthy amount of both. When we personally think about leaders we respect, we consider them competent and humble; not obnoxious, overbearing, destructive or unkind. Workplaces, however, often automatically assume the same person who is overly confident to be competent. Studies show that there is not a direct correlation between confidence and competence. In fact, overconfidence is inversely related to leadership talent.[168] And if you are overconfident, you are more likely to fail than if you are underconfident.[169] It is defeating when we see incompetence rewarded, ignored, and covered up.

WHY IS THIS SKILL HARD TO ACHIEVE?

- If you have low self-esteem and feel incompetent, you think you need to act overconfident.
- Systems and leaders continue to signal women and marginalized groups to adopt leadership styles defined by men, yet confidence is not interpreted positively in the workplace.
- You struggle to find the right degree of confidence.

WHAT ARE THE CRITICAL ACTIONS FOR THIS MICROSKILL?

BUILD YOUR CONFIDENCE: When you get positive feedback, take it and tell yourself *I believe it.*

ASK QUESTIONS: Normalize asking questions and clarifying knowledge gaps. This takes confidence, and shows that uncertainty is okay. Never think you know everything. We practice the same approach and notice the same in our competent colleagues.

SPEAK WITH FIRMNESS AND OPENNESS: There are ways to speak confidently—e.g. in stating a message, asserting an opinion, leading a meeting—without sounding obnoxious or overly confident. We want you to be clear and confident and kind. Be open to suggestions and dissenting opinions. The right tone complimented by open body language sends the message that you have a firm idea, and you are grounded with an openness to other considerations.

LESS IDEAL COMMUNICATION	MORE IDEAL COMMUNICATION
"She is the best person for the job. No other candidate deserves our vote.	"She struck me as the best person for the job given her personal story, resume, and interview. What were your thoughts?"

PAY ATTENTION TO LANGUAGE SOFTENERS: While we want you to be open to correction, we don't want you to lose all confidence in yourself. Try removing the excessive "I think," "I feel," "perhaps" and "maybe" when you speak and write. Especially if what you are saying is factual, we don't want you to devalue your intelligence. This is especially true for women and people of color who worry about being overly confident.[170]

LESS IDEAL COMMUNICATION	MORE IDEAL COMMUNICATION
"I think we should probably consider moving forward with the project."	"Let's move forward and let me know if that is a problem."

THANK PEOPLE WHO CORRECT YOU: If someone takes the time to offer a correction or even just a counterpoint, thank them. Pause and say "I appreciate you saying that" or "Thanks for that feedback." This opens space for others and keeps your demonstrated competence intact without harming your competence because no one expects you to know everything.

ASK FOR FEEDBACK: If you are unsure how you come across, go back to your board of directors. Ask trusted colleagues and friends. Remember they will be more subjective in their feedback. So ask people you trust at work too. Ask "How would you interpret my confidence? What about my competence?"

BE COMPETENT: At the end of the day, you need to know your expertise and your trade. Study, pass certifying examinations, go deep on learning and knowing the subject matter of your chosen field.

THE MICROSKILL:

8. KEEP A PAPER TRAIL

WHAT IS THE ACTUAL SKILL?

When navigating a conflict at work, keep an up-to-date paper trail.

ADAIRA

Emergency medicine doctors are shift workers. Because of this, it's easy to swap shifts, and we do it often. Once a colleague walked up to me and asked me to cover their twelve-hour shift. No problem. They emailed me a shift trade and I clicked the button, "accept." A few weeks later they said, "I need to pay you back for that shift you covered." However, they offered to cover an 8-hour shift as the payback—not a 12-hour shift. I assumed good intention and simply wanted to check on the 4-hour discrepancy. And luckily there was a digital paper trail of the trade. I logged on to look at the emails—whenever I do a trade I just move those emails to a folder called "Trades." I forwarded the email receipt and simply said, "Hey, just checking on this. I'd love it if you could cover a shift of a similar length. Can you take a 12-hour shift of mine?" Keeping a paper trail isn't to create controversy, it's to avoid disagreement.

WHY DO WE NEED THIS SKILL?

Keeping a paper trail is often discussed in the context of an employer tracking an employee's wrongdoings in case of a lawsuit after termination.[171] You should keep a paper trail for any complex issue at work. A paper trail documents a timeline of events. This can include emails, conversations via text, summaries of meetings, and exchanges among individuals. Importantly, it is not just for times of conflict. We recommend using it to *prevent* conflict. For instance, you can send an email after you meet with your boss to summarize key points or use it to delineate tasks and roles for projects. Documentation may never get shared or used again—or it will come in handy just when you need it. The larger issue arises if you never write anything down.

WHY IS THIS SKILL HARD TO ACHIEVE?

- It takes time and energy to collect and write down conversations and interactions.

- Details are lost and recall may be limited if you wait too long to write facts down.
- Recalling and rehashing difficult interactions are stressful and traumatizing.
- It feels uncomfortable and scandalous to document this sort of information.

WHAT ARE THE CRITICAL ACTIONS FOR THIS MICROSKILL?

WRITE IT DOWN: You may have heard the phrase "Get it in writing." to allude that nothing is guaranteed without receipts. It's a smart recommendation. And to be clear, not everything you document as a paper trail will be controversial. Some things are documented just for a friendly reference. Keep the system you build organized: use email, a document or folder. The most important part is that it is protected and easy to discover later. Avoid putting sensitive information on a paper that can be lost or discovered later, on your work computer or in your work email. Once you anticipate or recognize a conflict at work, start a document or folder or email to yourself on your personal laptop or mobile device. Write everything down in a protected place. Not on a sheet of paper that could be discovered later, not on your work computer, and not in your work email.

UPDATE IT IN REAL TIME: As things happen in real time, update your paper trail. Dates, times, quoted communications are all helpful. If you hold or participate in a difficult or even a positive high-stakes conversation e.g. salary increase, put a summary in writing. Send after careful review confirming that trusted stakeholders are aware of the final plan.

FROM:	
TO:	
CC:	
BCC:	
SUBJECT:	
MESSAGE:	Thank you for meeting today. I wish to be sure I understood our conversation correctly. My current salary is $75,000, and with the agreed upon increase of $5,000, my annual compensation will be $80,000, beginning July 1 this year. Can you please confirm that I got this right? Many thanks, Adaira

CHECK IN WITH AND TAKE CARE OF YOURSELF: Reduce stress in times of conflict. Writing emotions down and getting stress off your chest helps you maintain peace. Creating a paper trail should not need to be a regular occurrence. If so, there is a larger issue at play, and it would be worth evaluating your sense of psychological safety in the work environment. Ask yourself if this is the right workplace culture for you.

THE MICROSKILL:

9. LEARN WHO HUMAN RESOURCES SERVES

WHAT IS THE ACTUAL SKILL?

Learn the beneficiaries and functions of HR.

RESA

I was midcareer by the time I gained a real sense of what HR does and whom they serve. Up til then, I knew HR as a team who helped employees with benefits. I was in a department faculty meeting where the discussion got heated over sexual harassment in the workplace. One colleague said that if someone got harassed, they should go to HR and that HR would protect them and take care of it. "That's what they are there for." I was confused because women colleagues I knew did not have this experience when they went to HR with workplace-bullying and harassment complaints. I did some fact checking and asked friends who work in HR and they clarified: HR primarily serves and protects the institution, not individual employees.

WHY DO WE NEED THIS SKILL?

You may sense that HR is there to help serve you and protect employees. We want you to understand that HR is there to serve and protect the company.[172] Yes, the person on the call may be friendly, but they are not your friend. HR's goal is to reduce turnover. They are there to minimize negative attention to the company. Yes, HR is there to take complaints seriously. We do not want you to consider them an enemy. However, when you interact with HR, we want you to be aware and wise to their loyalty: it's not to you. The HR department is not an employee advocate. Take serious issues seriously, and that means protecting what you write and say. Communicate with the right people for your desired outcome.

WHY IS THIS SKILL HARD TO ACHIEVE?

- You have been given the wrong information about HR—or nothing at all.
- It's a mind-frame shift to learn that HR is there to protect the organization when you may have understood that HR is there for the employee.
- You need to seek alternative options for help, support, and answers.

WHAT ARE THE CRITICAL ACTIONS FOR THIS MICROSKILL?

GET TO KNOW HR AND A REPRESENTATIVE: This person can assist and support you in accessing and learning the specifics about the organization's policies and benefits. Add the name and contact to your address book. Remember HR may track and document your conversation; ask them if that is the case if you'd like to be certain. Gain comfort calling and asking questions anonymously, if your company is large enough.

LEARN THE RESOURCES AVAILABLE TO EMPLOYEES: An employee handbook, company website, or colleague who has been at your workplace for a while are good resources when you have questions. Some specifics: Do you have conflict about your contract? Consider hiring your own contract lawyer; the company lawyer does not work for you. Sex discrimination? You may have a Title IX office. General professionalism or ethical issues? Some workplaces have an office of professionalism. When it comes to reporting issues—we want you to be strategic, not impulsive or afraid.

COMMUNICATE THOUGHTFULLY: Be careful about your work-related postings on social media and in email. In general, avoid specifics like names of people, institutions, jobs, or customers or clients. Understand the potential consequences: defamation accusations, termination, legal action, professionalism remediation, or documentation in your employee file.

THE MICROSKILL:

10. REPORTING AND IGNORING BAD BEHAVIOR

WHAT IS THE ACTUAL SKILL?

Learn if, when and how to report bad behavior.

ADAIRA

Years ago I worked with a nurse who would always have conflict with residents, especially women. He would question their knowledge very aggressively, delay clinical orders that he disagreed with, say rude comments about patients. It was clear that he was toxic. I want to be clear about something—I've seen toxic doctors just as I've seen toxic nurses. No matter the position or title, we should be supportive. So, I told the resident I planned to report the nurse. And I did report the nurse to my boss. And then I circled back to my resident to let them know the steps I took and the response that I was given. Circling back with my resident trainee was most important as I wanted them to know that bad behavior must not be tolerated and normalized. From my understanding (details were not described in full) the nurse went through a professionalism coaching program and training on gender and cultural sensitivity. After my reporting his behavior improved.

WHY DO WE NEED THIS SKILL?

We want to be honest about something—just because you report someone does not mean further action will be taken. However, it is even easier for a workplace to retain toxic individuals if no one speaks up. Even if there are no repercussions, we still believe in advocacy and accountability—therefore we still recommend reporting, if safe to do so. Lack of reporting can normalize for that individual. "See, my actions are tolerated and effective, so I will keep doing them since no one stops me." This troubles us greatly. Because bad behavior not only affects the self, but it can affect the team and the work. We also know that reporting anyone at any time can be incredibly frightening and make you vulnerable. These are all reasons to be thoughtful about next steps when you witness bad behavior at work.

WHY IS THIS SKILL HARD TO ACHIEVE?

- You fear retaliation or other negative consequences if you speak up.
- You have seen no change occur in the past when addressing bad behavior.
- You have no one to teach you if, when, and how to report.
- You don't think it's your responsibility.
- You cannot afford the time and emotional investment to report everything and everyone.

WHAT ARE THE CRITICAL ACTIONS OF THIS MICROSKILL?

PROCESS YOUR EMOTIONS ALONE AT FIRST: Processing trauma or challenges at work can take many forms. There is no one way: journal it, sleep on it, go for a run or do some other exercise. The most important thing is that you address your needs before proceeding further.

PROCESS THE EXPERIENCE WITH TRUSTED OTHERS: Talk to your personal board. Or, identify the people in your work environment who make you feel safe. Remember, your friends and family may not be objective as they are biased in your favor. You want an objective or unbiased opinion from someone who really is also looking out for the best for you. Decide early, even before the conversation starts, if you need a conversation to get support or if you are seeking to act and get solutions. Start the conversation with, "I'm seeking support and/or solutions for this issue. This is what happened. Yesterday at work..."

SUPPORT	SOLUTIONS
I need to know that I'm not the only one this is happening to. I would like to get this off my chest and move on. I feel so lost going to work and seeing my supervisor now. I'm curious how you got the courage to report someone in the past.	I need to know how to file a complaint. I need to know how much notice I need to give before switching jobs. I am looking to join another team in my company. If I were to report this incident, what would be my next steps?

When you seek a meeting with a trusted person about a challenging situation let it be known what you are seeking.

PARSE THE FACTS: Once you have processed your emotions, share the specifics. This is hard to do—we know. But when it comes to preparing to report it is helpful for you to try to eliminate any bias or favoring. Try reporting the events to your trusted contact first, as facts with the data clearly mentioned.

SUBJECTIVE COMMENTS	OBJECTIVE COMMENTS
"He was incredibly mean to me."	"He stood in my face and spoke with a raised voice. He put his hand up four times to stop me from speaking. His hand was 2-3 inches from my face."
"I feel uncomfortable at our team meetings."	"At every meeting for the last month, he asks me to sit next to him, and texts me to get a drink with him after work."

DECIDE IF YOU WANT TO MOVE FORWARD: This is a personal decision. Once you process your emotions, and speak with trusted colleagues: Do you want to move forward? We certainly understand the fear and hesitation—if it doesn't feel right then pause. Keep reflecting and check in with yourself at a later date. It is normal to constantly reassess your psychological safety at your work. There is a balance to protecting yourself and also, we don't want you to have major regrets for foregoing self-advocacy.

AVOID EMAIL OR TEXT: Try your hardest to put little in writing. Have in-person meetings so you are aware who is listening. Be sure you have a clear plan about what you want to report and what is not relevant. And this should stay off of email and text.

CONCLUSION:

Colleagues may be difficult. You are not imagining what is likely longstanding.	Document and speak carefully. Understand the power of listening and providing space.	Recognize and remember your role in conflict.

SUPPLEMENTAL RESOURCES:

TEDTalk

HBR Guide for Women at Work

Forbes

10

MICROSKILLS TO ACTIVELY FIND NEW OPPORTUNITIES

RESA

I remember the emergency department shift when I realized that gaining professional experience and finding opportunities to do what we call "high risk low frequency procedures" was not going to just happen for me. The case was dramatic. A patient came in unable to breath and about to go into respiratory arrest. We could not intubate (put a tube down the throat to help the patient breathe) and all other options failed. We needed to do an emergent "cric." This is a cut to the front of the neck making a hole in the throat where we then place a tube to create an opening to breathe. It was my friend's patient. My friend was in her fourth and final emergency medicine training year. I was in my third year. The surgery team was at the bedside. They thought they would do the procedure. However, my friend stood at the head of the bed and confidently called out, "This is my patient and my procedure. I'm doing the cric." She did it. The airway was successful and the patient stabilized. In that moment, I realized I had not been speaking up for myself. I had taken a more passive approach to owning these procedures. I realized there were similar procedures that should have been mine; however, I did not seek the opportunities or self-advocate. Watching my friend taught me how to self-advocate and secure these opportunities for myself going forward.

At one point in your life, you may have looked around and thought, *How is everyone doing cool things but me?* Perhaps you wondered, *When will someone help me?* The truth is many of us wait for help that isn't coming. It's not that no one cares about you, it's just that people around you are occupied with their own lives. Of course, a few of us get professional opportunities with minimal effort. However mostly opportunities don't find us; we find opportunities.

Fear of Missing Out (FOMO) or a sense of longing, that others are having rewarding experiences without us is not completely a bad thing.[173] It pushes us to pay attention to other people and their careers in ways that can be educational. Through observation, you can witness the scale and potential scope of success possible.[174] Read, watch, listen to other people's success and stories and you get a free copy of the playbook of the workplace.

Unfortunately, FOMO has a downside. It can tip you into emotional stress, motivational stress, overwhelm, over commitment, insecurity, and envy. Social media and smartphone use add to the problem.[175] Admittedly, it is hard to avoid that feeling of missing out. Even we sometimes wonder why we don't get the opportunities others do. Though we know the availability is abundant.

Shaping your career to your liking is a gift you give to yourself. Your path and journey are yours. We want you to deliberately create space for change in your career. Actively work to find opportunities. New opportunities happen through curiosity, conversations, sharing, and listening. You are ambitious, and there is nothing wrong with that. In fact, it is this yearning to develop that allows you to push the self, the team, and the work.

Here we describe seven MicroSkills which are instrumental to finding your next opportunity.

MICROSKILLS FOR ACTIVELY FINDING NEW OPPORTUNITIES:

1. Learn how to convert your skills.
2. Catalog potential professional-growth opportunities.
3. Become comfortable talking about yourself.
4. Apply to out-of-reach opportunities.
5. Draft your own letters of recommendation.
6. Pause before accepting an opportunity.
7. Be mindful of your team as you take on new opportunities.

THE MICROSKILL:

1. LEARN HOW TO CONVERT YOUR SKILLS

WHAT IS THE ACTUAL SKILL?

Apply your current skill set to new opportunities.

ADAIRA

When I was training to be an emergency doctor, I assumed that my entire professional life would consist of going to work, caring for patients, and then going home. However, a particular mentor, Dr. Uché Blackstock, completely changed my understanding of what is possible with a medical degree. I was an intern, and we were sitting in a café in New York City when she asked me about my plans for my career. I was confused and said, "I guess I plan to see patients?" That was the main option I knew. She looked at me and said, "Oh, there is so much more you can do with your medical degree." I'll never forget that comment because it really normalized the idea that I can be a physician, founder, writer, speaker, and more. For instance, my training in medicine and ultrasound led to a consulting opportunity for a medical start-up. My experience as a mentor led to writing multiple topical articles and ultimately this book. My experience as a writer led to starting a non-profit focused on teaching people of color about writing. I have seen how the tools I acquired professionally built upon each other and help create new opportunities.

WHY DO WE NEED THIS SKILL?

When you understand the versatility and transferability of your skills you start to see more options. And you see how your professional attributes appeal to employers. In fact, many companies seek employees with competences that are "adjacent" to the specific roles for which they are advertising.[176] Companies are growing employee skills by training them for new tasks.[177]

WHY IS THIS SKILL HARD TO ACHIEVE?

- You may not be able to identify your skills.

- You may not know which skills translate to new opportunities.
- You may not know how to find opportunities with those skills.

WHAT ARE THE CRITICAL ACTIONS FOR THIS MICROSKILL?

IDENTIFY EXISTING PRACTICES YOU DO AT HOME REGULARLY: Brainstorm your everyday practices at home—even activities that don't see to directly apply to the workplace. Look at your resume. Ask your friends what they see you doing often. Brainstorm your list with your personal board of directors.

EXTRACT YOUR SKILL SET: From your list of everyday practices, take a moment to think about the skills you use to complete those tasks. Think of how these skills may be relevant at work.

EXISTING PRACTICE	SKILLS	APPLICATION AT WORK
Regular yoga and/or meditation practice	Breathing, Relaxation techniques, Stretching, Emotional maturity	Skills in crisis management strategy, leading difficult conversations
Podcast host and producer	Communication with strangers, Networking, Interviewing, Storytelling and curation	Capturing the story of a client or project. Able to lead meetings and conversations

Healthy eating	Understanding nutrition, self-care, self-compassion, and physical and mental health	Team morale and care through ensuring the team is not working through hunger or on empty calories
Improv comedy	Communication, Entertainment, Confidence-building	Increase comfort in speaking in front of large audiences, skilled at icebreakers
Gardening	Patient, nurturing, hopeful	Able to boost morale and by bringing comfort and compassion to work

TEACH SKILLS TO THE TEAM: Share your skills. "It sounds like you might need help with the spreadsheet. I used a lot of Excel in my last job, so I'm glad to help" or "It sounds like you might be stressed. I practice meditation and I'd be happy to teach you about it." This morale boost and sharing of skills helps everyone—including you and your reputation as a team player.

USE ACTION VERBS TO DESCRIBE YOUR SKILLS: Instead of saying "I did this" in a passive voice say, "I launched, organized, directed, discovered." When applying for any opportunity be sure to stop and think about your skill set in full. Report those skills using concrete, affirmative words, and action verbs.[178]

THE MICROSKILL:

2. CATALOG POTENTIAL PROFESSIONAL-GROWTH OPPORTUNITIES

WHAT IS THE ACTUAL SKILL?

Maintain a running list of opportunities and ideas that you may pursue in the future.

> **ADAIRA**
>
> On my web browser I have a bookmark folder called "Opportunities" which sits right beneath my search bar, and it's my most active tab. I use it when I'm on social media or reading an article or just doing random searches on the internet. Whenever I stumble across something—a writing course, development program, or scholarship—that I believe could be interesting or useful to explore later, I drag it into my Opportunities folder. It may remain there for a year or more. I keep links until I use them or realize that I am definitely not interested in exploring them further. The benefit of this approach is that I'm able to quickly catalog some of the opportunities that I stumble upon, without worrying about forgetting them or needing to explore it further in real time.

WHY DO WE NEED THIS SKILL?

Despite how you feel now, you may not be in the same position in a few years. Or you may be in the same position, but want more out of your career. Interests and ambitions shift and we want you to be prepared. This list can be a great reminder of the opportunities you once found interesting. They may take all different forms: a list of people to meet, a list of opportunities to apply to, a list of skills to learn. Use these catalogs to keep you action-oriented and armed with ready information.

WHY IS THIS SKILL HARD TO ACHIEVE?

- You have to create an organized filing system.
- You are just treading water and trying to keep up.
- Some opportunities require a network you don't have.

WHAT ARE THE CRITICAL ACTIONS FOR THIS MICROSKILL?

DEVELOP A TRACKING SYSTEM: Make it simple and easy. Start keeping a list of aspirations, interests, and opportunities in a journal, notebook, or the cloud, e.g. Google Drive. Be general. Or be more detailed. If you choose to be detailed and create a written or digital list, classify opportunities and information with descriptors, such as Jobs and Positions, Awards, Courses, or People to Meet. Add a column each for website, contact person, email address, and relevant timelines. Tailor your method to keep it sustainable.

ENGAGE WITH A WIDE AUDIENCE: Your local networking might not provide you with a comprehensive list of opportunities to pursue. Consider ways to find out about more. Social media is a great approach. Read and follow the people seeming to do well in your field. Look at their opportunities—where are they speaking, who is giving their team funding, what are their promotions. Note rising stars or people with a successful track record. What are they working on? If you don't know, ask to meet for guidance.

SIGN UP FOR LISTS: Follow newsletters and blogs in your field. They post announcements for training programs, courses, events, seminars and jobs. Be intentional as your inbox will overflood. Unsubscribe to anything unhelpful. Nearly every field or industry has a national organization and local chapters.

REVISIT AND REVISE THE LIST: Try not to get frustrated if you are adding items and only slowly checking the opportunities off. This takes time. Remember that some opportunities are more accessible through nomination. You can always pause or accelerate at different times of your career. You may lose interest, pivot away, or ultimately return to an opportunity.

THE MICROSKILL:

3. BECOME COMFORTABLE TALKING ABOUT YOURSELF

WHAT IS THE ACTUAL SKILL?

Normalize talking about yourself to gain professional opportunities.

ADAIRA

I won a mentoring award a few years ago. It was truly a deeply meaningful surprise. When the awards committee emailed me, they told me to prepare a brief speech about myself and my accomplishments for the ceremony. At the time I felt very uncomfortable talking about my accomplishments. As a result, I prepared two versions: one about 15 seconds and another about 2 minutes. When I got to the ceremony, the first awardee gave a brief speech with very little information. The hostess immediately moved on with the program. The second awardee gave a much fuller speech that lasted about three or four minutes. It was meaningful and very relevant for the audience. Parts of the speech felt inspiring and made me want to ask her questions. Afterwards the same hostess said, "Wow, you are amazing. Remind me later to talk to you about something that would be interesting to you." I sat in my table and thought, "Which speech do I want to give?" It was clear the longer speech would offer more opportunity. And it was the first time I learned the value of sharing my experiences. Opening up with the details and journey allows people to see where they can fit in your story.

WHY DO WE NEED THIS SKILL?

Assume most people in your network will want to help you and they might just not know how. The truth is that you have to start talking about yourself: what you do, what you have accomplished, and what you want. Sharing professional accomplishments and interests helps others keep you in mind. When they see an opportunity that matches what you want, they may share it your way.

WHY IS THIS SKILL HARD TO ACHIEVE?

- Some of us are less comfortable with self-promotion. We know there is a gender gap here. Women, starting as early as the sixth grade, are less comfortable with self-promotion.[179]

- It can feel obnoxious and self-centered to talk about and promote yourself.

- You may not know how much or how little to share.

WHAT ARE THE CRITICAL ACTIONS FOR THIS MICROSKILL?

PREPARE YOUR PITCH: Practice a bit. You should be able to sell yourself a bit more than *I'm looking for new opportunities.* Sharing specific and positive attributes help. In the pitch, tell who you are, what you do, and what you are looking for.

Who you are	"I'm Adaira Landry and I'm physician, writer, and mentor."	"I'm Resa Lewiss, a physician, health care designer, author, and podcaster."
What you do	"I coauthored a book called *MicroSkills*, and I'm a cofounder of a nonprofit, Writing in Color."	"I coauthored a book called *MicroSkills* and I share written and spoken stories on healthcare and equity."
What you are looking for	"I'm looking to teach more early-career people about writing and career development."	"I'm looking for sponsors and avenues to grow the audience and impact of the podcast episodes. This will amplify my guests, their work, and their stories."

PRACTICE SPEAKING ABOUT YOURSELF: Share your achievements with the team. Seek feedback. Incorporate feedback so what you say feels comfortable and authentic to you and to your personality.

PITCH YOURSELF THROUGH YOUR SIGNATURE: Use your email signature to talk about yourself. Place relevant links beneath your name and title. Be sparing as it shouldn't feel like your résumé.

Adaira Landry, MD, MEd
Assistant Professor, Harvard Medical School
Co-founder, Writing in Color
Twitter: @AdairaLandryMD
555-555-5555 (work)

Resa E. Lewiss, MD
Professor of Emergency Medicine
Pronouns: She/Her/Hers
Website | Instagram | LinkedIn

PITCH YOURSELF THROUGH YOUR BIO: Your social media username and bio are ways of pitching yourself. Be descriptive and intentional in what you write about yourself.

PITCH YOURSELF TO PEOPLE: Connecting with people through email or on social media is a strategy to dip your toes in the water. Send a direct message, e.g. "Hello, thanks for the connection. Congrats on your TEDx last year." Personalize the introduction before you begin sharing who you are and what you have done. See if or how they respond before you ask for something. If you don't hear back, try not to take it personally. There is no harm in circling back once, then moving on.

THE MICROSKILL:

4. APPLY TO OUT-OF-REACH OPPORTUNITIES

WHAT IS THE ACTUAL SKILL?

Accept that you do not need to meet every criterion to apply for an opportunity.

RESA

In high school and college, I did not do any laboratory research. But by medical school, I felt ready to test the waters. What would it be like to be a researcher? I learned about the Howard Hughes Medical Institute HHMI-NIH Research Scholars program from a classmate with a lot of laboratory research experience. They planned to be a career medical scientist and were experienced in writing grants and research papers. I had none of those skills. As an undergraduate, I studied Sociology Ethnoracial Studies. After hearing about how great their year was though, I told my medical school dean and that classmate that I would apply for the HHMI-NIH program year. The classmate discouraged me. They emphasized that I was not the typical applicant and I would certainly be the least experienced. And although Epidemiology was listed as a research option, nobody pursued that. (This was confirmed when I met my 49 other program mates.) I ended up being selected. I completed projects in cancer epidemiology. And I credit that year with so many important lessons, experiences, and opportunities.

The most important lesson? Just apply. Even if you know you are not the strongest candidate.

WHY DO YOU NEED THIS SKILL?

Self-sabotage is real. It's easy to take an opportunity off the plate before we even apply for it. We see an exciting opportunity, glance at the job requirements, and see a single item on that list can be enough to make us not pursue the position. Think about this often-quoted Hewlett-Packard report statistic: men will apply for a job even with only 60% of the qualifications. Women won't apply unless they meet 100%.[180] Why is that? A Harvard Business Review study found that unlike men, women assumed each criterion listed for the opportunity was mandatory.[181]

WHY IS THIS SKILL HARD?

- Sometimes it feels like we are lying, exagerating, or misrepresenting our abilities.
- We don't want to waste our own or other people's time.
- We fear rejection.

WHAT ARE THE CRITICAL ACTIONS OF THIS MICROSKILL?

REVIEW THE QUALIFICATIONS: Take a look at the qualifications that are listed in the description. If you meet the vast majority of the qualifications but perhaps miss one or two, go for it.

SPEAK WITH PEOPLE FAMILIAR WITH THE OPPORTUNITY: Send an email or place a quick call to someone who's had the position in the past. Ask about the experience, the qualifications, and how strict the hiring criteria are.

SET UP A MEETING OR ATTEND THE INFORMATION SESSION: If a contact person is listed, show interest by meeting and speaking with them. E.g., "Hello, I am interested in the position, and would like to ask a few clarifying questions. How is your calendar for a 20-minute conversation?" Sign up for the information sessions if they are offered.

APPLY: In the end, applying for an opportunity—any opportunity—is a great exercise no matter the outcome. The self-reflection involved in answering questions, sometimes writing essays, or attending an interview allows you to reflect upon your experience—and your expertise. This also exposes gaps you had not appreciated. Aside from the time and energy invested, there's very little downside.

MIND THE PAPERTRAIL: Remember emails sent via your work email address can be monitored and forwarded—and the law will often side with your employer if there is a breach in privacy.[182] Word may get out that you are applying for new opportunities. Be mindful and think about how you would respond if asked about this. Consider using a non-work email address.

DISCLOSE NEED FOR PRIVACY: Be honest about disclosure. During an interview disclose that you have not told your current employer so that your privacy is maintained. In some cases, the new opportunity may require you to let your current employer know that you are looking.

THE MICROSKILL:

5. DRAFT YOUR OWN LETTERS OF RECOMMENDATION

WHAT IS THE ACTUAL SKILL?

Remove obstacles around nomination for an opportunity by drafting your own letter of recommendation (LOR).

RESA

One of my favorite secrets of the workplace which is not so secret yet nobody tells you centers on letters of recommendation. I was applying for my first job and asked my supervisor for a recommendation letter. He said sure, then promptly asked me to write the first draft. My jaw dropped in shock. Was this legal? Was this office housework? Would I get in trouble? It felt underhanded. I asked around and found out that it's actually common practice and not taboo or violating a code of conduct at all—unless the rules specifically state so. I soon realized that it makes complete sense to draft my own letter: I know me best. I can more easily pull relevant objective items from my résumé and share specific anecdotes and details which the letter writer may not know or recall. Since this is one of those unspoken yet commonly done practices, I am sure to explain this to people when they ask me for letters.

WHY DO WE NEED THIS SKILL?

We wrote the Fast Company article "How to Write a Letter of Recommendation—for Yourself" which explains why you are the ideal person to write your own LOR because you know your accomplishments best.[183] People are busy, and your request adds work to their plate. The LOR is a summary of who you are, what you have done, and what you intend to do later. You know this information most accurately. Since you have already practiced pitching yourself, then this is just a MicroSkill which builds upon another.

WHY IS THIS SKILL HARD TO ACHIEVE?

- It's uncomfortable to write about yourself, self-nominate, and self-promote.
- It is hard to be specific not generic, to recall stories, and to not sound boastful.
- You find out that drafting your letter is actually not legal for the particular opportunity. This is a situation to not draft the LOR.

WHAT ARE THE CRITICAL ACTIONS FOR THIS MICROSKILL?

OFFER TO WRITE THE FIRST DRAFT: When you ask for a LOR, offer to write the first draft for them—not the complete final draft. Consider even having it ready to share. You could say e.g. "I am glad to draft the letter and share it by email."

AMPLIFY THE LETTER WRITER: Most letters open by speaking about the letter writer—the person who is submitting the nomination letter. Start by describing that person's relevant accomplishments, titles, and roles as related to you and the position you're seeking. Keep it objective and relevant to the purpose of the letter.

SHARE YOUR SPECIFIC HIGHLIGHTS: You know your most specific accomplishments that have occurred at work. Be concrete and specific. Keep what you share short, fact-based, and outcome-focused. Write in the third person, e.g. Resa is the host and creator of the award-winning podcast called, The Visible Voices. With over 150 episodes, she gained the attention of The Guardian newspaper, which highlighted her program in their weekend Culture section.

AVOID SUPERLATIVES: Keep the descriptors objective. Do not write that you are the *best*, *strongest*, or *fastest*. Let the letter writer convey this information about you with their edits. Your job is to give an objective and documented reporting of your career.

DESCRIBE THE IMPACT OF THE OPPORTUNITY: Describe what the position or opportunity will do for you, if selected. How will it help your career as a leader and collaborator? Be specific. What do you plan to do with this exposure, recognition, and inclusion? Also share what you plan to do for others.

SCREEN FOR ERRORS: Make sure you don't have any spelling or grammar errors. Proofread and check that you are using the correct names, dates, and contact information.

SUPPLY REFERENCES: In our experience some of the best LORs that we have read—and written—include quoted comments from notable people who can speak to your strengths. Curate a list of two to three people to provide a quotation for the letter. Include their contact information (name, email address) for the writer.

THE MICROSKILL:

6. PAUSE BEFORE ACCEPTING AN OPPORTUNITY

WHAT IS THE ACTUAL SKILL?

Perform due diligence upfront to vet an opportunity.

ADAIRA

I was once invited to speak on a national panel. I knew the five other panelists and two moderators. I had worked with many of them previously, they were all nice, intelligent, and organized. They were also all men. I had heard of the panel weeks prior to their email, because I saw the advertisements on social media. When I got the invitation, the panel was set to occur two weeks later. It felt weird to be asked so last minute. I would need to book a flight and a hotel. Some separate friends provided a bit of background. The panel organizers had received late feedback that the panel was too homogeneous. Instead of starting from scratch and developing a new panel they sought to add me, a Black woman, last minute. I had been an "add on" for many events in the past. Different variations of a "diversity hire." And at that stage of my career, I had drawn the line. It didn't feel good. Even though I suspect panelists believed their approach was right, I trusted my gut and decided that the panel would not help professionally, I had competing commitments, and the backstory made me unexcited. So, I declined after pausing to investigate the offer at a deeper level. And I'm glad I did.

WHY DO WE NEED THE SKILL?

Very rarely do you have to make a rush decision. Yet, saying no is difficult for many of us. Maybe its FOMO. This delayed realization can lead to resentment, disengagement, and overwhelm. You might tell yourself, "Why the heck did I sign up for this?" This MicroSkill falls in the self-care category. It's a healthy way to establish boundaries.

WHY IS THIS SKILL HARD?

- It's hard to poke holes and see flaws in advance. It takes time, experience, and discernment.
- It can feel uncomfortable to say no to an offer.
- You may not know what questions to ask or what to look for.
- You may explain away red flags, not trust your gut and rationalize a toxic culture.
- You don't want to disappoint people.
- You fear not being asked again.

WHAT ARE THE CRITICAL ACTIONS FOR THIS MICROSKILL?

PRACTICE PAUSING: Focus on being kind, straightforward, and providing an honest explanation.[184] Figure out clarifying questions or go-to phrases that you feel comfortable to employ when you are unexpectedly asked. Say, "Wow, thank you for thinking of me. Do you mind if I learn a bit more first?"

ASK FOR ADMIN SUPPORT: Depending on the opportunity, there might be work that you can do alone and there might be tasks that require additional hands and minds. Request information on administrative support, when relevant. Pay particular attention to opportunities that lack support—they have the potential to become a heavy lift. Say "This seems like a large event you want to host. May I have any administrative support to help with organization?"

DISCOVER IF YOU HAVE COLLABORATORS: Some opportunities are amazing not because of the content of the work but because of the people with whom you will work. Are they going to help you learn? Will you be able to mentor them—are you interested in mentoring? Ask if they plan to leave the job anytime soon. You would not want to arrive to find that they are leaving or have left.

CONFIRM THAT AN OPPORTUNITY MEETS A NEED: It's okay to be discerning. Is this something you need, want, and/or desire? If it's something potentially attractive or positive, then figure out what would make it good, better, or great, and ask for that. "This opportunity sounds amazing, but I would need a budget to support the recruitment of a diverse and inclusive team." If there is no obvious benefit, then decline.

CONSIDER THE RARITY OF THE POSITION: Some positions are truly once in a lifetime. Assess if this is the case. If yes, this opportunity will never come again, do a double take. Ask others who are familiar with the opportunity. We don't want you to have regrets.

CHECK WHAT SKILLS ARE NEEDED: If the new opportunity is a job, ask the person in charge of hiring or the supervisor whether coaching or a course is needed. You want to succeed. And pitch it like that: "I've noticed the job requires me to balance a significant budget. I've balanced a smaller budget without difficulty. I'd love to meet regularly with you or someone with similar experience to make sure I'm progressing correctly."

CHECK FOR EQUITY AND AVOID CONTROVERSY: Ask around whether the opportunity has had any historical controversy. Make sure the position has a reputation for being equitable. Ask trusted friends about salary equity—trust us, you want to know this early. Probe carefully to see just how much inequity exists. The internet is your friend here. Search and really explore the opportunity. Make sure there is nothing about the opportunity that would compromise your reputation if you joined.

GET ALL OFFERS IN WRITING: Sometimes your peer, supervisor, or recruiter will verbally offer you an opportunity. This is great...and this is not a guarantee. Ask for offers in writing. While a verbal promise seems trustworthy, it could easily be retracted. Resa has had experience being verbally offered a job, told the offer letter was coming, and it never did. Gulp.

CHECK THE LETTER: You won't always get a letter but for some big opportunities, you might. So when the offer letter does arrive, read it—before you sign be sure to read the offer to be sure it matches what was discussed. We have plenty of examples where the letter is not what was discussed and offered. It leaves a bad feeling for sure. Ask a trusted someone—a mentor, lawyer, with experience and ideally someone who has held a similar positions—to read it over.

THE MICROSKILL:

7. BE MINDFUL OF YOUR TEAM AS YOU TAKE ON NEW OPPORTUNITIES

WHAT IS THE ACTUAL SKILL?

Be deliberate in how you transfer tasks and transition roles.

RESA

I knew that to write this book, I needed time, and that meant taking a break from doing a lot of emergency-department shifts. But it was not only shifts, it was also the teaching and the administrative parts of the work: organizing workshops, teaching, running weekly meetings, and more. I knew that taking a leave would add work to other people's plates, and I brainstormed ways to ease the load for teammates. Two examples: we started rotating the person who organized, set the agenda, and led the weekly meeting. In doing so, I could coach and mentor that person as needed. Importantly, for professional development, this allowed younger teammates seeking the opportunity to gain experience in a supportive way. Secondly, 6 months ahead of my writing sabbatical, I scheduled and confirmed guests for our monthly lecture series for the entire academic year. In this way, last-minute invitations were not necessary, and the guest speaker series—an important education and networking opportunity for the group—was not interrupted.

WHY DO WE NEED THIS SKILL?

As we grow and develop, convert skills, and get ready for our next position, there is a risk of increasing demands beyond our current day-to-day work responsibilities. As a result, more work may fall on the team. By falling short on commitments, this could affect team productivity and morale. This is neither kind nor fair nor a good idea. Be mindful. Think of others as you build yourself. You have to think about how you transition tasks off your plate as well as communicate these requests with your supervisor. Be prepared for them to ask you to keep work on your plate.

WHY IS THIS SKILL HARD TO ACHIEVE?

- Distancing away from local responsibilities feels cold and isolating.
- Moving tasks to the team causes resentment.
- It is tempting to work only on tasks and projects that interest you and to avoid the less interesting and less inspiring work.

WHAT ARE THE CRITICAL ACTIONS FOR THIS MICROSKILL?

COMMUNICATE REGULARLY: Communicate with the team about your professional-growth plans. Check in the team to mitigate any resentments. Discuss the distribution of work by the team and aim for parity.

ORGANIZE YOUR CALENDAR: Use your calendar to organize your time and mark timelines so you don't miss tasks. Keep a list of work duties and projects that need completion. Run the list on a routine basis.

DELEGATE AND DIVIDE: Times of transition are good opportunities to take stock. Identify the work on your plate that should be delegated. Is there a teammate who would appreciate the opportunity for more responsibility? Can a project be divided into parts so a few people can help?

GIVE NOTICE THOUGHTFULLY AND INTENTIONALLY: Give a respectful amount of notice that you are building your career and transitioning to new opportunities. This ranges, is very situation dependent, and depends upon your contract and the workplace culture. Tell your supervisor in person rather than by email, text, or phone. Be enthusiastic, and remember that it's good to leave on a positive note, given that your next role may need your supervisor as a reference. And you never know what the future holds in terms of positions and people.

CONCLUSION:

Be active in thinking about your next opportunity and realizing it.	Brainstorm opportunities, keep a list, and speak with people about potential opportunities.	When gaining a new skill or considering a new opportunity, be mindful of the effect on your team.

SUPPLEMENTAL RESOURCES:

TEDTalk

Podcast

Forbes

CONCLUSION

When we started writing *MicroSkills*, three truths about the workplace crystallized.

- **TRUTH #1:** Time is only spent. We cannot deposit or withdraw time from a savings account—so we need to be intentional, thoughtful, even strategic with how we utilize such a valuable resource.

- **TRUTH #2:** The world is not equal. We are all different—where we start, the privilege we carry, and the advantages we hold. And importantly, some of us are more welcome and feel a greater sense of belonging in the workplace.

- **TRUTH #3:** Learning is limitless if it is accessible. When we make information accessible to all—there is no limit to what we can learn.

We want you to keep these three truths in mind as you use the MicroSkills from small actions to big impact. The professional growth and navigation journey is not all about you. It is about all three key components to any workplace: the self, the team, and the work. These should exist in harmony—not in conflict and not at the expense of another. MicroSkills are not isolated small steps with no overlap or applicability. They should build upon each other so any big task seems do-able. When you meet a large task, an overwhelming project, a big problem, a huge goal, we hope you pause. Think about the situation. And break it down. What MicroSkill applies here? Why do you need it? Why is it hard? What critical actions can I take?

Cumulatively, we have been in the workforce over fifty years. Our experiences range from medicine, academia, the private sector, the nonprofit sector to the arts. And we wrote *MicroSkills*, motivated to make the workplace easier, more transparent, and more straightforward for you.

Much of this book comes from our own lived experience, the teachings of our boards of directors, our workplaces, and all of our education resources. We would be nowhere without help. We wrote the book we wish we had available to us as we entered the workforce. We hope this serves as one of many important books in your professional life. We would love to hear from you. Please share your lessons learned on social media—follow us, tag us, message us, hashtag the book #MicroSkills.

★ ★ ★ ★ ★

ACKNOWLEDGMENTS

We acknowledge the too numerous to count and so many people who supported us and contributed to the production of this book. Thank you for the overwhelming love.

Abby Wambach
Abi Turano
Aditi Joshi
Al'ai Alvarez
Alex Soojung-Kim Pang
Alicia Maule
Alyson McGregor
Alister Martin
Almaz Dessie
Amie Varley
Amiera Landry
Amorina Lopez
Amy Bernstein
Amy Celico
Amy Edmondson
Amy Gallo
Amy Reiss
Anand Swaminathan
Andrea Austin
Anita Chary
Anne Maitland
April Dinwoodie
Ari Lipsky
Azita Hamedani
Barb Natterson-Horowitz
Beth Schonning
Beverly Landry
Bora Tekogul
Brad Johnson
Cara Natterson
Carl Preiksaitis
Catherine Fullerton
Celeste Mergens
Charlotte Sutton
Chase Landry
Chelsea Larsson
Christine Laine
Dan Egan
Daniel Goldman
Daniel Nava
Danielle Ofri
Darilyn Moyer
Darin Wiggins
Dan Dworkis
Dave Smith
David Bach
David Hem
David Landry Jr.
David Landry Sr.
Deborah Estrin
Devora Zack
Eden Railsback
Ellen Lupton
Emi Ikkanda
Emily Silverman
Eric Nadel
Eric Shappell
Erin Peavey
Eva Niyibizi
Everett Lyn
Farah Dadabhoy
Farrah Siganporia
Farah Siraj
Felix Ankel
Frances Schulz
Francesca Grossberg
Francesca Irene Decker
Gillianne Defoe
Gita Pensa
Giuliano de Portu
Gretchen Diemer
Hannah Wild

Helen Burstin
Hazar Khidir
Heidi Messer
Imoigele Aisiku
Jaidree Braddix
James Li
Janae Sharp
Jane Van Dis
Jason Han
Jason Woods
Jay Baruch
Jeff Liguori
Jeffrey Chou
Jeffrey Manko
Jennifer Freyd
Jenny Mladenovic
Jessica Meyer
Jessie Gold
Jiho Huang
Jill Baren
Jill Schlesinger
Jo Shapiro
Jordan Grumet
Jordana Haber
Joy Scaglione
Julie Silver
K. Anis Ahmed
Kali Cyrus
Karen Catlin
Kasturi Pananjady
Kathleen Brandenburg
Kaylah Maloney
Keivn Webb
Kemi Doll
Kim LaPean
Kim Newby
Kim Scott
Laura Rock
Laurence Amar
Linda Babcock
Lisa DiMona
Lisa McGann
Lissa Warren
Louise Aronson
Luke Messac
Lynn Fiellin
Maggie Apollon
Marc Harrison
Maria O'Rourke
Marianne Neuwirth
Marie-Carmelle Elie
Marina Catallozzi
Marina Del Rios
Mark Clark
Mark Foran
Mark Pearlman
Maureen Gang
Mavis Zondervaan
Maya Alexandri
Mecca Jamilah Sullivan
Megan Ranney
Michael Gottlieb
Michelle Finkel
Michelle Johnston
Michelle Lin
Mike Gisondi
Mike Van Rooyen
Minda Harts
Miriam Laufer
Nassim Assefi
Nikita Joshi
Noliwe Rooks
Ojeagbase Asikhia
Pat Pinckombe
Patrish Gagnon
Paula Johnson
Paule Joseph
Peilin Chou
Peter Joseph
Peter Tomaselli
Peter Weimersheimer
Phyllis Hwang
Pooja Lakshmin
Rana Awdish
Rehan Kapadia
Riss Hauptman
Robert Liguori
Robin Landry
Ron Walls
Ruchika Tulshyan
Sayantani DasGupta
Sean McGann
Serena Murillo
Seth Godin
Sharonne Hayes
Sheila Heen
Soledad O'Brien
Sree Natesan
Stesha Doku
Subha Airan-Javia
Susan Chon
Suzanne Koven
Suzanne Rivera
Tamieka Evans
Teresa Chan
Tess Jones
Tomas Chamorro-Premuzic
Tommy Wong
Tracy Sanson
Trish Henwood
Troy Foster
Uché Blackstock
Vanessa Kroll Bennett
Vanessa Wells
Veena Vasista
Venetia Dale
Vinny Arora
Wendy Coates

ENDNOTES

1 Kimber P. Richter, Lauren Clark, Jo A. Wick, et. al., "Women Physicians and Promotion in Academic Medicine," *N Engl J Med,* pp. 2148-2157, November 26, 2020, https://pubmed.ncbi.nlm.nih.gov/33252871/

2 Andrea C. Fang, Sharon A. Chekijian, Amy J. Zeidan, et. al., "National Awards and Female Emergency Physicians in the United States: Is the 'Recognition Gap' Closing?" *J Emerg Med*, pp. 540-549, November 2020, https://pubmed.ncbi.nlm.nih.gov/34364703/

3 Elizabeth Cooney, "Salary Gap between Male and Female Physicians Adds Up To $2 Million in Lifetime Earnings," *STATNews.com*, December 6, 2021, https://www.statnews.com/2021/12/06/male-female-physician-salaries-gap-2-million-lifetime-earnings/

4 "The Majority of U.S. Medical Students Are Women, New Data Show," AAMC.org, December 9, 2019, https://www.aamc.org/news/press-releases/majority-us-medical-students-are-women-new-data-show

5 "Faculty Roster: U.S. Medical School Faculty," AAMC.org, https://www.aamc.org/data-reports/faculty-institutions/report/faculty-roster-us-medical-school-faculty

6 Patrick Boyle, "What's Your Specialty? New Data Show the Choices of America's Doctors by Gender, Race, and Age," AAMC.org, January 12, 2023, https://www.aamc.org/news/what-s-your-specialty-new-data-show-choices-america-s-doctors-gender-race-and-age

7 Amy Paturel, "Why Women Leave Medicine," AAMC.org, October 1, 2019, https://www.aamc.org/news/why-women-leave-medicine

8 Cameron J. Gettel, D. Mark Courtney, Pooja Agrawal, et al., "Emergency medicine physician workforce attrition differences by age and gender," *Acad Emerg Med.,* pp. 1-9, June 14, 2023, https://onlinelibrary.wiley.com/action/showCitFormats?doi=10.1111%2Facem.14764

9 "Self-care," *Merriam-Webster.com Dictionary,* Merriam-Webster, https://www.merriam-webster.com/dictionary/self-care, accessed September 19, 2023.

10 Eva S. Schernhammer and Graham A. Colditz, "Suicide Rates Amont Physicians: A Quantitative and Gender Assessment (Meta-Analysis)," *Am J Psychiatry,* December 2004, https://ajp.psychiatryonline.org/doi/pdf/10.1176/appi.ajp.161.12.2295

11 Stacy Weiner, "Doctors forgo mental health care during pandemic over concerns about licensing, stigma," *AAMC News*, December 10, 2020, https://www.aamc.org/news/doctors-forgo-mental-health-care-during-pandemic-over-concerns-about-licensing-stigma

12 Jennifer J. Robertson and Brit Long, "Medicine's Shame Problem," *The Journal of Emergency Medicine*, vol. 57, issue 3, pp. 329–338, September 2019, https://www.sciencedirect.com/science/article/pii/S0736467919305505; Liselotte N. Dyrbye, Colin P. West, Christine A. Sinsky, et. al., "Medical Licensure Questions and Physician Reluctance to Seek Care for Mental Health Conditions," *Mayo Clinic Proceedings,* vol. 92, issue 10, pp. 1486-1493, October 2017, https://www.mayoclinicproceedings.org/article/S0025-6196(17)30522-0/fulltext

13 Joseph V. Simone, "Understanding Academic Medical Centers: Simon's Maxims," *Clin Cancer Res,* vol. 1, issue 9, pp. 2281-2285, September 1, 1999, https://aacrjournals.org/clincancerres/article/5/9/2281/287826/Understanding-Academic-Medical-Centers-Simone-s

14 Sara Moniuszko, "Want to live to 100? 'Blue Zones' expert shares longevity lessons in new Netflix series," *CBS News*, August 30, 2023, https://www.cbsnews.com/news/blue-zone-expert-longevity-lessons-netflix-series/

15 Susan Stelter, "Want to Advance in Your Career? Build Your Own Board of Directors." *Ascend,* May 9, 2022, https://hbr.org/2022/05/want-to-advance-in-your-career-build-your-own-board-of-directors

16 Sara Gray, "Fail Better with a Failure Friend," *feminem.org,* December 5, 2017, https://feminem.org/2017/12/05/fail-better-failure-friend/

17 Alex M. Wood, Stephen Joseph, Joanna Lloyd, and Samuel Atkins, "Gratitude Influences Sleep through the Mechanism of Pre-sleep Cognitions," *Journal of Psychosomatic Research*, vol. 66, issue 1, pp. 43–48, January 2009, https://pubmed.ncbi.nlm.nih.gov/19073292/

18 "How Much Sleep Do I Need?" Centers for Disease Control and Prevention, https://www.cdc.gov/sleep/about_sleep/how_much_sleep.html

19 "What Are Sleep Deprivation and Deficiency?" National Heart, Lung, and Blood Institute, https://www.nhlbi.nih.gov/health/sleep-deprivation#:~:text=Sleep%20deficiency%20is%20linked%20to,adults%2C%20teens%2C%20and%20children

20 Adaira Landry and Resa E. Lewiss, "Four Evidence-backed Reasons to Say 'No' to Early-morning Meetings," *Nature*, October 26, 2022, https://www.nature.com/articles/d41586-022-03461-6?utm_medium=Social&utm_campaign=nature&utm_source=Twitter#Echobox=1666871412

21 Ian M. Colrain, Christian L. Nicholas, and Fiona C. Baker, "Alcohol and the Sleeping Brain," *Handb Clin Neurol,* vol. 125, pp. 415-31, 2014, *https://www.ncbi.nlm.nih.gov/pmc/articles/PMC5821259/*; Timothy Fitzgerald and Jeffrey Vietri, "Residual Effects of Sleep Medications Are Commonly Reported and Associated with Impaired Patient-Reported Outcomes among Insomnia Patients in the United States," *Sleep Disord*, December 9, 2015, https://pubmed.ncbi.nlm.nih.gov/26783470/

22 Ravinder Jerath, Connor Beveridge, and Vernon A. Barnes, "Self-Regulation of Breathing as an Adjunctive Treatment of Insomnia,"

Front Psychiatry, vol. 9, p. 780, January 9, 2019, https://www.ncbi.nlm.nih.gov/pmc/articles/PMC6361823/

23 Virgin Pulse, "8 Ways to Quiet Your Mind and Sleep Better Tonight," 2020, https://hr.unc.edu/wp-content/uploads/sites/222/2020/04/8-Ways-to-Quiet-Your-Mind-and-Sleep-Better-Tonight.pdf

24 Will Stone, "Sleeping in a Room Even a Little Bit of Light Can Hurt a Person's Health, Study Shows," *NPR*, March 29, 2022, https://www.npr.org/2022/03/29/1089533755/sleeping-in-a-room-even-a-little-bit-of-light-can-hurt-a-persons-health-study-sh

25 Kenji Obayashi, Keigo Saeki, and Norio Kurumatani, "Bedroom Light Exposure at Night and the Incidence of Depressive Symptoms: A Longitudinal Study of the HEIJO-KYO Cohort," *American Journal of Epidemiology,* vol. 187, issue 3, pp. 427–434, March 2018, https://doi.org/10.1093/aje/kwx290

26 "Is Eating Before Bed Bad for You?" *Cleveland Health,* March 23, 2022, https://health.clevelandclinic.org/is-eating-before-bed-bad-for-you/

27 Christopher E. Kline, "The bidirectional relationship between exercise and sleep: Implications for exercise adherence and sleep improvement," *Am J Lifestyle Med,* vol. 8, issue 6, pp. 375-379, November 2014, https://www.ncbi.nlm.nih.gov/pmc/articles/PMC4341978/

28 Ferris Jabr, "Why Your Brain Needs More Downtime," *Scientific American*, October 15, 2013, https://www.scientificamerican.com/article/mental-downtime/

29 Alex Soojung-Kim Pang, *Rest: Why You Get More Done When You Work Less*, Basic Books, June 12, 2018

30 Arlie Russell Hochschild with Anne Machung, "Second Shift: Working Parents and the Revolution at Home," Viking Penguin, 1989.

31 Allison E. McWilliams, "The Critical Need for Intentional Rest," *Psychology Today,* June 9, 2023, https://www.psychologytoday.com/us/blog/your-awesome-career/202306/the-critical-need-for-intentional-rest.

32 Lawrence M. Berger and Jason N. Houle, "Parental Debt and Children's Socioeconomical Well-being," American Academy of Pe-

diatrics, February 1, 2016, https://publications.aap.org/pediatrics/article-abstract/137/2/e20153059/52721/Parental-Debt-and-Children-s-Socioemotional-Well?redirectedFrom=fulltext?autologincheck=redirected

33 Kat Tretina and Mike Cetera, "11 Student Loan Forgiveness Programs: How To Qualify," *Forbes Advisor,* updated September 27, 2023, https://www.forbes.com/advisor/student-loans/student-loan-forgiveness-programs/

34 Annika Olson, "Millenials have almost no chance of being able to afford a house. This is what can be done," *CNN*, March 23, 2021, https://www.cnn.com/2021/03/23/opinions/millennials-almost-impossible-to-afford-home-olson/index.html

35 "r/financialindependence," *Reddit*, https://www.reddit.com/r/financialindependence/

36 Liz Frazier, "11 Financial Advisor Red Flags That You Should Never Ignore," *Forbes*, May 15, 2017, https://www.forbes.com/sites/lizfrazierpeck/2017/05/15/11-financial-advisor-red-flags-that-you-should-never-ignore/?sh=547f71296cb1

37 Greg McFarlane, "Reasons Why Life Insurance May Not Be Worth It," *Investopedia*, https://www.investopedia.com/financial-edge/0312/when-life-insurance-isnt-worth-it.aspx

38 Tomas Chamorro-Premuzic, "Attractive People Get Unfair Advantages at Work. AI Can Help," *Harvard Business Review*, October 31, 2019, https://hbr.org/2019/10/attractive-people-get-unfair-advantages-at-work-ai-can-help

39 "What You Wear to Work May Be Preventing You from Getting a Promotion," Robert Half Talent Solutions, May 8, 2018, https://press.roberthalf.com/2018-05-08-What-You-Wear-To-Work-May-Be-Preventing-You-From-Getting-A-Promotion

40 Adaira Landry and Resa E. Lewiss, "Emergency doctors share 7 longevity foods they eat to stay 'healthy, full and energized' every day," *CNNBC Make It,* March 24, 2023, https://www.cnbc.com/2023/03/24/emergency-doctors-share-the-foods-they-eat-to-stay-healthy-full-and-energized-all-day.html

41 "Home Oral Care," American Dental Association, https://www.ada.org/resources/research/science-and-research-institute/oral-health-topics/home-care

42 "How to Quit Smoking," Centers for Disease Control and Prevention, https://www.cdc.gov/tobacco/campaign/tips/quit-smoking/index.html

43 "Only the overworked die young," *Harvard Health Publishing,* December 14, 2015, https://www.health.harvard.edu/blog/only-the-overworked-die-young-201512148815

44 Timothy J. Buschman, Markus Siegel, Jefferson E. Roy, and Earl K. Miller, "Neural substrates of cognitive capacity limitations," PNAS.org, July 5, 2011, https://www.pnas.org/doi/pdf/10.1073/pnas.1104666108

45 Lebene Richmond Soga, Yemisi Bolade-Ogunfodun, Marcello Mariani, Rita Nasr, and Benjamin Laker, "Unmasking the Other Face of Flexible Working Practices: A Systematic Literature Review," *Journal of Business Research*, vol. 142, pp. 648–662, March 2022, https://www.sciencedirect.com/science/article/pii/S0148296322000364

46 Brad Aeon, "The Philosophy of Time Management," TEDx, https://www.ted.com/talks/brad_aeon_the_philosophy_of_time_management

47 Greg Kihlstrom, "The ROI of Great Employee Experience," *Forbes*, October 16, 2019, https://www.forbes.com/sites/forbesagencycouncil/2019/10/16/the-roi-of-great-employee-experience/?sh=4aa37aaa4d7c

48 Dave Wendland, "Brainstorming More Effectively," *Forbes,* January 13, 2023, https://www.forbes.com/sites/forbesagencycouncil/2023/01/13/brainstorming-more-effectively/?sh=328dbac73252

49 Laura Hennigan and Cassie Bottorff, "How To Create a Simple, Effective Project Timeline In Six Steps," *Forbes,* updated July 19, 2023, https://www.forbes.com/advisor/business/software/create-a-project-timeline/

50 Laura A. Brannon, Paul J. Hershberger, and Timothy C. Brock, "Timeless demonstrations of Parkinson's first law," *Psychonomic Bul-*

letin & Review, pp. 148-156, March 1999, https://link.springer.com/article/10.3758/BF03210823

51 Rachel Layne, "For entrepreneurs, Blown Deadlines Can Crush Big Ideas," *Harvard Business School,* September 29, 2021, https://hbswk.hbs.edu/item/for-entrepreneurs-blown-deadlines-can-crush-big-ideas

52 Seth Godin, *The Dip: A Little Book That Teaches You When to Quit (and When to Stick),* Portfolio, May 10, 2007

53 Kristen Fuller, "The Joy of Missing Out," *Psychology Today,* July 26, 2018, https://www.psychologytoday.com/us/blog/happiness-is-state-mind/201807/jomo-the-joy-missing-out

54 David Lancefield, "Stop Wasting People's Time with Meetings," *Harvard Business Review,* March 14, 2022, https://hbr.org/2022/03/stop-wasting-peoples-time-with-bad-meetings

55 Linda Babcock, Maria P. Recalde, and Lise Vesterlund, "Why Women Volunteer for Tasks That Don't Lead to Promotions," *Harvard Business Review,* July 16, 2018, https://hbr.org/2018/07/why-women-volunteer-for-tasks-that-dont-lead-to-promotions#:~:text=Averaging%20across%20the%2010%20rounds,one%20of%20the%2010%20rounds.

56 Carmine Gallo, "How Great Leaders Communicate," *Harvard Business Review,* November 23, 2022, https://hbr.org/2022/11/how-great-leaders-communicate

57 Jeff Thompson, "Is Nonverbal Communication a Numbers Game?" *Psychology Today,* September 30, 2011, https://www.psychologytoday.com/us/blog/beyond-words/201109/is-nonverbal-communication-a-numbers-game

58 Daniel Goleman and Richard E. Boyatzis, "Emotional Intelligence Has 12 Elements. Which Do You Need to Work On?" *Harvard Business Review,* February 6, 2017, https://hbr.org/2017/02/emotional-intelligence-has-12-elements-which-do-you-need-to-work-on

59 Brené Brown, "Clear Is Kind. Unclear Is Unkind," Brené Brown, October 15, 2018, https://brenebrown.com/articles/2018/10/15/clear-is-kind-unclear-is-unkind/

60 Resa Lewiss, "How an Old Technology Became a Disruptive Innovation," TEDMED, https://www.tedmed.com/talks/show?id=293054

61 Paul J. Zak, "Why Your Brain Loves Good Storytelling," *Harvard Business Review,* October 28, 2014, https://hbr.org/2014/10/why-your-brain-loves-good-storytelling

62 Anne Gulland, "Men Dominate Conference Q&A Sessions—Including Online Ones," *Nature*, December 1, 2022, https://www.nature.com/articles/d41586-022-04241-y

63 Valerie Fridland, "First Came Mansplaining, Then Came Manterruptions," *Psychology Today*, January 31, 2021, https://www.psychologytoday.com/us/blog/language-in-the-wild/202101/first-came-mansplaining-then-came-manterruptions

64 Resa E. Lewiss, "Dave Smith and Brad Johnson: Men Can Be Better Allies," *The Visible Voices Podcast, https://www.thevisiblevoicespodcast.com/episodes/eI-ggkbFMIhi1rU9tVZJ1w*; David G. Smith and W. Brad Johnson, "Good Guys: How Men Can Be Better Allies for Women in the Workplace," *Harvard Business Review Press,* October 13, 2020.

65 "mansplain," *Merriam-Webster, https://www.merriam-webster.com/dictionary/mansplain*, accessed August 8, 2023

66 Jessica Bennett, "How Not to Be 'Manterrupted' in Meetings," *TIME,* January 14, 2015, updated January 20, 2015, https://time.com/3666135/sheryl-sandberg-talking-while-female-manterruptions/

67 ibid

68 Laurel Farrer, "The Art of Asynchronous: Optimizing Efficiency in Remote Teams," *Forbes*, December 10, 2020, https://www.forbes.com/sites/laurelfarrer/2020/12/10/the-art-of-asynchronous-optimizing-efficiency-in-remote-teams/?sh=6ffd2e88747c

69 "The 12 second Rule: How can you Plan your Emails Accordingly?" *Upland, https://uplandsoftware.com/adestra/resources/blog/12-second-rule/*; L. Ceci, "Average time people spend reading brand emails from 2011 to 2021," *Statista,* November 2, 2021, https://www.statista.com/statistics/1273288/time-spent-brand-emails/

70 Shep Hyken, "Sixty-Five Percent Of Emails Are Ignored," *Forbes*, October 4, 2020, https://www.forbes.com/sites/shephyken/2020/10/04/sixty-five-percent-of-emails-are-ignored/?sh=5d6737ec1e6a

71 Dan Bullock and Raúl Sánchez, "What's the Best Way to Communicate on a Global Team?" *Harvard Business Review*, Ascend, March 22, 2021, https://hbr.org/2021/03/whats-the-best-way-to-communicate-on-a-global-team

72 Carol Waseleski, "Gender and the Use of Exclamation Points in Computer-Mediated Communication: An Analysis of Exclamations Posted to Two Electronic Discussion Lists," *Journal of Computer-Mediated Communication*, vol. 11, issue 4, pp. 1012-1024, October 9, 2006, *https://onlinelibrary.wiley.com/doi/full/10.1111/j.1083-6101.2006.00305.x*; David Ruth, "Women use emoticons more than men in text messaging :-)," *Rice University*, October 10, 2012, https://news2.rice.edu/2012/10/10/women-use-emoticons-more-than-men-in-text-messaging/

73 Abigail Johnson Hess, "Here's How Many Hours American Workers Spend on Email Each Day," *CNBC*, Make It, September 23, 2019, https://www.cnbc.com/2019/09/22/heres-how-many-hours-american-workers-spend-on-email-each-day.html

74 Adaira Landry and Resa E. Lewiss, "What a Compassionate Email Culture Looks Like," *Harvard Business Review*, March 16, 2021, https://hbr.org/2021/03/what-a-compassionate-email-culture-looks-like

75 Zahid Saghir, Javeria N. Syeda, Adnan S. Muhammad, and Tareg H. Balla Abdalla, "The Amygdala, Sleep Debt, Sleep Deprivation, and the Emotion of Anger: A Possible Connection?" *National Library of Medicine*, Cureus, vol. 10, issue 7, July 2, 2018, https://www.ncbi.nlm.nih.gov/pmc/articles/PMC6122651/

76 Adaira Landry and Resa E. Lewiss, "What a Compassionate Email Culture Looks Like," *Harvard Business Review*, March 16, 2021, https://hbr.org/2021/03/what-a-compassionate-email-culture-looks-like

77 School of Infection and Immunity, "Core Hours Policy," University of Glasgow, https://www.gla.ac.uk/schools/infectionimmunity/athenaswan/athenaswaninitiatives/#corehourspolicy; "Athena Swan

Charter," *Advance HE,* https://www.advance-he.ac.uk/equality-charters/athena-swan-charter

78 Ryan Erskine, "20 Online Reputation Statistics That Every Business Owner Needs to Know," *Forbes*, September 19, 2017, https://www.forbes.com/sites/ryanerskine/2017/09/19/20-online-reputation-statistics-that-every-business-owner-needs-to-know/?sh=2a54a454cc5c

79 Kathleen L. McGinn and Nicole Tempest, "Heidi Roizen," Harvard Business School Case 800-228, January 2000, https://www.hbs.edu/faculty/Pages/item.aspx?num=26880; Daphna Motro, Jonathan B. Evans, Aleksander P. J. Ellis, and Lehman Benson III, "Race and Reactions to Women's Expressions of Anger at Work: Examining the Effects of the "Angry Black Woman" Stereotype," *Journal of Applied Psychology*, vol. 107, issue 1, pp. 142–152, https://psycnet.apa.org/record/2021-32191-001

80 Marshall Goldsmith, "Reducing Negativity in the Workplace," *Harvard Business Review*, October 8, 2007, https://hbr.org/2007/10/reducing-negativity-in-the-wor

81 Sabina Nawaz, "The Problem with Saying 'Don't Bring Me Problems, Bring Me Solutions,'" *Harvard Business Review,* September 1, 2017, https://hbr.org/2017/09/the-problem-with-saying-dont-bring-me-problems-bring-me-solutions?utm_medium=social&utm_campaign=hbr&utm_source=twitter&tpcc=orgsocial_edit

82 "Shame in Medicine," *The Nocturnists,* 2022, https://www.thenocturnists-shame.org/

83 Andrea K. Bellovary, Nathaniel A. Young, and Amit Goldenberg, "Left- and Right-Leaning News Organizations' Negative Tweets Are More Likely to be Shared," *Harvard Business School*, https://www.hbs.edu/ris/Publication%20Files/Left-%20and%20Right-Leaning%20News%20_3d45857a-8210-4d4a-83d5-01508848006a.pdf

84 Adaira Landry and Resa E. Lewiss, "7 Ways to Promote Yourself on Social Media without Bragging," *Fast Company*, February 15, 2022, https://www.fastcompany.com/90719543/7-ways-to-promote-yourself-on-social-media-without-bragging

85 Errol Morris, "The Anosognosic's Dilemma: Something's Wrong but You'll Never Know What It Is (Part 1)," *New York Times*, June 20, 2010, https://archive.nytimes.com/opinionator.blogs.nytimes.com/2010/06/20/the-anosognosics-dilemma-1/

86 Tomas Chamorro-Premuzic, "Why Do So Many Incompetent Men Become Leaders?" *Harvard Business Review*, August 22, 2013, https://hbr.org/2013/08/why-do-so-many-incompetent-men

87 ibid

88 Michael Seitchik, "Confidence and Gender: Few Differences, but Gender Stereotypes Impact Perceptions of Confidence," *Psychologist-Manager Journal*, vol. 23, issues 3–4, pp. 194–205, 2020, https://psycnet.apa.org/record/2020-87561-005

89 Stephanie Vozza, "How to Fix a Bad Reputation," *Fast Company*, May 6, 2019, https://www.fastcompany.com/90342095/how-to-fix-a-bad-reputation

90 Caroline Castrillon, "How Women Can Stop Apologizing and Take Their Power Back," *Forbes*, July 14, 2019, https://www.forbes.com/sites/carolinecastrillon/2019/07/14/how-women-can-stop-apologizing-and-take-their-power-back/?sh=538e0f1f4ce6

91 Tyler G. Okimoto, Michael Wenzel, and Kyli Hedrick, "Refusing to Apologize Can Have Psychological Benefits (and We Issue No Mea Culpa for This Research Finding)," *European Journal of Social Psychology*, vol. 43, issue 1, pp. 22–31, 2013, https://psycnet.apa.org/record/2013-03180-004

92 Elizabeth A. Segal, "When We Don't Apologize," *Psychology Today*, August 29, 2018, https://www.psychologytoday.com/us/blog/social-empathy/201808/when-we-don-t-apologize

93 Laurie A. Boge, Carlos Dos Santos, Lisa A. Moreno-Walton, Luigi X. Cubeddu, and David A. Farcy, "The Relationship between Physician/Nurse Gender and Patients' Correct Identification of Health Care Professional Roles in the Emergency Department," *Journal of Women's Health*, vol. 28, issue 7, pp. 961–964, July 16, 2019, https://www.liebertpub.com/doi/10.1089/jwh.2018.7571

94 "A History of Objectives and Key Results (OKRs)," Plai, https://www.plai.team/blog/history-of-objectives-and-key-results

95 Leslie Jamison, "Why Everyone Feels Like They're Faking It," *The New Yorker,* February 6, 2023, *https://www.newyorker.com/magazine/2023/02/13/the-dubious-rise-of-impostor-syndrome*; Pauline Rose Clance and Suzanne Imes, "The Imposter Phenomenon in High Achieving Women: Dynamics and Therapeutic Intervention," *Psychotherapy Theory, Research and Practice,* vol. 15, issue 3, 1978, https://www.paulineroseclance.com/pdf/ip_high_achieving_women.pdf

96 Sree Sreenivasan, "How to Use Social Media in Your Career, *New York Times*, https://www.nytimes.com/guides/business/social-media-for-career-and-business

97 Roxanne Calder, "5 Ways to Figure Out If a Job Is Right for You," *Harvard Business Review*, September 23, 2022, https://hbr.org/2022/09/5-ways-to-figure-out-if-a-job-is-right-for-you

98 Priya Fielding-Singh, Devon Magliozzi, and Swethaa Ballakrishnen, "Why Women Stay Out Of the Spotlight at Work," *Harvard Business Review*, August 28, 2018, https://hbr.org/2018/08/why-women-stay-out-of-the-spotlight-at-work

99 Adaira Landry and Resa E. Lewiss, "How to Write a Letter of Recommendation—for Yourself," *Fast Company*, June 11, 2022, https://www.fastcompany.com/90757084/how-to-write-a-letter-of-recommendation-for-yourself

100 Blair Williams, "Simple Ways Leaders Can Keep Learning and Growing," *Forbes*, April 2, 2020, https://www.forbes.com/sites/theyec/2020/04/02/simple-ways-leaders-can-keep-learning-and-growing/?sh=61839a8618b8

101 "U.S. Medical School Department Chairs by Chair Type and Gender," Association of American Medical Colleges, https://www.aamc.org/data-reports/faculty-institutions/interactive-data/us-medical-school-chairs-trends

102 Bryan Strickland, "Diversity among CEOs, CFOs Continues to Rise," *Journal of Accountancy*, August 23, 2022, https://www.journalofaccountancy.com/news/2022/aug/diversity-among-ceos-cfos-

continues-rise.html#:~:text=Overall%2C%2088.8%25%20of%20 CEOs%2C,%2C%20and%2088.1%25%20are%20men

103 "The Power Gap in Massachusetts K–12 Education," Women's Power Gap Study Series, 2021, https://www.renniecenter.org/sites/default/files/2021-11/K12%20Power%20Gap.pdf

104 Karen Gross, "How You Introduce Yourself Really Matters—Especially Now," Aspen Institute, September 12, 2016, https://www.aspeninstitute.org/blog-posts/introduce-really-matters-especially-now/

105 David M. Mayer, "How Not to Advocate for a Woman at Work," *Harvard Business Review,* July 26, 2017, https://hbr.org/2017/07/how-not-to-advocate-for-a-woman-at-work

106 Mary Sharp Emerson, "Is Your Workplace Communication Style as Effective as It Could Be?" Harvard Division of Continuing Education, February 4, 2022, https://professional.dce.harvard.edu/blog/is-your-workplace-communication-style-as-effective-as-it-could-be/

107 "13 Times In-Person Communication Is Better than Electronic Exchanges," *Forbes*, July 17, 2020, https://www.forbes.com/sites/forbescoachescouncil/2020/07/17/13-times-in-person-communication-is-better-than-electronic-exchanges/?sh=756e87652eb7

108 "Organization Chart," Inc.com, https://www.inc.com/encyclopedia/organization-chart.html

109 Christine Organ and Cassie Bottorff, "Employee Handbook Best Practices in 2023," *Forbes Advisor,* updated October 18, 2022, https://www.forbes.com/advisor/business/employee-handbook/

110 Melissa Dahl, "Can You Blend in Anywhere? Or Are You Always the Same You?" *The Cut,* March 15, 2017, https://www.thecut.com/2017/03/heres-a-test-to-tell-you-if-you-are-a-high-self-monitor.html

111 Resa E. Lewiss, Julie K. Silver, Carol A. Bernstein, et. al., "Is Academic Medicine Making Mid-Career Women Physicians Invisible?" *Journal of Women's Health,* vol. 29, no. 2, February 7, 2020, https://www.liebertpub.com/doi/10.1089/jwh.2019.7732?url_ver=Z39.88-2003&rfr_id=ori%3Arid%3Acrossref.org&rfr_dat=cr_pub++0pubmed

112 David G. Smith and W. Brad Johnson, *Good Guys*, Harvard Business Review Press, October 13, 2020

113 Rebecca Boone, "Attacks at medical centers contribute to health care being one of nation's most violent fields," *PBS,* August 7, 2023, https://www.pbs.org/newshour/health/attacks-at-medical-centers-contribute-to-health-care-being-one-of-nations-most-violent-fields

114 Hildegunn Sagvaag, Silje Lill Rimstad, Liv Grethe Kinn, and Randi Wågø Aas, "Six Shades of Grey: Identifying Drinking Culture and Potentially Risky Drinking Behaviour in the Grey Zone between Work and Leisure," *Journal of Public Health Research*, vol. 8, issue 2, p 1585, September 5, 2019, https://www.ncbi.nlm.nih.gov/pmc/articles/PMC6747020/

115 Kim Elsesser, "These 6 Surprising Office Romance Stats Should Be a Wake-Up Call for Organizations," *Forbes*, February 14, 2019, https://www.forbes.com/sites/kimelsesser/2019/02/14/these-6-surprising-office-romance-stats-should-be-a-wake-up-call-to-organizations/?sh=23d6ff3223a2

116 "Culture Transformation," *Gallup*, https://www.gallup.com/workplace/229832/culture.aspx?utm_source=google&utm_medium=cpc&utm_campaign=workplace_non-branded_cuture&utm_term=organizational%20culture&utm_content=culture_audit&gclid=Cj0KCQjwlumhBhClARIsABO6p-ztKCzeFrnCpWpnDa6C7-mHgs7MD-nWYe88RMPgUgpeXWW_MGVrAHAQaAgH7EALw_wcB

117 Donald Sull, Charles Sull, and Ben Zweig, "Toxic Culture Is Driving the Great Resignation," *MIT Sloan Management Review,* January 11, 2022, https://sloanreview.mit.edu/article/toxic-culture-is-driving-the-great-resignation/

118 "Visual Thinking Strategies (VTS)," Milwaukee Art Museum, http://teachers.mam.org/collection/teaching-with-art/visual-thinking-strategies-vts/

119 Abby Wambach, *Wolfpack: How to Come Together, Unleash Our Power, and Change the Game*, Celadon Books, April 9, 2019

120 Joseph V. Simone, "Understanding Academic Medical Centers: Simone's Maxims," *Clin Cancer Res,* vol. 5, issue 9, pp. 2281-2285, September 1,

1999, https://aacrjournals.org/clincancerres/article/5/9/2281/287826/Understanding-Academic-Medical-Centers-Simone-s

121 Robert Waldinger and Marc Shulz, "The Good Life: Lessons from the World's Longest Scientific Study of Happiness," Simon & Schuster, January 10, 2023

122 Amy Edmondson, "Psychological Safety and Learning Behavior in Work Teams," *Administrative Science Quarterly,* vol. 44, no. 2, pp. 350-383, June 1999, https://journals.sagepub.com/doi/10.2307/2666999

123 Julia Rosovski, "The five keys to a successful Google team," *re:Work,* November 17, 2015, *https://rework.withgoogle.com/blog/five-keys-to-a-successful-google-team/*; "Understand team effectiveness," *re:Work,* https://rework.withgoogle.com/print/guides/5721312655835136/

124 Sian Ferguson, "Yes, Mental Illness Can Impact Your Hygiene. Here's What You Can Do about It," *Healthline*, October 28, 2019, https://www.healthline.com/health/mental-health/mental-illness-can-impact-hygiene#Why-is-it-so-hard-to-brush-my-teeth-or-shower?

125 Amy Morin, "7 Scientifically Proven Benefits of Gratitude," *Psychology Today*, April 3, 2015, https://www.psychologytoday.com/us/blog/what-mentally-strong-people-dont-do/201504/7-scientifically-proven-benefits-of-gratitude

126 James Cook, "More than two-thirds of female employees believe they deserve more recognition," *Business Leader,* July 20, 2022, https://www.businessleader.co.uk/more-than-two-thirds-of-female-employees-believe-they-deserve-more-recognition/; Ruchika Tulshyan, "Women of Color Get Asked to Do More 'Office Housework.' Here's How They Can Say No," *Harvard Business Review,* April 6, 2018, *https://hbr.org/2018/04/women-of-color-get-asked-to-do-more-office-housework-heres-how-they-can-say-no*

127 Jennifer J. Freyd, "Institutional Betrayal and Institutional Courage," Freyd Dynamics Lab, https://dynamic.uoregon.edu/jjf/institutionalbetrayal/

128 Art Markman, "How to Help a Colleague Who Seems Off Their Game," *Harvard Business Review*, September 25, 2018, https://hbr.org/2018/09/how-to-help-a-colleague-who-seems-off-their-game

129 Rebecca Knight, "When You're Stuck Working with a Slacker," *Harvard Business Review*, May 14, 2021, https://hbr.org/2021/05/when-youre-stuck-working-with-a-slacker

130 School of Infection and Immunity, "Core Hours Policy," University of Glasgow, https://www.gla.ac.uk/schools/infectionimmunity/athenaswan/athenaswaninitiatives/#corehourspolicy

131 Adaira Landry and Resa E. Lewiss, "Four Evidence-backed Reasons to Say 'No' to Early-morning Meetings," *Nature*, October 26, 2022, https://www.nature.com/articles/d41586-022-03461-6?utm_medium=Social&utm_campaign=nature&utm_source=Twitter#Echobox=1666871412

132 Holley Linkous, "How Can We Help? Adult Learning as Self-Care in COVID-19," New Horizons in Adult Education and Human Resource Development, vol. 33, issue 2, pp. 65–70, May 29, 2021, https://www.ncbi.nlm.nih.gov/pmc/articles/PMC8207015/

133 Pam Belluck, "Long Covid Is Keeping Significant Numbers of People Out of Work, Study Finds," *New York Times*, January 24, 2023, https://www.nytimes.com/2023/01/24/health/long-covid-work.html

134 The Officevibe Content Team, "Statistics on the Importance of Employee Feedback," *Officevibe*, October 7, 2014, updated December 1, 2022, https://officevibe.com/blog/infographic-employee-feedback

135 Douglas Stone and Sheila Heen, *Thanks for the Feedback: The Science and Art of Receiving Feedback Well*, Penguin Books, March 31, 2015

136 Melissa Summer, "Introverts and Leadership – World Introvert Day," *The Myers-Briggs Company*, January 2, 2020, https://www.themyersbriggs.com/en-US/Connect-With-Us/Blog/2020/January/World-Introvert-Day-2020

137 Rebecca Knight, "How to Be Good at Managing Both Introverts and Extroverts," *Harvard Business Review*, November 16, 2015, *https://hbr.org/2015/11/how-to-be-good-at-managing-both-introverts-and-extroverts*; Susan Cain, *Quiet: The Power of Introverts in a World That Can't Stop Talking*, Crown, January 29, 2013; Devora Zack, *Networking for People Who Hate Networking, Second Edition: A Field Guide for Introverts, the Overwhelmed, and the Underconnected*, Berrett-Koehler Publishers, May

21, 2019; Susan Cain, "The Power of Introverts," *TED2012,* 2012, https://www.ted.com/talks/susan_cain_the_power_of_introverts

138 Devora Zack, "Networking for People Who Hate Networking: A Field Guide for Introverts, the Overwhelmed, and the Underconnected," Berrett-Koehler Publishers, May 21, 2019

139 Ben Dattner, "The Psychology of Networking," *Psychology Today,* May 4, 2008, https://www.psychologytoday.com/intl/blog/credit-and-blame-at-work/200805/the-psychology-of-networking

140 Lewis Schiff, "The Most Influential People Only Have 6 People in Their Inner Circles," *Insider,* April 28, 2013, https://www.businessinsider.com/successful-people-have-small-network-2013-4

141 Adaira Landry and Resa E. Lewiss, "7 Ways to Promote Yourself on Social Media Without Bragging," *Fast Company,* February 15, 2022, https://www.fastcompany.com/90719543/7-ways-to-promote-yourself-on-social-media-without-bragging

142 Adaira Landry and Resa E. Lewiss, "Is Good Mentorship Found on Twitter? We Think So," *European Journal of Emergency Medicine,* vol. 28, issue 1, pp. 9–10, January 2021, https://journals.lww.com/euro-emergencymed/Citation/2021/01000/Is_good_mentorship_found_on_Twitter__We_think_so.5.aspx

143 "Your Network and Degrees of Connection," LinkedIn, updated February 23, 2022, https://www.linkedin.com/help/linkedin/answer/a545636/your-network-and-degrees-of-connection?lang=en

144 Cathy Paper, "3 Tips for Sharing Your Business Network," *The Business Journals,* October 18, 2016, https://www.bizjournals.com/bizjournals/how-to/marketing/2016/10/3-tips-for-sharing-your-business-network.html

145 CPP Inc., "Workplace Conflict and How Business Can Harness It to Thrive," July 2008, https://img.en25.com/Web/CPP/Conflict_report.pdf

146 Elizabeth Leiba, *I'm Not Yelling: A Black Woman's Guide to Navigating the Workplace,* Mango, December 13, 2022; Paula A. Johnson, Sheila E. Widnall, and Frazier F. Benya, "Sexual Harassment of Women:

Climate, Culture, and Consequences in Academic Sciences, Engineering, and Medicine," National Academies Press, Washington, DC, 2018

147 Associated Press, "It's No Trick: Merriam-Webster Says 'Gaslighting' Is the Word of the Year," *NPR*, November 28, 2022, https://www.npr.org/2022/11/28/1139384432/its-no-trick-merriam-webster-says-gaslighting-is-the-word-of-the-year#:~:text=April%202%2C%201962.-,%22Gaslighting%22%20%E2%80%94%20mind%20manipulating%2C%20grossly%20misleading%2C%20downright%20deceitful,Merriam%2DWebster's%20word%20of%202022

148 Jennifer J. Freyd, "What is DARVO?" https://dynamic.uoregon.edu/jjf/defineDARVO.html

149 Resa E. Lewiss, David G. Smith, Shikha Jain, W. Brad Johnson, and Jennifer J. Freyd, "Who's Really the Victim Here?" *MedPage Today*, June 2, 2022, https://www.medpagetoday.com/opinion/second-opinions/99015

150 Resa E. Lewiss, W. Brad Johnson, David G. Smith, and Robin Naples, "Stop Protecting 'Good Guys,'" *Harvard Business Review*, August 1, 2022, https://hbr.org/2022/08/stop-protecting-good-guys

151 "Workplace Conflict and How Business Can Harness It to Thrive," July 2008, https://img.en25.com/Web/CPP/Conflict_report.pdf

152 Kyoko Yamamoto, Masanori Kimura, and Miki Osaka, "Sorry, Not Sorry: Effects of Different Types of Apologies and Self-Monitoring on Non-verbal Behaviors," *Frontiers in Psychology*, vol. 12, August 26, 2021, https://www.ncbi.nlm.nih.gov/pmc/articles/PMC8428520/

153 Kyoko Yamamoto et al., ibid.

154 Leanne ten Brinke and Gabrielle S. Adams, "Saving Face? When Emotion Displays during Public Apologies Mitigate Damage to Organizational Performance," *Organizational Behavior and Human Decision Processes*, vol. 130, pp. 1–12, September 2015, https://www.sciencedirect.com/science/article/abs/pii/S0749597815000540?via%3Dihub

155 Amy Edmondson, *The Fearless Organization: Creating Psychological Safety in the Workplace for Learning, Innovation, and Growth*, Wiley, November 20, 2018

156 Kelly Lockwood Primus, "Why the Most Successful Leaders Create a Psychologically Safe Workplace," *Forbes*, March 17, 2023, https://www.forbes.com/sites/forbeshumanresourcescouncil/2023/03/17/why-the-most-successful-leaders-create-a-psychologically-safe-workplace/?sh=33a5d7867c2c

157 Donald Sull, Charles Sull, and Ben Zweig, "Toxic Culture Is Driving the Great Resignation," *MIT Sloan Management Review*, January 11, 2022, https://sloanreview.mit.edu/article/toxic-culture-is-driving-the-great-resignation/

158 Avraham N. Kluger and Angelo DeNisi, "The Effects of Feedback on Performance: A Historical Review, a Meta-Analysis, and a Preliminary Feedback Intervention Theory," *Psychological Bulletin*, vol. 119, no. 2, pp. 254–284, 1996, https://mrbartonmaths.com/resourcesnew/8.%20Research/Marking%20and%20Feedback/The%20effects%20of%20feedback%20interventions.pdf

159 "People Underestimate Others' Desire for Constructive Feedback," March 24, 2022, https://www.apa.org/news/press/releases/2022/03/constructive-criticism

160 Daphna Motro, Debra R. Comer, and Janet A. Lenaghan, "Examining the Effects of Negative Performance Feedback: The Roles of Sadness, Feedback Self-efficacy, and Grit," *Journal of Business and Psychology*, March 13, 2020, https://sci-hub.ru/10.1007/s10869-020-09689-1

161 Minda Harts, *The Memo: What Women of Color Need to Know to Secure a Seat at the Table*, Seal Press, August 20, 2019

162 Amy Gallo, "Getting Along: How to Work with Anyone (Even Difficult People)," *The Visible Voices Podcast,* February 8, 2023, https://www.thevisiblevoicespodcast.com/episodes/OLWhRaEjTp-inK-fXQpRiww

163 "MBTI® personality types," *The Myers-Briggs Company, https://eu.themyersbriggs.com/en/tools/MBTI/MBTI-personality-Types*; "Clifton Strengths," *Gallup,* https://www.gallup.com/cliftonstrengths/en/home.aspx?utm_source=google&utm_medium=cpc&utm_campaign=us_strengths_branded_cs_ecom&utm_term=cliftonstrengths&gclid=Cj0KCQjwlPWgBhDHARIsAH2xdNe40mvF8ZxDc1GBjT_oft7zSnCU2tgX18e4a3xu05kuLeUTCdBUaNMaAvw-zEALw_wcB

164 "The 16 MBTI® Personality Types," *The Myers & Briggs Foundation,* https://www.myersbriggs.org/my-mbti-personality-type/the-16-mbti-personality-types/

165 Matthias R. Mehl, Simine Vazire, Nairán Ramírez-Esparza, Richard B. Slatcher, and James W. Pennebaker, "Are Women Really More Talkative Than Men?" *Science*, vol. 317, issue 5834, p. 82, July 6, 2007, https://www.science.org/doi/10.1126/science.1139940

166 Douglas Stone, Bruce Patton, and Sheila Heen, "Difficult Conversations: How to Discuss What Matters Most," Penguin Books, November 2, 2010

167 Kierstin Kennedy, Teresa Cornelius, Aziz Ansari, et. al., "Six steps to conflict resolution: Best practices for conflict management in health care," *Journal of Hospital Medicine,* vol. 18, issue 4, December 22, 2022, https://shmpublications.onlinelibrary.wiley.com/authored-by/Ansari/Aziz

168 Tomas Chamorro-Premuzic, "Why Do So Many Incompetent Men Become Leaders?" *Harvard Business Review*, August 22, 2013, https://hbr.org/2013/08/why-do-so-many-incompetent-men

169 Steven Stosny, "Self-Confidence, Under Confidence, Overconfidence," *Psychology Today*, November 29, 2022, https://www.psychologytoday.com/us/blog/anger-in-the-age-entitlement/202211/self-confidence-under-confidence-overconfidence

170 Gwen Moran, "Women still feel they have to soften their communication at work," *Fast Company,* October 11, 2019, https://www.fastcompany.com/90413951/women-still-feel-they-have-to-soften-their-communication-at-work

171 Gwen Moran, "The Right Way to Fire Someone," *Fast Company*, January 12, 2017, https://www.fastcompany.com/3066961/the-right-way-to-fire-someone

172 Joanna York, "Is HR Ever Really Your Friend?" *BBC*, October 24, 2021, https://www.bbc.com/worklife/article/20211022-is-hr-ever-really-your-friend

173 Andrew K. Przybylski, Kou Murayama, Cody R. DeHaan, and Valerie Gladwell, "Motivational, Emotional, and Behavioral Correlates

of Fear of Missing Out," *Computers in Human Behavior*, vol. 29, issue 4, pp. 1841–1848, July 2013, https://www.sciencedirect.com/science/article/abs/pii/S0747563213000800?via%3Dihub

174 Andrew K. Przybylski et al., ibid.

175 Pengcheng Wang, Xingchao Wang, Jia Nie, Pan Zeng, Ke Liu, Jiayi Wang, Jinjin Guo, and Li Lei, "Envy and Problematic Smartphone Use: The Mediating Role of FOMO and the Moderating Role of Student-student Relationship," *Personality and Individual Differences*, vol. 146, pp. 136–142, August 1, 2019, https://www.sciencedirect.com/science/article/abs/pii/S0191886919302363

176 Kathy Gurchiek, "Address Skills Gap by Identifying 'Skill Adjacencies,'" *SHRM*, March 5, 2021, https://www.shrm.org/resourcesandtools/hr-topics/organizational-and-employee-development/pages/address-skills-gap-by-identifying-skill-adjacencies-.aspx

177 McKinsey & Company, "Five Fifty: The Skillful Corporation," *McKinsey Quarterly*, https://www.mckinsey.com/capabilities/people-and-organizational-performance/our-insights/five-fifty-the-skillful-corporation

178 Indeed Editorial Team, "150 Business Resume Buzzwords (With Tips)," Indeed.com, updated June 24, 2022, https://www.indeed.com/career-advice/resumes-cover-letters/business-resume-buzzwords

179 Christine L. Exley and Judd B. Kessler, "The Gender Gap in Self-Promotion," *Quarterly Journal of Economics*, vol. 137, issue 3, pp. 1345–1381, August 2022, https://academic.oup.com/qje/article/137/3/1345/6513425

180 Curt Rice, "How McKinsey's Story Became Sheryl Sandberg's Statistic—and Why It Didn't Deserve To," *HuffPost UK*, April 24, 2014, https://www.huffingtonpost.co.uk/curt-rice/how-mckinseys-story-became-sheryl-sandbergs-statistic-and-why-it-didnt-deserve-to_b_5198744.html?guce_referrer=aHR0cHM6Ly93d3cuZ29vZ2xlLmNvbS8&guce_referrer_sig=AQAAAJ4BfyBCOz1CMcpRBTbA45LxMTbi0Yq-In6EjNuUH-d7fRatlRcNmELW5XC_J_Jgr8ZmWYFZFs8CUTEVPCjVKUPV5JgrAVX_HTKlhQ3x-lOgX9tGGg7OcKwst6fs_oiGQ-ibOoLry-GGfUkC1DZlw4WavVnR86g51bL0Ez0kxkKht&guccounter=2